KENNETH POWELL WITH CATHY STRONGMAN

NEW LONDON ARCHITECTURE 2

MERRELL

LONDON · NEW YORK

First published 2007 by Merrell Publishers Limited

Head office:
81 Southwark Street
London SE1 0HX

New York office:
49 West 24th Street, 8th Floor
New York, NY 10010

merrellpublishers.com

British Library Cataloguing-in-Publication Data:
Powell, Kenneth, 1947–
New London architecture 2
1. Architecture, Modern – 21st century
2. Architecture – England – London – 21st century
3. Buildings – England – London 4. London (England) – Buildings,
structures, etc.
I. Title II. Strongman, Cathy
720.9'421'0905

ISBN-13: 978-1-8589-4360-2
ISBN-10: 1-8589-4360-4

Produced by Merrell Publishers
Design concept by Maggi Smith
Layout by Karen Wilks
Edited by Sarah Yates

Printed and bound in China

Front jacket: View of the River Thames looking east, showing
   the London Bridge Tower and New London Bridge House
   (pp. 226–27). Image by Hayes Davidson and John Maclean
Back jacket: Kew Gardens Alpine House (pp. 54–55). Image
   © Dennis Gilbert/VIEW
Page 2: Bankside 123 (pp. 214–15). Image © Dennis Gilbert/VIEW

Merrell Publishers is grateful to the architecture and interior-design
photographic agency VIEW for providing the majority of the
photographs published in this book. Founded in 1997, VIEW
now represents over forty photographers. The emphasis of its
collection is on contemporary architecture from around the world;
iconic modern buildings and historic structures are also covered.
VIEW also distributes the work of other architectural photographic
agencies and overseas photo libraries. Its collection includes
images of buildings by such leading architects as Renzo Piano,
Jean Nouvel, Frank Gehry, Herzog & de Meuron, Zaha Hadid,
Norman Foster and Richard Rogers. **www.viewpictures.co.uk**

ACKNOWLEDGEMENTS

I should like to thank Julian Honer of Merrell for commissioning this book, and Rosanna Fairhead for seeing
the project to fruition; also at Merrell, Paul Shinn and Sadie Butler. Isabel Allen and Paul Finch kindly advised
on the selection of projects. It has been a pleasure working with Cathy Strongman: her knowledge and
enthusiasm have provided a vital catalyst. Catherine Langford was a great help with research and fact-
finding. Architects, clients and building users too numerous to mention provided the information, drawings
and a selection of the photographs that have made the book possible, and the contribution of VIEW
photographers was equally vital to the project.

With the millennium building boom over, and National Lottery funds being shamelessly diverted away
from good causes to plug gaps in public finance, new building in London is dominated by the commercial
sector, and it is refreshing to see it turning to new talent as well as seasoned hands. Though public buildings
(notably in the education sector) feature strongly in this book, London continues to face huge problems as a
result of inadequate investment, above all in its transport system. The capital's success in 2005 in securing
the 2012 Olympics was widely welcomed, but unless the Olympics produces lasting benefits for London as
a whole that success may come to be regretted. A buoyant world city, London is riding high but faces major
challenges, which architects and their clients have a vital role in meeting.

Kenneth Powell
London, 2007

I am grateful to Kenneth Powell for giving me the opportunity to write this book with him, and for his
generous encouragement throughout. I should like to thank Julian Honer of Merrell for commissioning the
book, and the brilliant Rosanna Fairhead who has patiently completed all the nuts and bolts. Peter Murray,
curator of the unrelated New London Architecture exhibition at the Building Design Centre in central London,
kindly gave his time to advise on the selection of projects, as did Anna Strongman, Associate at Arup. Thank
you to the numerous architects who have provided information, plans and images, and to VIEW photographers
for capturing so well the spirit of these buildings. Finally, thank you to Duncan Donaldson for putting up with
cancelled dinners and spending Sundays with a workaholic.

Cathy Strongman
London, 2007

CONTENTS

Close to Lloyd's Register and the Willis Building, Richard Rogers Partnership's dramatic Leadenhall Tower, also known as the 'Cheese Grater', is another tall City building to have been recently approved.

In the first decade of the twenty-first century London has become the capital of the European, and arguably the global, architectural scene, and British architecture is more diverse and varied than it has been at any time in the last hundred years. It is from London that such world-renowned British architects as Richard Rogers, Norman Foster, Nicholas Grimshaw, Zaha Hadid, David Chipperfield, Will Alsop, Caruso St John and Foreign Office Architects are working on projects for cities as far afield as Beijing, Melbourne, Toronto and Des Moines, Iowa. London also attracts architects from abroad of the stature of Jean Nouvel, Daniel Libeskind, Herzog & de Meuron, Rem Koolhaas, Renzo Piano and Rafael Viñoly, all of whom have built or are building in the city. The capital's architectural schools – the Architectural Association School of Architecture and The Bartlett at University College London among them – are powerhouses of new ideas. Such architecture festivals as the London Architecture Biennale, launched in 2004, and the Open House weekend every September, in which six hundred buildings are open to the public for free, attract thousands of visitors. Fifteen years into its existence, the Architecture Foundation is to get a permanent home, designed by Zaha Hadid.

After years of uncertainty, during which Britain appeared unwilling to embrace radical new architecture, public opinion is warming to tall buildings (largely because of Norman Foster's 30 St Mary Axe, or 'Gherkin'), and traditionally cautious planning authorities welcome the new and experimental. Young practices, accustomed to making a living from modest bar fit-outs and private apartment refurbishments, find themselves building schools, housing and health centres, and fielding enquiries from a new generation of developers prepared to take risks and not to rely on the same tried, trusted – and too often tired – list of 'commercial' practices.

Emerging from the recession of the early 1990s, London acquired a new energy as the Labour government was elected in 1997 and preparations were made to celebrate the new millennium. The National Lottery, established in 1993 by John Major's Conservative government, allowed the British Museum, Tate, National Portrait Gallery, Royal Opera House and smaller institutions, such as the Royal Court Theatre and Dulwich Picture Gallery, to complete building projects that previously seemed unachievable. (In contrast to so many other projects around Britain, the National Lottery funds seem to have been invested to good effect in London.) It was Major, too, who, while responsible for the disastrous privatization of the nation's rail system, gave the green light to London Underground's Jubilee Line Extension, an essential foundation for the regeneration

of a swathe of south and east London, and a lifeline to Canary Wharf. In contrast, Tony Blair's 'New Labour' government has dithered over the future of such vital infrastructure schemes as Thameslink and Crossrail. Ken Livingstone, elected as Mayor of London against the opposition of the Blair government, took the courageous steps of imposing the central London congestion charge for traffic – partly as an environmental measure – and of pressing ahead with the partial pedestrianization of Trafalgar Square. The latter was part of a programme launched in 2002 to create one hundred new public spaces across London.

Since reconciled to the Labour government, which has augmented the power of the Mayor of London to intervene and approve projects of "strategic" significance, Livingstone has had a huge impact on planning and development in London. Working alongside him, Richard Rogers – Livingstone's architectural guru – has championed the cause of architecture and urban design, and in 2006 was appointed chairman of an advisory group for Design for London. This new agency was established by the Mayor to make London "a world leader in sustainable urban planning, design and architecture", and its new director, Peter Bishop, was appointed in the autumn of 2006.

Livingstone's support for tall buildings in the capital seems to have overwhelmed the defenders of the historic London skyline. Its opposition to the Heron Tower on Bishopsgate and Piano's 'Shard of Glass' at London Bridge having been brushed aside, English Heritage (the government's adviser on the historic environment) has been less vociferous in this direction. The Commission for Architecture and the Built Environment (CABE), another New Labour creation, came out in favour of a number of high-rise projects while calling for a London-wide strategy to protect the skyline. Deputy Prime Minister John Prescott's long stint in overall charge of the planning system reinforced the cause of building high. Such projects as Kohn Pedersen Fox's DIFA Tower, Richard Rogers Partnership's Leadenhall Tower and the Bishopsgate Tower by Skidmore, Owings & Merrill (SOM) all gained planning approval, as did Broadway Malyan's residential tower at Vauxhall. The last project was perhaps more controversial than the others because it was not the work of a critically approved practice. Here, as in the case of Terry Farrell's Lots Road project, Prescott rejected the findings of a public inquiry in order to approve the proposals. The borough of Southwark, however, while revelling in its record as a focus of regeneration over two decades, appeared disconcerted by the prospect of a new clump of towers around

Left

The Music Box at White City is a rehearsal space and concert hall designed by Foreign Office Architects for the BBC, and was the subject of a competition in 2003.

Opposite

The Willis Building on Lime Street is a large office development by Foster + Partners on the site of the Lloyd's '1958' building, opposite Richard Rogers Partnership's Lloyd's Register (seen on the right). It is one of a large number of office projects in London by Foster + Partners in recent years.

Blackfriars Road, including, most prominently, the proposed 180-metre-high One Blackfriars Road designed by Ian Simpson (pp. 188–89). With proposals for more tall buildings upstream in Lambeth, the case for a strategy for tall buildings that extended across borough boundaries appeared unchallengeable. The stance of the Conservative-run borough of Westminster in central London, however, remained one of dogged opposition to high buildings, along with an unenthusiastic attitude to innovative design in general.

The advent of the Labour government led to renewed investment in housing, schools and hospitals, but the way in which those buildings were procured was contentious. Once into its second term, the Blair government began to recognize the drawbacks of the Private Finance Initiative (PFI) method hitherto consistently backed by the Treasury (in which private consortiums are contracted to construct and, in some cases, run buildings that are then leased by a public authority), and there were moves at least to reform it. The saga of the St Bartholomew's and Royal London hospitals rebuilding project highlighted the problems with PFI, though government indecision only added to the spiralling costs, while patients endured a hospital environment that was among the worst in western Europe. Noting, not before time, that PFI can lead to a huge waste of resources, Chancellor of the Exchequer Gordon Brown appeared to have endorsed the Royal Institute of British Architects' 'Smart PFI' model, which gives greater weight to design quality, in his 2006 budget.

London may be a world architectural capital, but it is still a place where outstanding ideas founder on practical and political realities. Thanks to the British Airports Authority's obsession with 'value engineering' (which strictly limits the cost of a project's elements according to their perceived usefulness), the long-delayed Terminal 5 at Heathrow Airport (pp. 32–33) lacks the outstanding quality of the new terminal at Madrid's Barajas Airport, though both are the work of Richard Rogers Partnership. Richard MacCormac's visionary plans for rebuilding the BBC's Broadcasting House look set to emerge badly compromised from a complex process of project management. Another prestigious BBC commission, the 'Music Box' at White City, was firmly on hold three years after Foreign Office Architects won the competition to design it. Ian Ritchie's proposals for a shopping centre at White City represented a potential reinvention of the building type, but have been abandoned, though Ritchie is still involved in the public transport elements of the scheme.

It will be a few years yet before London's ability to respond to the greatest architectural and planning challenge it has faced in fifty years – the 2012 Olympic and Paralympic Games – can be judged. The capital won the contest to stage the Games in July 2005, and Zaha Hadid was commissioned to design the Aquatic Centre, the first major building on the Lower Lea Valley site in east London, soon afterwards (pp. 86–87).

The appointment early in 2006 of the architecture/landscape team that had underpinned London's winning bid (Edaw/Allies and Morrison/HOK Sport Architecture/Foreign Office Architects) as masterplanners for the 500-hectare Olympic Park was encouraging, but the emphasis in commissioning buildings appeared to be firmly on a construction-led, design-and-build approach. The chief executive of the Olympic Delivery Authority (ODA) – the agency responsible for

completing the Olympic venues – promised a limited number of design competitions, but for most building projects, including the six major commissions, the onus will be on contractors to select outstanding architects. Whether this process will produce buildings of the quality of Herzog & de Meuron's stadium for the Beijing Olympics of 2008 remains to be seen. The problems in building the new Wembley Stadium underline the risks involved in a design-and-build contract, though HOK Sport Architecture's Emirates Stadium is an example of such a project delivered on time and to cost.

The ODA endorsed a series of "construction commitments", a series of worthy intentions relating to issues of employment practice, health and safety, and sustainability, as much as to design, but the commitment to encourage "emerging designers" did not seem in tune with the chosen procurement route. In any case the requirement to advertise projects via notices in the *Official Journal of the European Union* typically excludes practices lacking experience of big projects: the scope for London's young architects is confined to the design of kiosks, toilet blocks and other minor structures. The Games did not seem to presage the "spectacular ten years" for British architects predicted by Graham Morrison of Allies and Morrison in July 2005. The long-term prospects of development in the Thames Gateway, however, where there could be at least 40,000 new homes, could indeed offer a bonanza for the profession – or conversely it could lead to the creation of a vast tract of architecturally undistinguished suburbia. Meanwhile, Londoners, already alarmed by the potential financial burden of the Games, wait to see if it will be a triumph or a rather more modest achievement.

Halfway through the first decade of a new century, the hierarchy of British architecture was remarkably stable. Norman Foster and Richard Rogers, both life peers and in their seventies, remained at the helms of practices founded in the 1960s. Nicholas Grimshaw, enthroned as President of the Royal Academy, and Michael and Patty Hopkins were still major players with their roots in High-tech. Zaha Hadid, Pritzker Prize winner with large built projects across the globe, had yet to complete a building in London: her premiere in the capital will be the modest Architecture Foundation headquarters in Southwark (pp. 40–41). Another international superstar, David Chipperfield, had built little in London. Will Alsop had yet to attain the heights some critics had predicted twenty years ago and was forced to merge his practice with a large commercial firm. Yet his recent London buildings – a medical school in the East End (pp. 118–19), a teaching block for Goldsmiths at New Cross (pp. 98–99), a children's centre in Stonebridge Park (pp. 108–09) and a large office scheme in Southwark (pp. 228–29) – are all distinctive and inventive (yet far from extravagant) projects. Alsop will make his mark still further on London, it is to be hoped; so, too, will Future Systems, the practice whose Media Centre at Lord's Cricket Ground was one of the truly popular London buildings of the late 1990s.

A very different tradition of design is represented by Dixon Jones, the partnership Jeremy Dixon and Edward Jones formed in the late 1980s, and which is best known for the Royal Opera House reconstruction. Other projects include a building for University College London, the remodelling of Exhibition Road and a mixed-use building at King's Cross that will house the offices of *The Guardian* and *The Observer* newspapers. Terry Farrell, Grimshaw's former partner, is still associated with the Post-modernist projects he completed in the late 1980s and early 1990s. More recently his architecture has lacked a specific stylistic stamp – the new Home Office in Marsham Street is a mainstream corporate building in appearance, though the project is interesting as an exercise in repair of the urban environment (pp. 224–25). Farrell's considerable abilities as an urban designer and masterplanner remain underused, though his proposals for recasting the Euston Road corridor as a spectacular, enjoyable city boulevard typify the boldness of his thinking, as does the proposal for a national park in the Thames Estuary, envisaged as a showcase for sustainable industry.

Among the younger practices with roots in the Foster and Rogers offices, Wilkinson Eyre and John McAslan + Partners are conspicuously big players, though the special interest of McAslan's work remains in the conversion and reuse projects that have given the practice a high profile – the Roundhouse at Chalk Farm is an outstanding example (pp. 64–65). The High-tech roots in Rogers's own work continue to show through, for example in the dramatically expressive diagram of the proposed Leadenhall Tower. Foster's work is more diffuse. Of a dozen or more recent and ongoing City office projects (apart from 30 St Mary Axe), only the Bishop's Square development at Spitalfields – actually beyond the City boundary – stands out as a fresh look at the office building in the context of urban fabric and life (pp. 218–19). The forthcoming office scheme at Lime Street, replacing the Lloyd's '1958' building, is a more typical product, highly efficient and tailored to its site. The scale of Foster's practice makes it difficult sometimes to detect the master's touch on a project, though it is possible that the great arch of the new Wembley Stadium reflects his instinct for the symbolic and memorable (pp. 92–93).

Competing with Foster in the commercial field, practices with transatlantic origins remain strong: Kohn Pedersen Fox (KPF) has the Heron and DIFA Tower projects in hand, HOK designed headquarters for Barclays Bank – breaking the mould for office buildings at Canary Wharf – and SOM is back on form with the Bishopsgate Tower (though this was partly designed from Chicago). London remains an important base for Americans dealing with Europe and the Middle East, as prospective Arab clients are increasingly reluctant to visit the USA after the terrorist attacks of 11 September 2001. In the 1980s there was talk of an 'invasion' of American architects and of London being wrecked by developments alien to its traditions. Yet all these practices have developed a distinctly European identity: HOK, for example, was responsible for a superb restoration of the King's Library in the British Museum, as well as big office projects. Swanke Hayden Connell's complex for Merrill Lynch is often cited as a model of how large spaces for the financial industry can be accommodated within the historic context of the City.

While commercial practices with their origins in the 1950s and 1960s, such as Aukett Fitzroy Robinson, EPR, RHWL and Sheppard Robson (responsible for the excellent Salvation Army building in the City; see pp. 232–33), remain prominent, firms of more recent vintage have invaded the field. Allies and Morrison, a partnership dating from the 1980s, is working as masterplanner for the Olympic

site, the Royal Arsenal (pp. 26–27) and King's Cross Central (pp. 20–21). It is also architect of the Bankside 123 development in Southwark (pp. 214–15) as well as for the comprehensive £91,000,000 redevelopment of the Grade I-listed Royal Festival Hall, scheduled for completion in the summer of 2007. Allford Hall Monaghan Morris (AHMM), a practice founded in 1989 by four young graduates of Sheffield University, has also made the transition from young and upcoming to the big league. AHMM's architectural approach is, like that of Allies and Morrison, mainstream modern, highly rational but with a strong interest in materials, and appears to be highly attractive to developers and other clients. The practice's masterplan for the town centre of Barking, Essex, provides the framework for injecting civic character into a decayed area and includes the refurbishment of a 1960s library as well as new housing and the transformation (by Tim Foster) of the existing civic hall into the stylish Broadway Theatre. The new town square is being designed by AHMM in association with Muf. 'Mainstream modern' might also be a fair description of the work of two former architects in partnership, Terry Pawson and Keith Williams, who established separate practices in 2001. Pawson's lovingly detailed office building in Vernon Street, Hammersmith, was described, somewhat spitefully, by the *RIBA Journal* as "weak modernism", wanting "to make a statement while simultaneously trying not to say anything", but his parish hall in Wimbledon is an assured exercise in modern contextualism (pp. 90–91). Williams has made his mark on London with the Unicorn Theatre in Southwark, a building that looks too elegant and grown-up for its purpose – it stages plays for children – but seems to work well for its clientele (pp. 70–71). The architecture of Stanton Williams, a firm that established its reputation in the 1980s with exhibition design projects, is broadly in the same spirit. Consistently well-detailed, it eschews the pursuit of form in favour of the sort of understatement found in its recent building for City University in Clerkenwell and its landscape scheme for the environs of the Tower of London (pp. 34–35).

'Materiality' is one of the over-used buzzwords of recent architectural criticism. It is a quality, however, that is always present in the work of Caruso St John, a practice that seems to take its cue from the ethos of Team X and the New Brutalism of the late 1950s. The partnership of Adam Caruso and Peter St John made its name with the new art gallery in the West Midlands town of Walsall but has since won major commissions outside the UK. Its Brick House in Westbourne Grove, west London, was critically acclaimed even before it was built (pp. 160–61). The practice was not an obvious choice to extend Denys Lasdun's Hallfield School in Paddington, but the recent additions have a strength and dignity of their own (pp. 112–14). Caruso St John's exquisite reworking of a former industrial space in King's Cross for the Gagosian Gallery provides one of the best new venues for displaying contemporary art since Tony Fretton's highly influential Lisson Gallery. Sergison Bates is another London practice whose work harks back to the era of Team X and the work of Peter and Alison Smithson in particular. Caruso St John and Sergison Bates have both had a strong influence on

A product of London's adventurous post-'Gherkin' period, Skidmore, Owings & Merrill's Bishopsgate Tower is a classic design that refers to the practice's iconic John Hancock Center in Chicago.

young architects and the new generation in the schools. Very different in character but equally fashionable is the work of David Adjaye. Making his name with a series of flats and houses, mostly commissioned by figures in the art world, Adjaye completed his first big London project, the Idea Store in Whitechapel, in 2005: this tough, economical building is glamorous but not condescending to the far-from-affluent area in which it stands (pp. 52–53).

The traditionalist lobby, represented by such architects as Quinlan Terry, John Simpson, Robert Adam and Julian Bicknell, seems to be on the retreat in London, though none of these practitioners lacks commissions in Britain and abroad. The Classical masterplans for London Bridge City and Paternoster Square are now a distant – and not very happy – memory. Office projects by Terry (in Baker Street) and Adam (on Piccadilly; see pp. 210–11) demonstrate, however, the potential for marrying load-bearing masonry façades, replete with ornament, with modern workspaces. At the Royal Hospital, Chelsea, Quinlan Terry won a planning battle that involved local resident Richard Rogers as an objector, to build a new infirmary wing in the Classical style, boldly challenging the historic architecture of Sir Christopher Wren (pp. 150–51). Liam O'Connor's Commonwealth War Memorial at Hyde Park Corner is a dignified, rather dull exercise in a sub-Lutyens manner, but it is the best of a series of relatively poor recent memorials in London. These projects are conspicuously at odds with prevailing fashions predicated on a revisiting of Modern Movement, rather than Classical, themes.

It is in urban planning that the traditionalist message has had more impact. The appointment of Demetri Porphyrios to masterplan the King's Cross Central development (with Allies and Morrison) underlines the degree to which the thinking of Leon Krier and the American Congress for the New Urbanism, which has its enthusiasts in New Labour political circles, has become prevalent. King's Cross Central will have streets and squares in the tradition of Mayfair and Belgravia – and no tall buildings (pp. 20–21).

At the beginning of the twenty-first century, London is a breeding ground for new architectural talent and a place where that talent is finding scope to build as well as to dream. Architects need clients, and young practices, such as Meadowcroft Griffin, Ash Sakula, Azman Owens, Piercy Conner, Peter Barber, Amin Taha, Tonkin Liu, Lynch Architects and Michaelis Boyd, have benefited from the revival of investment in 'social housing' as well as from a booming market in one-off private houses. Peter Barber's Donnybrook Quarter (pp. 166–67), commissioned by the Circle 33 Housing Trust, and the Peabody Trust developments at Evelyn Road (by Niall McLaughlin; see pp. 180–81) and Boxley Street (by Ash Sakula; see pp. 178–79), both in the borough of Newham, reflect the high aspirations of clients in the social-housing sector. They are continuing to back innovative design, including the use of prefabrication, and to emphasize the need for sustainable, low-energy construction.

Prefabricated construction, a method that engaged Modernist pioneers from Walter Gropius to Buckminster Fuller, is an obvious response to the urgent need for affordable housing, as London's economy booms and levels of immigration rise. It is predicted that forty per cent of all households in London will be occupied by a single person by 2011. Cartwright Pickard's Murray Grove housing for the Peabody Trust, completed in 1999, was a pioneering exercise in this direction, constructed – or, to be more accurate, assembled – in twenty-seven weeks. Peabody pursued the theme at the AHMM-designed Raines Dairy site in Stoke Newington. Piercy Conner (established in 1999) has pursued the possibilities of prefabrication in its 'Microflat' concept and in projects for Circle 33 and Newham Council. PCKO's housing at Wyndham Road, Southwark, completed in 2005 for Hyde Housing Association and following on from a smaller scheme at Barling Court, Stockwell, is designed to be dismantled and re-erected: the modular units sit on screw-pile foundations that can be removed easily. An even more radical approach is reflected in the Micro-Compact Home project, developed by Horden Cherry Lee with the German practice Haack & Höpfner. The first of these transportable residential units are already being inhabited by students in Munich, Germany. At Trinity Buoy Wharf, across the River Thames from the Millennium Dome, Urban Space Management has created Container City, a mix of residential development and workspaces forged from redundant freight containers by architects Nicholas Lacey and Ahrends Burton Koralek at a cost (in 2006) of around £72 per square foot, or £775 per square metre. Each 6-metre-long container was then sold for £700.

The conspicuous consumption by London's wealthy includes, thankfully, the commissioning of architecturally interesting one-off houses. Woolf Architects' Double House, an RIBA Award winner in 2004, is a spectacular recent example, occupying a magnificent site on the edge of Hampstead Heath. But many of the most interesting private residential commissions of the last few years are conversions or extensions of existing buildings, or insertions into 'gaps' in the city's fabric. Alex Michaelis of Michaelis Boyd managed to slot his own new home into a tiny site between two existing houses in north Kensington by sinking most of the house to basement level, where an indoor swimming pool (supplied with water via a borehole) acts as a heat sink, helping to maintain an even temperature inside the house (pp. 192–93). Given the project's weighty environmental credentials, it is not surprising that David Cameron, Conservative Party leader, subsequently commissioned Michaelis to adapt his own house in line with sustainable design principles. Graham Bizley's house on Newington Green (pp. 186–87) occupies a site of 60 square metres, and makes ingenious use of the available space, views and natural light to create a dwelling that combines privacy with an openness to the street. Alison Brooks Architects' exquisite Wrap House in Chiswick extends the living space of an Edwardian house into the garden (pp. 202–03), while Gianni Botsford's Light House in Notting Hill uses an abandoned back yard to create living spaces naturally lit from above. The house in Primrose Hill designed by Richard Paxton of Paxton Locher (who sadly died in 2006) slots into a narrow mews. Contemporary London architects enjoy the confrontation with the realities of city living. The old division between home and workplace is being eroded as many architects and other professionals opt for a combination of both: examples include an artist's studio in Kentish Town by Sanei Hopkins (pp. 212–13), DSDHA's house and studio in Deptford (pp. 172–73), and

The elegant and carefully detailed Vernon Street office by Terry Pawson Architects is an example of the practice's 'mainstream modern' style.

Christ Church Spitalfields, a historic
Hawksmoor church, has been beautifully
restored after a long battle to save it.

Meadowcroft Griffin's 319 Portobello Road (which fits comfortably
into an existing terrace; see pp. 38–39).

Education buildings have been a major source of work for
London architects, including a number of youngish firms. The
government's Sure Start programme generated new nursery/family
centre projects by DSDHA, John McAslan + Partners (pp. 134–35),
Greenhill Jenner (p. 132), Meadowcroft Griffin (p. 133) and others.
A more contentious new element of the Blair administration's
educational programme, the city academies, has produced buildings
by Foster, Rogers, Feilden Clegg Bradley and AHMM (pp. 138–39).
An announcement by the government agency Partnerships for
Schools that up to forty future academy projects across Britain
would be procured on a contractor-led, design-and-build basis led
to fears that a degree of standardization, at least, seemed likely. Of
London's higher-education institutions, Imperial College and Queen
Mary, University of London, were particularly interesting patrons. The
former commissioned a clutch of new buildings by Foster + Partners
and a residential development by KPF, and the latter a science
institute by Will Alsop (pp. 118–19), an engaging graduate centre by
Surface Architects (pp. 124–25) and a large development of student
housing by Feilden Clegg Bradley (pp. 136–37).

Although London is a city in constant flux, it appears to cherish
its history, and long-neglected historic buildings are being given new
life. Christ Church Spitalfields, among the most important works of
one of England's greatest architects, Nicholas Hawksmoor, was the
subject of a thirty-year rescue campaign, brought to fruition with the
aid of National Lottery funding and with Purcell Miller Tritton as
architects. Hawksmoor's St George's, Bloomsbury, has also been
restored from near dereliction by architects Molyneux Kerr, with
assistance from the World Monuments Fund. St Luke, Old Street,
which has an extraordinary obelisk spire by Hawksmoor, was
abandoned by the Church of England in the 1950s and left as a
roofless shell for nearly half a century. Today, with a strikingly
contemporary new interior by Levitt Bernstein, it houses a rehearsal
and performance space for the London Symphony Orchestra. St
Martin-in-the-Fields at the corner of Trafalgar Square has never been
anything less than a thriving place of worship, but its mission, and
particularly its social work for the homeless and others, will benefit
greatly from an ambitious development project by Eric Parry that
reuses and extends the crypt and vaults.

It is not only buildings most widely perceived as 'historic'
that are benefiting from imaginative repair and reuse schemes.
Wells Coates's Isokon Flats in Lawn Road, Hampstead, an iconic
1930s Modern Movement landmark where Agatha Christie, Walter
Gropius, Marcel Breuer and James Stirling all once resided,
has been restored as a mix of rented and privately owned
accommodation after years of neglect (pp. 176–77). The work was
carried out by Avanti Architects, a practice with an unequalled
record for resuscitating tired Modernist buildings. This is not to
suggest that conservation battles are yet a thing of the past.
Proposals by KPF for the demolition of the western end of Smithfield
Market in favour of an office-led redevelopment were hotly opposed
by SAVE Britain's Heritage, the group that has been campaigning to

The Micro-Compact Home by Horden Cherry Lee is a small but impeccably organized house that could be a model for high-density living in the future.

retain historic buildings in London since the mid-1970s. In 2006 these proposals were subjected to a public inquiry.

With the age of the big National Lottery hand-outs that funded the Great Court at the British Museum, the Royal Opera House rebuilding and the creation of Tate Modern seemingly over – though Tate director Sir Nicholas Serota expects a subvention for Tate Modern's phase 2, designed by Herzog & de Meuron – London's cultural institutions are looking at ways of using their existing buildings more efficiently. For a few years the Victoria and Albert Museum (V&A) was preoccupied by the 'Spiral', a striking but in practical terms rather irrelevant – and very costly – project designed by Daniel Libeskind. After the scheme, which was refused National Lottery funding, was abandoned, the V&A began to re-examine its sprawling collection of buildings. New galleries for British art and design, Islamic art, sculpture and the medieval and Renaissance collections have opened or are planned. Architecture has its own gallery, designed by Gareth Hoskins (pp. 42–43), while the study rooms that house the RIBA's Drawings Collection were designed by Wright & Wright. There is a new shop and a new café, located in the original Victorian refreshment rooms. The replanned garden at the heart of the museum, known as the John Madejski Garden and designed by Kim Wilkie, is a model of simple elegance. Dixon Jones's work at the National Gallery is ongoing, with the opening up of large areas of the ground floor previously used as offices and stores, and a new ground-level entrance (pp. 60–61). The extension to the Whitechapel Art Gallery by Robbrecht en Daem (pp. 74–75)

makes use of the existing Passmore Edwards Library, which became redundant when Adjaye's Idea Store (pp. 52–53) opened close by. King's College, one of the oldest in the University of London, is progressively rehabilitating its buildings in the eastern quadrant of Somerset House. The BDP-designed project also extends public routes through the site between the Strand and the Thames, building on the success of Somerset House, which has been transformed into an arts and education complex by one of London's most successful National Lottery projects. The new academic building for the London School of Economics is a radical conversion of a large Edwardian commercial block (pp. 128–29).

Good architecture needs good clients. The fabric of London is the product of private investment and speculative development, rather than royal or imperial decree. Compared with Paris, Vienna or Madrid, London lacks spectacular monuments. It has always been a commercial capital, built by developers, who created the squares and terraces of Mayfair, Belgravia, Pimlico and Kensington. In the post-war era, however, developers were widely reviled as the despoilers of London, destroyers rather than creators. A new generation who came to the fore in the 1980s, including Stuart Lipton and Geoffrey Wilson, began to change that image. Lipton, who insisted that "good design pays", was the prime mover behind Broadgate, a City office development with high-quality architecture, an ample budget for public art, and generous public spaces, a response to the growing challenge of Canary Wharf in Docklands. Today such long-established developers as British Land, Land

Cardinal Place, an unusual mixed-use development by EPR Architects near Victoria station in central London, has opened up an inaccessible site in a prime location near the Houses of Parliament.

Securities and Hammersons are commissioning architects of the calibre of Foster, Rogers, Viñoly and Nouvel to work on City office projects. Rem Koolhaas is working with Stanhope on a new headquarters for Rothschild Bank and an urban masterplan at White City in west London. Such major developments as Plantation Place in the City (pp. 230–31), Cardinal Place in Westminster and Regent's Place on Euston Road are new urban quarters in their own right, not just collections of office blocks.

A newer generation of London developers is pioneering mixed-use and city-centre residential development. They include Harry Handelsman of the Manhattan Loft Corporation, Crispin Kelly of Baylight (an Architectural Association graduate whose first venture was an outstanding Sloane Avenue project by Stanton Williams) and Simon Silver of Derwent Valley (which commissioned Broadwick House in Soho from Richard Rogers and the Johnson Building in Hatton Garden from AHMM). The London development scene is open to newcomers. In the last few years, for example, the Candy brothers, who formed their company in the late 1990s, have become property's new wunderkinds, working on projects with Rogers, Foster and Chipperfield. The Liverpool-based Beetham Organization, a family-owned business, commissioned Ian Simpson to design a high-rise hotel and apartment tower on the south end of Blackfriars Bridge (pp. 188–89), having completed high-profile projects with him in Manchester and Birmingham. Acquiring a site at Aldgate, east London, from Hammersons, Beethams held a design competition for the office complex Trinity EC3; won by Foreign Office Architects, it is likely to be the practice's first built project in London (pp. 234–35). The Australian mega-developer Westfield has become, in a few years, a huge presence in London, taking over the vast Stratford City project in the east (pp. 30–31) and developing the White City shopping centre in the west.

Ken Livingstone's vision of future London as a "compact, accessible and greener city", equipped with transport, housing and public services to accommodate a growing population, remains at odds with the results of much of government policy: the Treasury's decision to sell the management of the Underground to private companies has already proved a disastrous mistake, for example. London is the engine of the British economy, generating the subsidies that some other regions expect as a right. New Labour's decision to create a measure of cross-London government was a positive development, but further radical reform may be needed to equip the city for its continuing role as a major global centre. Do the boroughs still have significance as units of government? Does the planning system, as presently constituted, work for London? Why has Terminal 5 at Heathrow Airport taken twenty years to complete when Madrid can build a much larger project in half the time? London is enjoying a period of almost unprecedented growth and prosperity (in which, admittedly, many of its inhabitants do not share), reflected in an extraordinary diversity of new architecture. However, the "metropolis of social and ecological harmony" for which Richard Rogers has campaigned remains, for the moment, a vision that has yet to become reality.

INFRASTRUCTURE

EXHIBITION ROAD
DIXON JONES

KING'S CROSS CENTRAL
ALLIES AND MORRISON/PORPHYRIOS ASSOCIATES

KING'S CROSS STATION
JOHN MCASLAN + PARTNERS

LOTS ROAD
FARRELLS

ROYAL ARSENAL
ALLIES AND MORRISON

ST PANCRAS STATION AND CHAMBERS
RHWL/RICHARD GRIFFITHS ARCHITECTS

STRATFORD CITY
FLETCHER PRIEST ARCHITECTS/ARUP URBAN DESIGN/WEST 8

TERMINAL 5, HEATHROW AIRPORT
RICHARD ROGERS PARTNERSHIP

TOWER OF LONDON ENVIRONS SCHEME
STANTON WILLIAMS

EXHIBITION ROAD, SOUTH KENSINGTON, SW7

DIXON JONES, 2003–

Below
Dixon Jones's proposals for Exhibition Road provide a new pedestrian spine for 'Albertopolis', one of London's prime cultural quarters.

Opposite
The project removes the existing road and pavement and associated clutter in favour of all-over paving with extended tree-planting.

Exhibition Road is the central spine of 'Albertopolis', the cultural and educational quarter in Kensington developed with the proceeds of the Great Exhibition of 1851, under the inspiration of Prince Albert. The Victoria and Albert and Natural History museums flank the southern end of the road. The Science Museum, Imperial College, Royal Albert Hall, Royal College of Art and Royal College of Music are located to the west of Exhibition Road. Every year, more than ten million people come here to visit the museums and other institutions. A high proportion of them arrive via the nearby South Kensington Underground station, which handles thirty million passengers annually.

The inadequacy of the public realm around these institutions has long been recognized. Parked and moving cars, manoeuvring buses and traffic islands leave pedestrians scuttling at the margins of the wide street, and the route from South Kensington Underground station to the museums is not for the faint-hearted. In the mid-1990s, an ambitious plan by Foster + Partners was commissioned by a coalition of these institutions. It provided for new buildings, squares, a radical redevelopment of the existing (and rather depressing) tunnel that connects the museums to South Kensington station, and the landscaping of Exhibition Road as

a primarily pedestrian thoroughfare, but the scheme was subsequently abandoned. Dixon Jones's £35,000,000 project, the largest of the '100 Public Spaces' proposed by Mayor Ken Livingstone, shares many objectives with the Foster scheme, while omitting some of the more costly ingredients.

The project involves the creation of a broad new pedestrian route extending from South Kensington station to Kensington Gardens, with new crossings on Cromwell Road and Kensington Gore, and travelators serving a much refurbished museum tunnel. The tunnel will also provide access to the gardens of the Natural History Museum. Although still open to traffic, which will include new bus services, Exhibition Road will be entirely paved in a diagonal pattern, with kerbs removed in order to limit vehicle speeds, and parking areas reduced. Extensive tree-planting will strengthen the visual connection with Hyde Park. Thurloe Street, which connects the Underground station to Exhibition Road, will become the focus of 'South Kensington Village', a public space largely given over to pedestrians, with bus routes diverted.

The project went to public consultation during 2005, and in 2006 it underwent further development and refinement in readiness for an application for substantial National Lottery funding.

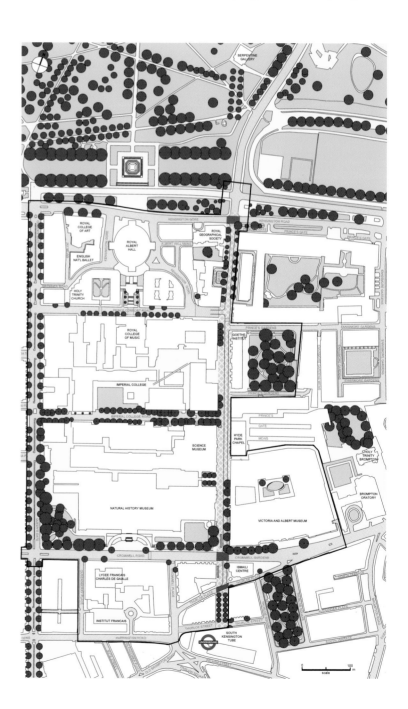

KING'S CROSS CENTRAL, N1

ALLIES AND MORRISON/PORPHYRIOS ASSOCIATES, 2002–

The lands alongside the railway to the north of King's Cross station have been the subject of a series of ambitious development proposals over the last twenty years, following the closure of the huge goods depot that occupied the site. In 1987 plans to redevelop the area primarily as a new 'office city' became public, and four developers, each working with an architectural practice, were invited to submit proposals. By the summer of 1988, the London Regeneration Consortium, in conjunction with Foster + Partners (then known as Foster Associates), had been selected as developer. The process coincided with the decision to build a new Foster-designed station for Channel Tunnel Rail Link (CTRL) trains, served by subterranean tracks. Backed by a private Act of Parliament, the masterplan for the entire area was further developed and, by

1991, took the form of a generously scaled new public park at the centre of the old goods yard, ringed by office and apartment buildings, and with landmark towers at the northern end of the site. The recession of the early 1990s killed the project, although the construction of the CTRL, via Stratford in east London, subsequently went ahead. St Pancras station was also adapted and extended to serve the Eurostar trains, and its 1860s hotel, which had been closed since 1935, restored as a new hotel and flats (see pp. 28–29).

In 2001 developer Argent, known for the successful Brindleyplace development, a mix of office and residential buildings by various architects on a brownfield site in central Birmingham, commissioned Allies and Morrison and Porphyrios Associates to prepare an entirely new masterplan for the goods-yard site. It takes account of the

new CTRL station and the proposed redevelopment of King's Cross by John McAslan + Partners (see pp. 22–23), but its approach is far removed from that of Foster. The great park has gone, as have the towers: this is to be a new city quarter linked to the districts surrounding it, a place of streets, squares and urban gardens in a recognizable London tradition. Connectivity is the principle, and new routes north from Euston into Camden Town and Islington traverse the site. The aim is to create that ever-elusive 'sense of place', with a proper balance of public and private spaces. The listed buildings, the most important of which is the magnificent granary by Lewis Cubitt (completed in 1852), are to be 'embedded' in the new fabric, not conspicuously preserved. There are hopes that the granary may be put to educational or cultural use.

The new masterplan provides for a mixed-use development, with offices concentrated towards the southern end of the site and housing to the north, along with extensive retail space. Buildings are to be low- to medium-rise. The masterplan won outline planning approval in 2006. The indications are that this will be a quarter in the Brindleyplace tradition, where many styles and schools of thought will be represented; as many as sixty architectural practices will be appointed to design buildings, working within the discipline of the masterplan. The entire scheme, one of the largest urban regeneration projects in Europe, will take at least a decade to realize. It will be judged not on its architectural variety, however, but on the degree to which it reinvents a tradition of urban design established by John Nash and the Cubitts in the nineteenth century.

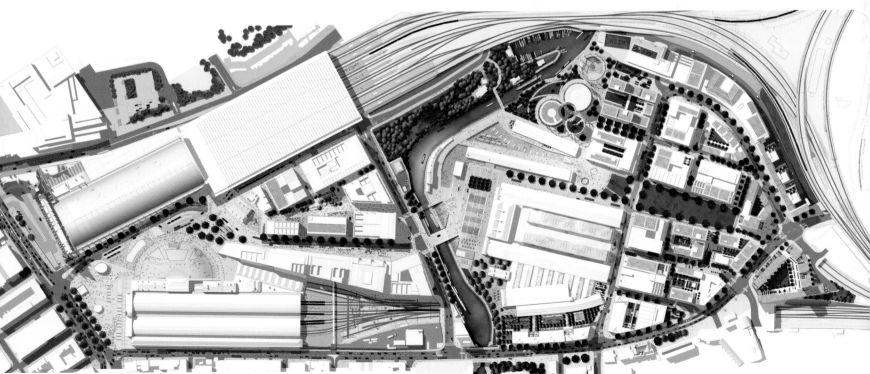

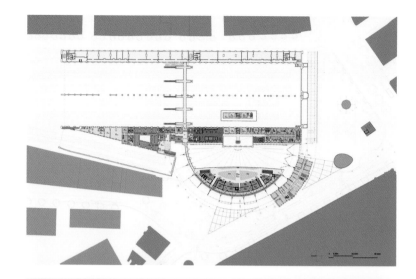

KING'S CROSS STATION, N1

JOHN MCASLAN + PARTNERS, 1998–2011

Commissioned by Railtrack (a body replaced by Network Rail), the King's Cross project is one of a number of major development schemes for London's historic railway termini, others of which appear to be currently in limbo. The reconstruction of the adjacent St Pancras station (see pp. 28–29) as the terminus of the Channel Tunnel Rail Link and as the departure point of the express shuttle link to the 2012 Olympics site has, however, provided impetus to the King's Cross station redevelopment project. In addition, King's Cross Central looks set finally to realize the development potential of the former railway lands immediately to the north of the station, the subject of abortive planning proposals over the last twenty years (see pp. 20–21).

King's Cross is the terminus of the east-coast main line from Scotland and the north. The station was built in 1851–52 to designs by Lewis Cubitt, its severely functional form contrasting – in a way that met with the approval of Modernist critics – with the florid mass of George Gilbert Scott's later Midland Grand Hotel. The original diagram of the station placed departures on the western side and arrivals on the eastern, with the space between used as sidings for railway carriages. Even after the addition of more platforms, the layout of the station presented operational challenges, and passenger facilities

were minimal. In the 1970s the clutter of temporary buildings that had developed at the southern end of the station was replaced by a new concourse that – although improving on what had existed previously – was banal in design and a poor addition to the Grade I-listed Victorian station.

John McAslan's project removes the 1970s concourse and opens the splendidly austere southern façade fully to view. A new concourse on the western side of the station incorporates the listed Great Northern Hotel and provides connections to St Pancras and the rebuilt King's Cross St Pancras Underground station. Developed in partnership with Arup, the roof of the new concourse is a structural *tour de force*: extremely lightweight, column-free, and a worthy successor to the great station roofs of the nineteenth century. Cecil Balmond of Arup, who advised on the designs, describes the new roof as "a retina of diamond cells, capable of opacity, transparency, and a widening and narrowing horizon as the curvature changes from outer rim into plunging interior tunnel. As the roof converges, the pattern closes and slips down like a mantle to the station entrance." The site of the 1970s concourse is laid out as a new public square, with the previously busy road in front of the station narrowed and tamed. Inside the station, public spaces have been extended and the entire structure renovated.

Opposite, top, and below

Opposite, middle and bottom

The new southern concourse forms a broad arc
extending towards the reconstructed St Pancras
Channel Tunnel Rail Link terminal and
incorporating the listed Great Northern Hotel.
Its lightweight roof is a modern version of the
great Victorian station roofs.

The redevelopment includes the remodelling of
the cluttered and claustrophobic Underground
station, with reorganized circulation, double-height
spaces and clean, pared-down finishes.

LOTS ROAD, CHELSEA, SW10

FARRELLS, 1996–

Terry Farrell's £500,000,000 Lots Road project in west London was finally approved in February 2006, after a long planning battle and ten years of work by the practice. During this time, the scheme changed form more than once. One of the complications of the site is that it straddles two boroughs (Hammersmith & Fulham and Kensington & Chelsea), separated by Chelsea Creek. Kensington & Chelsea strongly opposed the scheme, but, with the emphatic backing of Mayor Ken Livingstone, the application was approved by Deputy Prime Minister John Prescott, who set aside the findings of a public inquiry. For Livingstone, the fact that nearly half of the more than eight hundred flats there are to be affordable housing was a deciding factor, along with his conviction that tall buildings, provided that they are of suitable quality, are appropriate along the banks of the River Thames.

At the heart of the scheme is the former Lots Road power station, opened in 1905. Fuelled by coal brought on barges to a riverside wharf, it was built by the American financier C.T. Yerkes to power the Underground system, and continued to do so into the 1990s, when the Underground switched to electricity from the National Grid. Securing a suitable new use for this London landmark was one of the objectives of the project, although at one stage there was the possibility that it might be demolished. Farrell's final, approved scheme, exemplary in its respect for the historic structure, converts the power station to residential use, with the great turbine hall reconfigured as a full-height, glass-roofed galleria accommodating shops, restaurants and bars. The two

surviving chimneys – two others were demolished in the 1960s – will be retained, the exterior cleaned, and the elevation to Lots Road, currently a solid wall of brick, opened up to form a covered arcade, a public route into the heart of the building. Chelsea Creek, alongside the former power station, will become a new linear park and water garden.

Two new towers flank the entrance to the creek and frame the power station: the southern tower is thirty-seven storeys high, and that to the north twenty-five storeys. These buildings were inevitably the cause of prolonged debate, though the fanciful tower of nearby Chelsea Harbour, and the towers of local-authority housing at World's End, long ago set a precedent for high-rise development in the vicinity. Not everyone accepted Farrell's idea of them as "a dancing couple". They are sleek, highly glazed structures on trapezoidal plans conceived to provide extensive views from the flats. A lower-rise development south of the creek, intended to form a connection with the surrounding neighbourhood, incorporates new public routes through to the river, which was previously inaccessible at this point. It is claimed that forty-five per cent of the total development is devoted to public space, a generous allowance made possible by the use of the high-rise buildings for residential accommodation.

The new towers will inevitably have a major visual impact on Chelsea's riverside, with its run of old houses along Cheyne Walk, and on the views made famous in paintings by James Abbott McNeill Whistler – though in the early twentieth century the building of the power station itself changed

the character of the area dramatically. Upstream of Battersea Bridge, a series of recent developments has transformed the banks of the Thames, generally with regrettable results. Terry Farrell has a reputation as an inspired urbanist, however, and the success, or otherwise, of the Lots Road project may depend less on the new architecture than on the connections forged with the surrounding area, and the public gain in terms of enjoyable space and accessibility.

CONNECTIONS
The scheme provides major new pedestrian linkages through the Powerstation, linking the residential streets adjoining Lots Road with Chelsea Creek and the River Thames, providing access to a good range of local facilities and reclaiming the riverside for an enhanced urban quarter

ROOF-TOP TERRACES
Wonderful landscaped spaces will be created at roof level, like the Kensington Roof Gardens, which will reveal superb views over London and the Thames from a sheltered and safe location

VIEWS
Glazing will be restored to the huge window openings in the south facade of the Powerstation, replacing the forbidding blank appearance with light and animation, and opening up wonderful views of the Thames

PUBLIC STREET
Recreating the scale and grandeur of The Galleria in Milan, a new glass-roofed street with public access will provide a vibrant space with a mix of new uses and good local facilities, linking Lots Road to the river beyond

SCREENING PLANTING
Extensively landscaped roof areas on the northern wing of the Powerstation will prevent over-looking of the houses and gardens in the Lots Road area

RIVERSIDE APARTMENTS
Exciting living spaces will be formed out of the superb historic fabric of the Powerstation

LANDSCAPING
The cleaning of the Powerstation external facades, planting of new trees, new pavement and road surfaces, traffic calming and crossing points will all help to create a more pedestrian-friendly domain in Lots Road

CONNECTIONS
New pedestrian bridges and connections through the Powerstation will link the new public space in the heart of the building with Chelsea Creek and the River beyond

CHELSEA CREEK
A new landscaped environment will be created along a cleaner, safer Chelsea Creek, promoting new wildlife habitats and a linear park fully accessible to the public

COMMUNITY FACILITIES
Housed in the lower level of the Powerstation at one end of the street will be flexible community space for use by local residents

COLONNADE
A covered colonnade at street level will be created inside the Lots Road facade of the Powerstation along the whole length of the building, providing a safe and sheltered walkway and allowing more space in Lots Road for buses to pass

CONNECTIONS
New pedestrian connections through the Powerstation will link Lots Road and surrounding streets with the new public space in the heart of the building

Above

The existing Lots Road power station is to be converted to residential and retail use, with its chimneys retained.

Opposite

The project controversially includes two residential towers, which were given planning consent in 2006.

ROYAL ARSENAL, WOOLWICH, SE18

ALLIES AND MORRISON, 2005–

The manufacture and storage of arms and explosives began at Woolwich Warren, close to the naval dockyard, as early as the sixteenth century. By the early twentieth century, the Royal Arsenal covered more than 485 hectares, and during World War I it employed 75,000 people. After World War II the Arsenal declined rapidly, and in the late 1960s and 1970s almost half the site was cleared for new housing. Fortunately some fine historic buildings, including early eighteenth-century structures sometimes attributed to Vanbrugh, survived, and after a long era of neglect a programme of regeneration began in the mid-1990s. Key historic buildings have been retained and restored, and the "eerie and desolate scene" described by Nikolaus Pevsner's *The Buildings of England* no longer exists. Indeed, Woolwich, long perceived as a shabby and remote area of London, is now central to the development plans for the Thames Gateway.

Developer Berkeley Homes' first proposal for the Warren site, a masterplan by Broadway Malyan, was attacked by the Commission for Architecture and the Built Environment (CABE) as "depressing", and faced a public inquiry. Its response to surviving historic buildings on the site was felt to be less than sensitive. In 2005 Allies and Morrison was commissioned by Berkeley and the London Development Agency to draw up a new masterplan, including 2500 new homes, associated mixed-use buildings and open public spaces. The density of the development has been reduced, with high-rise buildings confined to the south-eastern corner of the site. CABE has welcomed the revised plans, feeling that they would create an agreeable new district. Certainly the balance between formal order and flexibility appears much improved, notwithstanding the unpredictable nature of the relationships between old and new buildings. The masterplan will be developed into detailed designs by a number of architects, but Allies and Morrison has sought to establish design codes that will protect the site's integrity and reduce the chance of the project becoming standardized in the process.

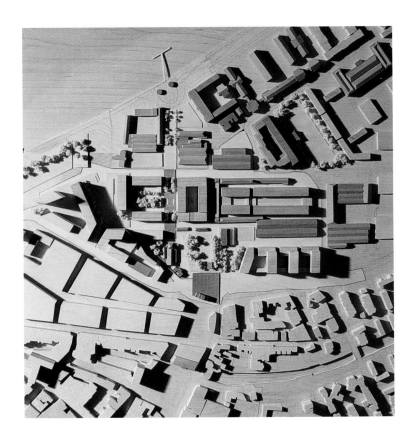

Above and opposite

The project involves the creation of a number of residential and mixed-use buildings, with a tree-filled public space at its heart (opposite, top right). Key to the design is the integration of the new buildings with historic structures, which are clustered at the centre; higher-rise construction is reserved for the edges of the site.

ST PANCRAS STATION AND CHAMBERS, N1

RHWL/RICHARD GRIFFITHS ARCHITECTS, 1996–2009

The Channel Tunnel opened in 1994 – after seven years of construction, two years late and heavily over-budget – carrying Eurostar rail services from Paris and Brussels to Grimshaw's Waterloo International station. On the English side of the Tunnel Eurostar trains used existing tracks, rather than dedicated high-speed routes, which had been created on the continental side. The decision to route Britain's own high-speed link to the east of London, serving a new station at Stratford and terminating at either King's Cross or St Pancras stations, was made as early as 1991 and subsequently confirmed by the governments of both John Major and Tony Blair.

The regeneration of the East End and the Thames estuary was seen as a major spin-off of the proposal (which originated in studies by Arup) and there was also the possibility of providing through services to the Midlands and the north, although this seems today to have been abandoned. The Channel Tunnel Rail Link (CTRL) was procured by the Private Finance Initiative route, and the London and Continental Railways (LCR) consortium won the bid to build the 108-kilometre link, which involved extensive tunnelling and other engineering challenges. Construction work began in 1998 and is due for completion late in 2007, when Eurostar services will begin to use St Pancras, and Waterloo International will close.

St Pancras was confirmed as the final destination of Eurostar in 1994, with the final abandonment of Norman Foster's proposal for a station below King's Cross, to be partly funded by development of the disused goods yard site to the north (now the site of King's Cross Central, see pp. 20–21).

Designs for an extended St Pancras were produced by Nick Derbyshire, who had headed the British Rail architectural team for the rebuilding of Liverpool Street station. The plans were subsequently developed in a new masterplan by Foster + Partners, the principle being that of a straightforward, flat-roofed shed 220 metres long, extending north of the arched shed designed by William Barlow and completed in 1876. Foster's proposals have been taken to detailed design and construction stage by the Rail Link Engineering (RLE) team, led by Alastair Lansley (who worked on the Liverpool Street project). RLE is responsible for the construction of the entire £5,000,000,000-plus CTRL project.

Impressive for its scale and generous natural light, and a genuine piece of railway architecture, the new train shed may nonetheless seem a little prosaic alongside Barlow's magnificent creation. But the strategy for adapting the latter for its new role is both highly imaginative and rigorously logical. The platforms at St Pancras are elevated above street level as a result of a decision made in the 1860s to route the new Midland line above Regent's Canal rather than under it. The station's vaulted undercroft, originally used to store beer barrels brought from Burton on Trent, will house the new check-in facilities for Eurostar, with the Channel Tunnel trains running the full length of the extended train shed above. A cut-out section allows views down into the undercroft. Trains serving the Midlands and suburban services, including fast Kent commuter trains using the CTRL route, are restricted to the new shed. The Underground station has been reconstructed in line with this strategy and in anticipation of the reconstruction of King's Cross station (see pp. 22–23).

The great hotel that forms a frontispiece to St Pancras was designed by George Gilbert Scott, closed as long ago as 1935 and long used as railway offices. Once vacated by British Rail, it was in a very poor condition and had to be stabilized by an external restoration and cleaning programme in 1993–95. This revealed the sheer splendour of Scott's building, which had been little altered inside since it opened. Work began in 2006 on a refurbishment and conversion project developed by Manhattan Loft Corporation at a cost of £100,000,000. The Marriott International chain of hotels is creating a 254-bedroom hotel in the building, restoring all the principal original interiors, with Richard Griffiths Architects overseeing conservation works. The overall scheme, for which RHWL is responsible, includes sixty-seven luxury flats in the upper levels of the building. The future of the hotel is finally assured: forty years ago, its demolition was seriously proposed.

With a direct, express rail service from the new station to the 2012 Olympics site, St Pancras will soon emerge as the focus of a regenerated London quarter. And travellers arriving in London by Eurostar will certainly have a spectacular introduction to the capital.

Opposite

Stratford City transforms neglected industrial land into a mixed-use quarter, focusing on the new International station.

Below

The project will include new waterside public spaces and parks, providing suitable surroundings for those expected to flood into the area for the Games, and lasting improvements for residents.

STRATFORD CITY, E15

FLETCHER PRIEST ARCHITECTS/
ARUP URBAN DESIGN/WEST 8
2004–12

The 73-hectare Stratford City site is one of the most extensive exercises in urban regeneration in Europe. The planning application lodged in 2004 and subsequently approved was the largest ever submitted in London. Developers Stanhope, Multiplex and Westfield, partners with London & Continental Railways in the development consortium for the site, proposed 1,200,000 square metres of residential, retail and commercial development. More than 30,000 people are likely to work there, and there will be homes for 11,000.

The impetus to develop the site west of Stratford town centre, which was formerly occupied by a railway works and freight yards, came from the routing of the Channel Tunnel Rail Link (CTRL) through Stratford (which already has mainline, Underground and Docklands Light Railway connections). The focus of the project is the new Stratford International station, which is to be served by Eurostar and will also act as the principal means of access for spectators at the 2012 Olympic Games. London's victory in July 2005 in the contest to stage the Games created fears of a conflict of interest between the developers of Stratford City and the Olympic organizers (now the Olympic Delivery Authority), who were charged with masterplanning the selected Games site in the lower Lea Valley, extending from

Stratford to the Thames. An agreement between the two parties, however, neatly integrated the Olympic Village with the residential element of Stratford City, so that construction of the athletes' housing (with accommodation for 17,000 competitors) could begin promptly. By the summer of 2006 it appeared that the two massive projects were moving forward in tandem, and a planning application was submitted for Zone I of Stratford City (140,000 square metres of retailing, 93,000 square metres of offices and five hundred homes, plus leisure and hotel developments). This phase includes a new boulevard to connect the new railway station to the existing town centre.

The masterplan by Fletcher Priest, Arup and West 8 is based on the idea of a series of distinct neighbourhoods and will involve commissioning a number of architectural practices, with the emphasis on high-quality architecture and landscaping. The latter has already been modelled using the huge amounts of spoil excavated from the CTRL tunnel and station box: if spread evenly, it was estimated, it would raise the ground level across the whole site by around 6 metres. Good connections, mixed-use provision and the creation of generous public spaces are the stated aims of the project. Construction of the first buildings at Stratford City is scheduled to begin in the summer of 2007.

TERMINAL 5, HEATHROW AIRPORT, TW6

RICHARD ROGERS PARTNERSHIP, 1989–2008

Richard Rogers's new terminal at Madrid's Barajas Airport, winner of the 2006 Stirling Prize, opened eight years after it was commissioned in 1997. In comparison, the twenty years from commissioning to opening at Terminal 5, Heathrow Airport, seems to underline the perversity of the British planning system. There were widespread objections to a new terminal and also to the expansion of air traffic into London, but ultimately a hugely expensive public inquiry convened in 1993 resulted in approval for the project, given in 2001.

The character of the project has changed radically over time, with the single-level terminal proposed in Rogers's 1989 competition-winning scheme abandoned after the public inquiry ruled against the use of greenbelt land, beyond the A3044, for parking. A redesign produced a scheme in which arriving and departing passengers were segregated on two levels, with 'canyons' (a device used also at Barajas) drawing natural light into the heart of the building. By 1999 these, too, had been removed in favour of a 'shed' in the tradition of the Centre Georges Pompidou in Paris by Rogers and Renzo Piano, completed more than thirty years ago. The scheme, recognizing the realities of air travel in the twenty-first century, caters for the dramatic changes that will inevitably arise as security tightens, airlines come and go, new check-in technologies are introduced, larger aircraft are put into use, and retailing – the prime source of income for airport operators – expands inexorably. Shops, offices, passenger lounges and other facilities in the new terminal are conceived as freestanding units that can be dismantled and reconfigured as required – like a theatre, where the scenery changes regularly.

This is a shed on a dramatic scale that will handle thirty million passengers annually. The vast majority of them will arrive by public transport, using the Underground and bus services, and it is planned that mainline high-speed rail services will connect the airport with Europe via the Channel Tunnel. One 85,000-square-metre satellite building is being constructed in tandem with the terminal, and there is provision for a second when needed.

Architecturally, Terminal 5 will be a spectacular experience for passengers in the tradition of the great nineteenth-century train sheds: the departure area, contained under the elegant double-curve roof, will be as dramatic as any comparable space in the world, a far remove from the cramped spaces found in some of the older Heathrow terminals (which face redevelopment). The terminal is designed to be easily navigated by outgoing and incoming passengers: it will take two minutes to reach the check-in zone from the rail platform.

There were moments when it appeared that Terminal 5 could be 'value-engineered' beyond recognition, with any exciting features dropped at the request of cost consultants, and the role of Richard Rogers Partnership reduced to the provision of an external envelope. Indeed, four other architectural practices are involved with various aspects of the project. The completed terminal, however, will be recognizably a Rogers building and an impressive gateway to London, though not quite the expression of national pride that other nations might have created.

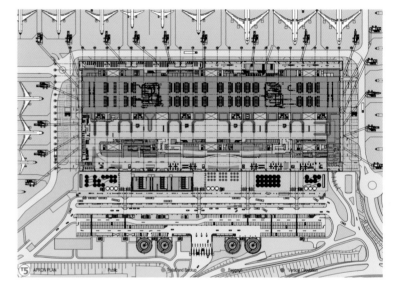

Above

Rationally (though conventionally) organized, Heathrow's new Terminal 5 is a spectacular shed in the tradition both of Richard Rogers's earlier work and of nineteenth-century rail termini.

Opposite

The terminal includes impressive new public spaces and convenient links to public transport, which will be the principal means of access for travellers.

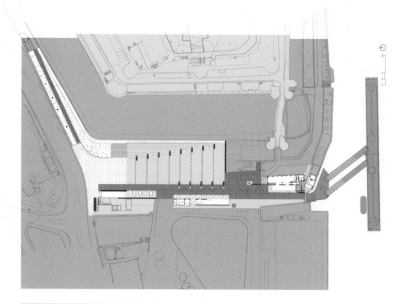

TOWER OF LONDON ENVIRONS SCHEME
TOWER HILL, EC3

STANTON WILLIAMS, 1999–2004

"The most important work of military architecture in England" is the unequivocal verdict of Nikolaus Pevsner's *The Buildings of England* on the Tower of London. After a series of restorations, however – notably that begun by Anthony Salvin in 1852 – parts of the great complex appear as exercises in fanciful mock medievalism, sometimes obscuring the much older structures. The draining of the moat in the mid-nineteenth century and the ever-increasing scale of development in the eastern sector of the City have further reduced the visual impact of this legendary monument, beloved of tourists but sadly not visited by many Londoners. (The wonderful Romanesque chapel in the White Tower is alone worth the admission charge.)

The design competition organized in 1999 by Historic Royal Palaces (the independent charity that manages the site) for a new public space and visitor facilities immediately west of the Tower reflected a recognition of the practical inadequacies – and sheer tackiness – of the existing clutter of kiosks, variegated paving and street furniture. The five-year, £14,500,000 project involved complex issues of archaeology and exhaustive consultation with interested parties before planning consent was given at the end of 2000. The new square opened in the summer of 2004.

Stanton Williams, a practice that made its reputation initially with fastidious exhibition and interior design, was selected because of the straightforwardness and simplicity of its proposals. These qualities characterize the finished product, which is certainly one of the best new public spaces created in London in decades. The plan is remarkable for the way in which it integrates the Tower and the City, creating a free flow of space into the adjacent Tower Place office development by Foster + Partners – no masterpiece, but a vast improvement on what it replaced – and framing views of Edwin Cooper's monumental Port of London Authority building to the north.

The architects have essentially created a public square, around 200 metres long and 50 metres wide, sloping down to the Thames and providing a clear and accessible visitor route – simply paved in granite – into the Tower. Street furniture and planting have been kept to a minimum, and lighting and seating integrated into the paving scheme. This approach is rare in Britain, where every new public space seems to end up cluttered with seats, light fittings, planters and other extraneous bric-a-brac. The new buildings, which contain ticket offices, cafés and shops, are conceived as a family of pavilions using a minimalist aesthetic of steel, glass and polished granite. Everything is sober, elegant and made to last, if a little corporate in feel. But it is the sheer quality of the space that makes quibbles about such details irrelevant.

Above and opposite
The scheme offers a simple but pleasant and welcoming space in the heart of a tourist-crowded area of London. Elegant and hard-wearing granite is the predominant material, and clutter has been kept to a minimum.

CULTURE

319 PORTOBELLO ROAD
MEADOWCROFT GRIFFIN ARCHITECTS

THE ARCHITECTURE FOUNDATION BUILDING
ZAHA HADID ARCHITECTS

ARCHITECTURE GALLERY, VICTORIA AND ALBERT MUSEUM
GARETH HOSKINS ARCHITECTS

CAMDEN ARTS CENTRE
TONY FRETTON ARCHITECTS/MUF

DARWIN CENTRE, PHASE TWO, NATURAL HISTORY MUSEUM
C.F. MØLLER ARCHITECTS

GORMLEY STUDIO
DAVID CHIPPERFIELD ARCHITECTS

HACKNEY EMPIRE
TIM RONALDS ARCHITECTS

IDEA STORE WHITECHAPEL
ADJAYE/ASSOCIATES

KEW GARDENS ALPINE HOUSE
WILKINSON EYRE

KINGS PLACE
DIXON JONES

LONDON LIBRARY EXTENSION
HAWORTH TOMPKINS

NATIONAL GALLERY, EAST WING, PHASE 2
DIXON JONES

OPEN-AIR THEATRE, BARRA HALL PARK
BRADY MALLALIEU ARCHITECTS

PUMP HOUSE
DE PAOR ARCHITECTS

THE ROUNDHOUSE
JOHN MCASLAN + PARTNERS

ROYAL GEOGRAPHICAL SOCIETY EXTENSION
STUDIO DOWNIE

SIOBHAN DAVIES STUDIOS
SARAH WIGGLESWORTH ARCHITECTS

UNICORN THEATRE FOR CHILDREN
KEITH WILLIAMS ARCHITECTS

VICTORIA AND ALBERT MUSEUM OF CHILDHOOD
CARUSO ST JOHN

WHITECHAPEL ART GALLERY EXPANSION
ROBBRECHT EN DAEM ARCHITECTEN

YOUNG VIC
HAWORTH TOMPKINS

319 PORTOBELLO ROAD, NOTTING HILL, W10

MEADOWCROFT GRIFFIN ARCHITECTS, 2001–05

Located at the scruffier northern end of Portobello Road in west London – beyond the Westway and the endurance of most tourists visiting the famous market – Meadowcroft Griffin's gallery and house for Simon Finch, a dealer of art and rare books, replaces a decrepit nineteenth-century property on the end of a short terrace. The exterior of the new building preserves the integrity of the terrace, typical of those lining Portobello Road, with its regular fenestration and use of white render. Inside, the architects have created four levels where there were previously three – including a new basement gallery – and increased floorspace by a remarkable fifty per cent. This is an example of the Victorian terraced house radically rethought, and is an interesting debut for the young practice, founded in 2001 by Philip Meadowcroft (a former employee of Eric Parry) and Ann Griffin (who worked for Haworth Tompkins).

The traditional design formula of the terraced house starts to break down at the corner of the new building, where a window, providing views of the market below, wraps around on to a side façade clad in steel mesh. A narrow slit of glazing extends around the corner at attic level. The shop window to the street collides with the residential space above, with a lowered floor level providing greater height for the first-floor living area. A glazed section, located where a shop sign would normally be placed, exposes the concrete structure of the lower areas of the building, giving way to a steel frame for the upper floors, and makes a connection between the public and private spaces. Internal finishes – exposed concrete, render, timber and metal – are very straightforward, providing an appropriate setting for works of art.

At once contextual and subversive, this project – "urban editing", as the architects describe it – 'collages' materials and uses in a way that reflects the interest of young London architects in the life of the city and their respect for the abiding strengths of its timeworn fabric.

Right and opposite

At the northern end of Portobello Road, Meadowcroft Griffin have transformed a run-of-the-mill Victorian house into a stylish gallery and residence. The external alterations provide some hint of the extensive reconfiguration of the interior, where exposed concrete and render provide a neutral setting for works of art.

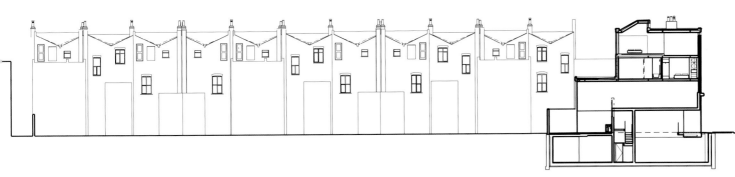

THE ARCHITECTURE FOUNDATION BUILDING
SOUTHWARK STREET, SOUTHWARK, SE1

ZAHA HADID ARCHITECTS, 2006–08

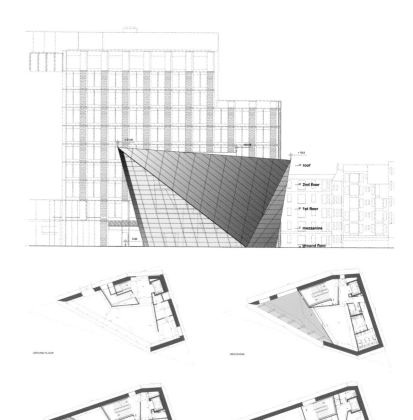

The Architecture Foundation has been an important player on the London architectural scene since its launch in 1991, with Richard Burdett as director and Richard Rogers as chairman. It is finally getting a permanent home (courtesy of Land Securities, developer of Bankside 123, with which it is to share a site), one purpose-built, moreover, to the designs of one of the world's leading architects.

In the 2004 competition for the new building, Zaha Hadid beat, among others, Caruso St John and Foreign Office Architects. For Hadid, who is now building on a large scale internationally, the commission was modest but highly prestigious, as it is her first building in London.

The site is at the junction of Southwark Street and Great Guildford Street, a triangle at the south-eastern tip of the Bankside 123 development (designed by Allies and Morrison). Tate Modern is a short walk away. The competition brief asked for a building that was "something between a chapel and a billboard", an eye-catcher with exceptional exhibition spaces and offices for the Foundation. A post-competition review of the project revealed some shortcomings in the original brief, and the size of the building (and its budget) were increased, with consequent delays to its completion; Allies and Morrison was

appointed as "co-ordinating architect". A planning application was submitted in the summer of 2006, and completion is scheduled for 2008.

If something of the impact of Hadid's competition scheme has been lost in all this, the building will still have a sensational presence on a rather depressing thoroughfare. Hadid conceives it as "a sculptural element, mysterious and intriguing, and not referable to traditional architectural typologies". Its shape, a mirror-clad diamond engineered by Adams Kara Taylor as "a pure architectural statement", responds to the triangular site. The 640-square-metre building is organized on three levels, with a mezzanine between ground and first floors. Flexible exhibition and lecture spaces extend over the ground, mezzanine and first floors, and the offices and boardroom are on the top floor. Traditional divisions using floors, walls and ceilings are lost in favour of a single abstract sculptural continuity.

The "dematerializing" qualities of the scheme are deliberate, giving the building a distinctive identity in its predominantly commercial context. With a front door on the street, it is well placed to lure in visitors to Tate Modern and infuse a potent architectural element into the cultural brew of Bankside.

Opposite

The building includes exhibition and lecture spaces, and offices, spread over three levels, with an additional mezzanine between ground- and first-floor levels.

Right and below

Zaha Hadid's first London building, slotted into a tight corner site, forms a striking presence amid intensive commercial development on Southwark Street.

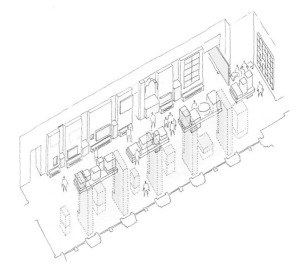

ARCHITECTURE GALLERY, VICTORIA AND ALBERT MUSEUM, SOUTH KENSINGTON, SW7

GARETH HOSKINS ARCHITECTS, 2001–04

The abandonment of Daniel Libeskind's fanciful (and, in practical terms, rather irrelevant) 'Spiral' project drove the Victoria and Albert Museum (V&A) to look seriously at its existing vast, sprawling complex of buildings, some of which was under-used. Under its director, Mark Jones, the museum has seen radical changes, among them the redesign of the entrance sequence from Exhibition Road, including a shop, sculpture galleries, and the John Madejski Garden by Kim Wilkie; and an education centre designed by Softroom Architects, in the Henry Cole Wing, which opens in 2007.

Within the buildings (their mix of styles and dates concealed by Aston Webb's ebullient Cromwell Road frontage, completed in 1909), the collections are being rearranged into themed 'quarters', with the aim of breaking down the old divisions between departments.

Gareth Hoskins Architects won a competition in 2001 to design an architecture gallery for the museum. Though relatively modest in cost, the project is prestigious, being Britain's first permanent architecture gallery. It also marks the launch of a groundbreaking collaboration between the V&A and the Royal Institute of British Architects (RIBA), which has rehoused its drawings collection in the Henry Cole Wing. The exhibits in the architecture gallery are drawn from the collections of both institutions, and reflect the history of British architecture from the seventeenth century to the present day.

The space given over to the new gallery formerly contained a rather frigid display of ceramics, which was relocated. Hoskins' installation is designed to have a minimum impact on the historic fabric, with new display cases (the old ones were ripped out) conceived as free-standing structures within the space. The lighting scheme is intended to highlight and dramatize the rich detail of Aston Webb's gallery. The revamped gallery is seen as a 'street', offering a variety of routes exploring the course of architecture in Britain from Christopher Wren to Norman Foster. Over the last half-century, new gallery fit-outs have paid scant respect to the architecture of the building; here, Hoskins set out to celebrate it.

Above, below and opposite
The product of a collaboration between the V&A and the RIBA, the Architecture Gallery transforms an existing space within the museum to form a showcase for a changing display of historic and contemporary architecture.

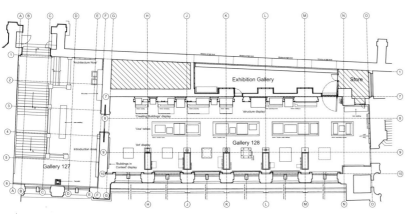

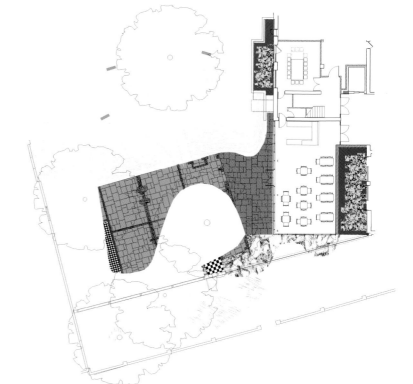

CAMDEN ARTS CENTRE
ARKWRIGHT ROAD/FINCHLEY ROAD
CAMDEN, NW3

TONY FRETTON ARCHITECTS/MUF, 2004–05

The building now housing Camden Arts Centre was designed by Arnold S. Tayler and opened in 1897 as the Hampstead Central Library. It is an attractive, if modest, building in an Arts and Crafts Tudor manner, although the original interiors were largely lost when it was gutted during World War II. The library closed after the new central library at Swiss Cottage, designed by Basil Spence, opened in the mid-1960s. The building was converted into an arts centre, a role it has fulfilled with considerable success for more than thirty years, attracting up to 45,000 visitors annually.

Tony Fretton's project has provided additional facilities for the centre's users, without changing the essential character of the place as an exhibition and education venue with close links to the local community. As a prelude to the project, the centre commissioned Muf to interview building users and staff, to research the history of the site and to include their findings in the brief. Muf was subsequently responsible for the new layout of the garden to the rear of the centre, which had previously not been accessible to the public.

The key element in Fretton's project is the provision of a new step-free, ground-floor public entrance area facing Finchley Road – the former entrance on Arkwright

Road, up steep steps, has been closed – with direct access to the café and bookshop and views right into the building. This radical intervention involved cutting large openings into the existing façade. Upstairs, at gallery level, the project assumed a very different character, one of renovation of the fabric and renewal of the services, with the spaces remaining essentially unchanged. Work was completed in time for the centre's reopening early in 2004. The final phase of the £4,600,000 project – the installation of a wall comprising ten panels of 40-millimetre-thick glass, each 2.8 metres high, facing Finchley Road and forming an acoustic barrier – was completed in the autumn of 2005.

Muf's garden scheme makes reference to the history of the area, revealing the footprints of houses that once stood on the garden site, and using a mix of paving and planting to explore the interface between nature and architecture. A paved terrace extends from the café into the sloping garden.

At quite modest cost (funding came from the National Lottery, local authority and private donors), this exemplary project has re-equipped an important local amenity not only to continue in its established role but also to expand its constituency and influence.

Right, top
Previously disused garden space has been transformed to a design by Muf.

Right, middle, and opposite
A glazed wall facing Finchley Road screens the refurbished Camden Arts Centre from the noise of traffic and forms a public marker for the project.

Right, bottom
The gallery spaces have been have been re-equipped and renovated, but are essentially unchanged.

DARWIN CENTRE, PHASE TWO
NATURAL HISTORY MUSEUM
CROMWELL ROAD, SOUTH KENSINGTON, SW7

C.F. MØLLER ARCHITECTS, 2002–07

The first phase of the Natural History Museum's Darwin Centre, designed by HOK, opened in 2002. The centre houses the museum's vast zoological archive – more than twenty million specimens of animals, birds and fish preserved in alcohol, some of which were collected two hundred and fifty years ago – and allows, for the first time, a degree of public access to this internationally renowned collection. The second phase of the project will contain the entomological and botanical collections, as well as laboratories and offices. Danish practice C.F. Møller Architects won the commission in competition in 2001. Its new building replaces a utilitarian interwar block tacked on to Alfred Waterhouse's masterpiece.

With a project cost of around £70,000,000, and covering 19,500 square metres, the building forms an effective link between the original museum and the HOK block. Externally, it is highly transparent, a relatively neutral neighbour to the Waterhouse building. Behind is an eight-storey-high atrium overlooking the museum's Wildlife Garden. Through the all-glass, west-facing façade, the 'cocoon' that forms the core, indeed, the *raison d'être*, of the building is visible. The cocoon is a massive structure that cannot be seen in its entirety from any one point. It symbolizes the collections it contains and dominates the public spaces that surround it. Inside it is a series of environmentally controlled storage spaces for the precious specimens. A route for visitors winds up, over, around and through the archives, offering glimpses into the laboratories and allowing the public to see and experience spaces that were previously out of bounds, without disturbing the scholarly research work going on inside them. One of the benefits of the scheme is improved circulation within the museum.

The design of the cocoon involved intensive exploration of its geometry and structure. It is constructed of walls nearly 0.4 metres thick to ensure stable environmental conditions inside. The storage spaces are necessarily mechanically cooled and ventilated, but the emphasis in the project has been on a low-energy agenda, with a hierarchy of servicing solutions.

Following on from Richard MacCormac's addition to the Science Museum, and work by Norman Foster and Kohn Pedersen Fox for Imperial College, not to mention HOK's Darwin Centre, Phase I, this building adds significantly to the sum of high-quality new architecture in 'Albertopolis', the group of cultural institutions in Kensington.

Below and opposite, top, and bottom right
The second phase of the Darwin Centre consists of a cocoon housing the museum's entomological and botanical collections set in a glazed box containing day-lit public spaces, offices and services.

Opposite, bottom left
The new building contrasts spectacularly with the ornate architecture of Waterhouse's museum.

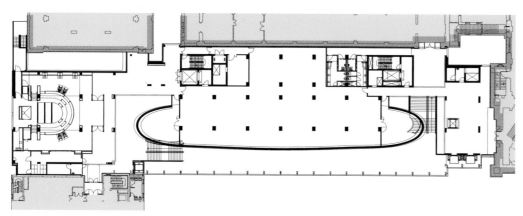

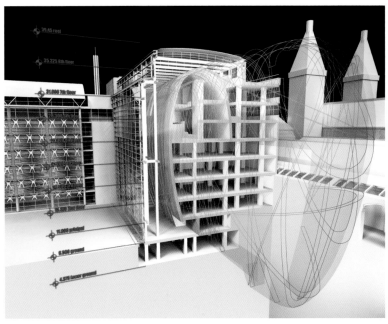

GORMLEY STUDIO, ISLINGTON, N7

DAVID CHIPPERFIELD ARCHITECTS, 2003

The continued paucity of built works by David Chipperfield in Britain – the Henley Rowing Museum, Oxfordshire, is his largest completed to date – is extraordinary, given the formidable international reputation of an architect whose work seems continually to scale new heights in terms of both refinement and inventiveness. Chipperfield's work has an apparently effortless appropriateness that reflects his intuitive feeling for materials and strong sense of place.

Antony Gormley is not only one of the most celebrated of living British sculptors, but also an artist with a remarkable facility for communicating with the public: his *Angel of the North* is a popular landmark in the north-east. Gormley's studio is located above the railway cutting that leads into King's Cross, in an area of industrial sheds, and its design was clearly strongly influenced by the no-nonsense character of the locality. The studio is a workplace – Gormley does not live on the site – and at first glance appears to be simply a highly functional container for the conception and production of works of art, though it is soon obvious that it is something altogether more sophisticated. Gormley's work is often very large in scale, so some generous spaces were vital, but smaller, more intimate studios and offices were also specified in the brief. The work that goes

on here may range from sketching and discussion to the assembly of large pieces of sculpture. The galvanized steel staircases that are the most distinctive feature of the exterior lead up from the enclosed entrance yard to upper-floor studios at both ends of the building, book-ending the full-height main studio. All these spaces benefit from even light from the north, while the main façade of the building is punctuated by a series of window openings, irregularly but far from artlessly disposed.

The Gormley studio can be read as Chipperfield's passionate counterblast against the fad for 'icons' that gripped the architectural world at the beginning of the twenty-first century. The building was the outcome of a very close collaboration between architect and client, a relationship that was both fertile and, at times, tense. Chipperfield's first instinct was for a flat-roofed structure, but it was the absolute need for perfect daylight that drove him back to the classic saw-toothed factory form. He has described the completed building as "a pastiche of a nineteenth-century building, a kind of perfect version of a building that you should be able to find, but when you start looking it is actually very difficult". But the studio is less pastiche than a fascinating commentary on London's neglected industrial vernacular.

Right
The main internal space is lofty and highly functional, a workshop for the fabrication of artworks in heavy-duty materials.

The first-floor studios are accessed via metal staircases.

Opposite
The studio takes its cue from the simple industrial sheds found in this area of London, with saw-toothed roofs providing ample north light.

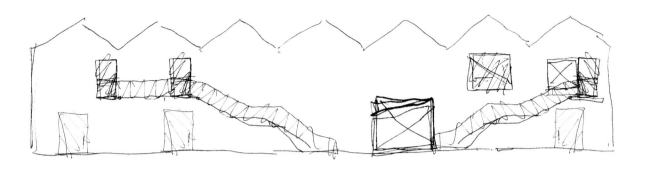

HACKNEY EMPIRE, MARE STREET
HACKNEY, E8

TIM RONALDS ARCHITECTS, 1999–2004

London is full of lost theatres. The Hackney Empire in east London could well have been one of them, had it not been for the local community, which loved the place and did not want to lose it, and a cast of prominent outsiders who rallied to the cause of saving and reinvigorating it. The playwright and actor Harold Pinter, for example, who was born yards from the "wonderful" theatre, recalled his parents taking him to see the comedian Max Miller on stage there. Comedian Paul Merton commented of the Empire: "It's been an absolute joy and has reminded me of why I do what I do." Famous performers from Marie Lloyd to Ralph Fiennes have trod its boards.

The Empire is a significant work of the great theatre architect Frank Matcham. It was constructed (in thirty-eight weeks) in 1901, with seats for 2800, and launched some of the greatest stars of music hall. By the 1980s, however, after years in use as a bingo hall, it faced demolition. Impresario Ronald Muldoon started a rescue operation, with the building vested in a charitable trust. A mixed programme was presented, ranging from stand-up comedy and world music to traditional pantomime and opera. An architectural competition held in 1997 was won by Tim Ronalds, with Homa and Sima Farjadi. After it became apparent that the project was too costly to get National Lottery backing, Tim Ronalds Architects developed a somewhat reduced version (costing under £20,000,000), and the actor and comedian Griff Rhys Jones led a successful fund-raising campaign. The auditorium reopened early in 2004 and the scheme was fully completed in the autumn of that year.

The project combines restoration of the historic theatre with new build. Services needed total renewal, and facilities for both audience and performers were dire. Issues that did not trouble Matcham, for example access for the disabled, had to be addressed. A key requirement was gaining more space on the cramped site in Mare Street. Fortunately it was possible to acquire the corner site next to the theatre; the undistinguished pub that stood there was demolished and a new block constructed, with a large bar on the ground floor and a hospitality/function room and small studio theatre on the upper levels. The new building also provides additional access to the auditorium, and its exterior features the first use in London of large supergraphics in the style of American architect Robert Venturi. The 3.5-metre-high letters spelling out the name of the theatre are made of terracotta, like the external ornament on Matcham's building.

Although the Empire is listed Grade II*, English Heritage (the government's adviser on the historic environment) allowed a radical reconstruction of the entire backstage domain, with a big new flytower clad in fritted glass panels. A new get-in area gives trucks direct access to the stage to install and remove scenery. The new dressing-rooms finally offer performers reasonably decent accommodation. The Matcham auditorium and front-of-house areas remain fundamentally unchanged. A restoration of the 1901 colour scheme was considered, but research revealed that the original hues were extremely pale and at odds with the current taste among the public for rich and warm theatre interiors, so a revised version of the scheme done in the 1960s was carried out. One of the great strengths of the project is the fact that the Empire appears to have been little altered, instead merely freshened up. This is a transformation operation that wears its colours lightly.

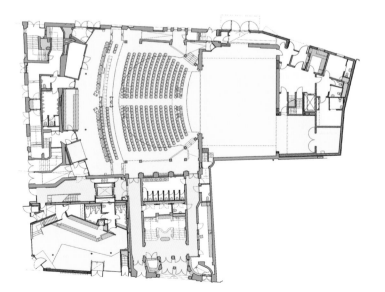

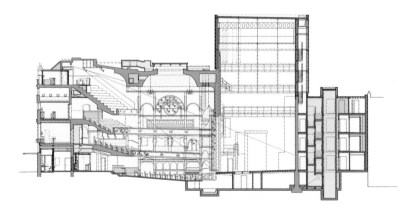

IDEA STORE WHITECHAPEL
WHITECHAPEL ROAD, WHITECHAPEL, E1

ADJAYE/ASSOCIATES, 2001–05

The 'Idea Stores' developed in east London by the borough of Tower Hamlets represent an attempt to reinvent the public library as a building that contains extended learning and community facilities as well as books, and that is open at weekends and late into the evening. The first Idea Store (a conversion of an existing building) opened in 2002 in Bow, with that in Chrisp Street, Poplar, designed by David Adjaye, following in 2004. The Whitechapel Idea Store, located opposite the Royal London Hospital and close to a Sainsbury's supermarket, is the flagship building of the programme. It replaces Whitechapel's Victorian library, incorporated into the extended Whitechapel Art Gallery (see pp. 74–75). With about 450,000 square metres of space over five storeys, this is a large building with, Adjaye argues, an appropriate civic presence. It is, he says, "a glamorous place that's open to everybody". Its full-height glazed façades, with panels of blue and green glass providing shading as well as an element of animation, take their cue from commercial architecture.

Unlike Will Alsop's Peckham Library in south London, opened in 2000 – itself a pioneering attempt to rethink the library – the Idea Store connects seamlessly to the street, with the children's library at ground level. A projecting glazed screen in front of the façade provides some insulation from the noise of Whitechapel Road. It also shields the escalator that scoops up passers-by from the pavement and rises to the second floor (in an echo of Rogers and Piano's iconic Pompidou Centre in Paris).

Interiors are straightforward and made to be hard-wearing, with details that are basic and sometimes a little crude, but have a reassuring generosity of scale that underwrites the civic objectives of the project. The top-floor space includes a café with fine views of the City, the East End and the towers of Canary Wharf. To the rear of the building, a lower block contains a double-height dance studio and therapy suite, spaces that would not be found in a traditional library.

The Idea Store may not be quite the major work that admirers of David Adjaye's architecture had hoped for. However, it is a building that provides an enjoyable, highly sociable atmosphere and that seems to fit comfortably into the Whitechapel scene. It is genuinely populist – and popular – though rich in ideas. It succeeds where a more cerebral project, such as Venturi Scott Brown's Sainsbury Wing at the National Gallery, which had similar objectives, falls flat.

Above and far left
The lively market, despite being both the setting and, to some degree, the inspiration for the building, provides a startling contrast to its clean, modern glazed façade.

Left
The interiors are straightforward but colourful and house a range of activities not found in a conventional library.

Opposite
Essentially a reinvention of the public library, the Idea Store is entered from Whitechapel Road via a broad slot containing escalators, behind a colourful glazed façade.

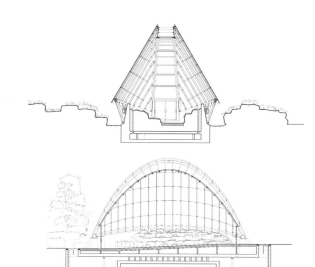

KEW GARDENS ALPINE HOUSE, KEW, TW9

WILKINSON EYRE, 2002–06

Kew Gardens, which now attracts one million visitors annually, has constructed a series of glasshouses since it opened to the public in 1841, the most famous being the Palm House (1841–48), designed by Decimus Burton and Richard Turner. The previous Alpine House, completed in the late 1970s, was not one of Kew's more successful commissions. It was badly sited, in a 'back of house' area, needed major refurbishment, and, more to the point, provided an unsuitable habitat for alpine plants, which had to be nurtured elsewhere.

A generous donation by Edwin Davies made it possible for Kew to develop a new alpine house, opened in March 2006. The commissioning of Wilkinson Eyre followed on from the practice's strategic development plan for the gardens, completed in 2002. Wilkinson Eyre was also appointed to build an extension to Kew's Jodrell Laboratory on the site of the former alpine house. There are memories in this landmark structure of Wilkinson Eyre's most famous project to date, the 2002 Stirling Prize-winning Millennium Bridge at Gateshead in north-east England. But why should a glasshouse resemble a bridge?

The form of the building is anything but arbitrary. Designed in conjunction with greenhouse specialist Green Mark International, structural engineer Dewhurst Macfarlane and services engineer Atelier 10, the new alpine house addresses the environmental failings of the previous structure as well as offering vastly improved public access to the internationally important plant collection. The provision of controlled light, with adequate shading in summer, and of the constant flow of cool air typical of alpine habitats, was fundamental to the demanding technical brief. The site is in the Rock Garden, close to an existing glasshouse complex, and to which the building forms a new gateway.

The twin arches that define the structure enclose a tall, narrow space ventilated using the 'stack effect', by which fresh air is drawn in at low level and exhausted through opening vents at the top of the building. (A supplementary mechanical ventilation system provides a back-up and supplies low-level heating in very cold weather.) Internal environmental conditions are strictly controlled by faceted cladding panels, using clear, low-iron glass on a structural glazing system; an automatic retractable blind system; and the orientation of the building, with the long elevations facing east and west. Just 144 square metres in area and 10 metres tall at its highest point, this is a small building with a big presence. Its complete transparency is stunning, though this is the outcome of a practical and technical, rather than an aesthetic, agenda. It is a building in a fine tradition of metal and glass architecture, pioneered in Britain, and a notable addition to the landscape of Kew.

Right
Striking in form and resembling a bridge, the structure of the alpine house reflects a sophisticated environmental strategy. Air is drawn in from underneath the building and cools the interior, exiting through vents at the top.

Opposite
The glazing system includes a series of blinds to control temperatures within the building.

KINGS PLACE, YORK WAY, N1

DIXON JONES, 2002–08

Dixon Jones's work shows a remarkable diversity, extending from the refurbishment of historic buildings to major infrastructure projects, such as that for Exhibition Road in Kensington (see pp. 18–19) and large commercial buildings. The practice won the commission for Kings Place in competition in 2002 – Demetri Porphyrios and John McAslan were among the other architects on the shortlist. Construction started in 2006 with occupation scheduled for early 2008.

The highly unusual nature of the £96,000,000 project reflects the interest of the developer, Peter Millican of Parabola Land, in cultural regeneration. Alongside 28,000 square metres of office space, much of it already let to *The Guardian* and *The Observer* newspapers (which are quitting their existing unattractive premises on Farringdon Road), the building contains a 425-seat concert hall, teaching and practice rooms, and a full-size rehearsal hall. These facilities will be used by two leading orchestras, the Orchestra of the Age of Enlightenment and the London Sinfonietta, which until now have both lacked a permanent base. The ground floor and basement contain art galleries, restaurants and cafés open to the public, capitalizing on the building's location next to Battlebridge Basin on the Regent's Canal. The stone-clad rotunda on the north-eastern corner provides a dramatic canalside landmark and helps to break down the building's large volume into distinctly separate elements. To the south, the masonry-framed Pavilion, with a generously scaled waterfront arcade, provides a point of transition to the surviving nineteenth-century warehouses, now converted to office use, along the western side of the basin.

The western edge of the development abuts York Way, a road with heavy traffic, and looks across the railway tracks into King's Cross station and the site of the forthcoming massive King's Cross Central scheme (see pp. 20–21). The elevation of the building here is triple-glazed, its outer layer an undulating, reflecting glass screen (a "crinkle-crankle wall" as Edward Jones describes it) that forms its principal public face. This slick, if slightly bland, feature is an expression of the offices behind, which are accessed from an entrance foyer at ground-floor level.

Office developments in Britain are customarily inaccessible to the public – more so than ever, in the light of the terrorist attacks on London in 2005 – so that the innovative approach of Kings Place is refreshing. Stealing a march on King's Cross Central, but part of an ongoing renaissance of the surrounding area, the scheme could before long form part of an enjoyable urban promenade linking Camden Town to the East End.

Above and opposite, top left
The external form of Kings Place responds both to the heavily trafficked York Way and to the more tranquil context of the canal behind.

Opposite, top right and bottom
Containing offices for two national newspapers, the building is innovative in also housing extensive public spaces, and a concert hall and rehearsal space for two leading orchestras.

LONDON LIBRARY EXTENSION
ST JAMES'S SQUARE, SW1

HAWORTH TOMPKINS, 2007–08

Below

The project involves the simplification and rationalization of the library building, resulting in a more logical arrangement of departments, as well as the construction of extra space for readers and for storage. Central to the design is the light well (left), which is opened up, improving the basement, in which the Periodicals and Societies section will be housed.

Opposite

A new reading room and members' room, complete with an external terrace, will be constructed on top of the existing building.

The 1930s Art Room will be restored as the new link between Duchess House and the original library building. The art collection is to be housed on specially made semi-transparent shelving.

The London Library is Britain's pre-eminent private subscription library, and has been famous as the haunt of writers and scholars for one hundred and fifty years. Founded by Thomas Carlyle, it moved to St James's Square in 1845. The present, Grade II-listed building by J. Osborne Smith was constructed in the 1890s – a pioneering example of steel-framed construction – with a series of extensions dating from the 1920s to the 1990s. The library is now chronically short of space: it acquires more than 8000 books annually and accommodation for readers is in short supply, as is office and workshop space.

The £25,000,000 development project by Haworth Tompkins – perhaps best known for its work on theatres, including the Royal Court and the Young Vic (see pp. 76–77) – involves the reconstruction of Duchess House, a 1970s block in Mason's Yard, just to the north of the library. This building, which was acquired in 2004, will provide thirty per cent more shelf space, catering for at least a quarter of a century of future expansion, and a second entrance into the library from Mason's Yard (also the location of the new White Cube gallery). The existing book stacks, remarkable for their use of cast iron on an open-grilled grid, will be extended upwards by three storeys, with the existing structure replicated as far as possible. A new reading room will be constructed at roof level, with a new members' room below and a terrace overlooking the square. All of this will involve emptying the library of books during 2007, decanting them into Duchess House, then moving them back during 2008. The recast Duchess House will link through at all levels to the 1890s building.

The project involves not only new construction but also a complete overhaul of the library's historic premises, with the renewal of aged services and installation of new environmental controls, a new lift and staircase in a light well, and the stripping out of unsightly accretions. The main staircase will remain the principal route through the library, and the issue hall and reading room are to be carefully restored.

Some members of the London Library may be concerned that the unique ambience of the place will be affected by all these changes (though it is hard to see how the library could survive in the long term without the alterations). But Haworth Tompkins has, on the strength of its Royal Court project, a sure touch when it comes to marrying old and new, and a particular feeling for materials and textures. Preserving the character of the library is a key aim in the project – for the architects, a building of this calibre is a historical palimpsest: every layer counts.

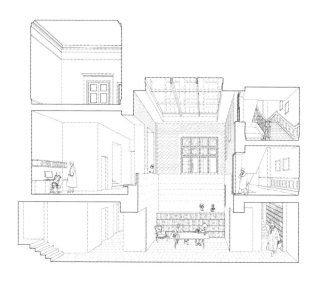

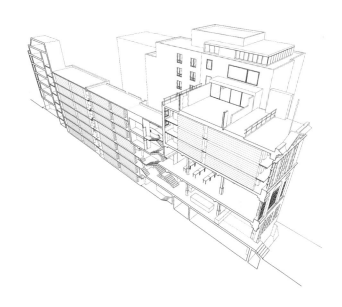

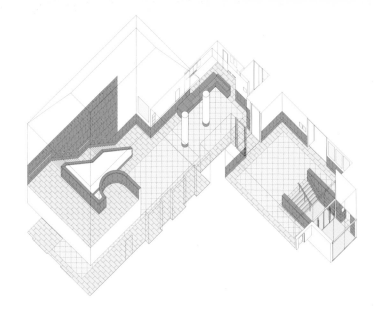

NATIONAL GALLERY, EAST WING, PHASE 2
TRAFALGAR SQUARE, W2

DIXON JONES, 1998–2004

The long frontage of William Wilkins's National Gallery (1832–38) forms a familiar backcloth to Trafalgar Square, but the building behind it grew by accretion: further rooms were added from the 1860s to the 1930s, all on a regular grid and in a congruous classical style. In recent years the historic interiors have been faithfully restored. The gallery's continuing need for additional space was addressed by the dismal 1970s Northern Extension and by Venturi Scott Brown's Sainsbury Wing, opened in 1991.

While hanging space is its most basic requirement, an art museum today aims to offer visitors far more than the edification of studying works of art. Shops, cafés and restaurants, decent lavatories and, increasingly, educational and IT facilities are now fundamental elements of museums from Walsall to Washington, D.C.

Dixon Jones's masterplan for the National Gallery, commissioned in 1998 to address the building's shortcomings, capitalizes on space on the ground floor, below gallery level, that was previously occupied by offices and stores. A new entrance has been created at ground level in the eastern wing of the building, with a new shop and large café. Beyond is the Walter and Leonore Annenberg Court, an impressive, generously day-lit space (roofed in lightweight ETFE, the strong, light and transparent material used for the

Eden Project's domes) with a new stair to the main galleries. A comfortable lounge, with computer terminals and a coffee bar, is heavily used by weary visitors – and the lavatories have been brought into the modern age.

In the autumn of 2005 the second phase of the project began. It involved opening up the previously cramped vestibule behind the main portico and restoring the entrance hall and main staircase beyond to a late Victorian colour scheme by J.D. Crace (largely painted over during World War II). Dixon Jones's client at the National Gallery is its Director, the architectural historian Charles Saumarez Smith. He was previously Director of the National Portrait Gallery, where he commissioned the outstanding Ondaatje Wing from the practice. Abandoning plans to turn the central gallery beyond the staircase into a reception and information area, Saumarez Smith has reinstated it as a place to display pictures, the heart of the building.

Dixon Jones's idea of constructing a grand set of steps extending down from the portico into Trafalgar Square remains under discussion. It would be a wonderful place to sit and watch London go by; the steps in front of New York's Metropolitan Museum of Art are an obvious inspiration. But would it give out the right message in an age where museums aim to be more accessible than imposing?

Above

Accessed from the newly reorganized entrance hall (top), the top-lit central gallery has been retained as an impressive place in which to display art (bottom).

Opposite

The pillared staircases and ceilings have been restored to their sumptuous original finishes.

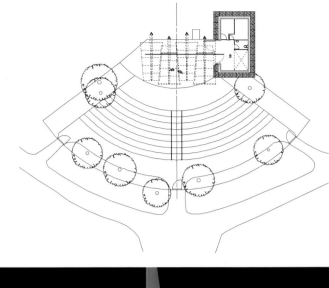

OPEN-AIR THEATRE, BARRA HALL PARK HAYES, UB3

BRADY MALLALIEU ARCHITECTS, 2003–05

London's parks used to contain innumerable small buildings – bandstands, tea rooms, sports pavilions, for example – many of which have succumbed to the ravages of time, neglect and vandalism, or have simply been tidied away by economy-minded local authorities. The open-air theatre in Barra Hall Park, Hayes (in the borough of Hillingdon), was originally constructed in 1951, a product of the Festival of Britain that year. By the 1990s, as a result of municipal cost-cutting (which resulted in the withdrawal of the park wardens), it had fallen into a state of dereliction, vandalized beyond repair, with the park itself sadly unkempt, a no-go area by night where muggings had become commonplace. Barra Hall, a listed building, stood empty and faced sale or even demolition. Fortunately, there was a strong feeling locally that the park should be restored and reclaimed for community use, and, in 1998, the Barra Hall Regeneration Committee was founded, chaired by the local MP.

The restoration campaign, raising most of its funds locally, has been remarkably successful, and the conversion of Barra Hall into a community and children's centre is now in hand. It was decided to construct a new theatre as part of the programme. Brady Mallalieu began work on the project in 2003, and the structure was completed in 2005 at a cost of £200,000. The aim was to create something that was not only useful but also a work of art in its own right. The existing raked seating was retained and upgraded. The new stage and backstage block, with changing rooms, WC and prop store, are designed to withstand the efforts of vandals while not appearing too defensive. The enclosing walls and canopy of the stage area are made of Cor-ten steel, its pre-rusted appearance suitably mellow in the parkland setting. The backstage block is constructed of concrete enclosed by stone-filled gabions. As the theatre is used only in the summer, no heating is provided and there is only basic lighting in the backstage block. The theatre, brought into use in the summer of 2005, is seen as a symbol of the renaissance of Barra Hall Park.

Right, top and middle
Replacing a dilapidated 1950s building, the open-air theatre at Barra Hall Park is a tough structure designed to resist vandalism.

Right, bottom
The structure is essentially an open-air stage, intended for use principally in the summer months. It forms an enigmatic presence in the setting of a municipal landscape.

PUMP HOUSE, MOVERS LANE, BARKING, IG11

DE PAOR ARCHITECTS, 2003

Irish architect Tom de Paor's concept for *Artscape*, one of Britain's largest public art projects, takes as its raw material a three-mile stretch of the A13 through Barking and Dagenham, one of the grimmest and most heavily trafficked roads in Greater London. His aim was "to choreograph serial and individual objects in space and produce a unified temporal experience – a perpetual rhythmic form whose movements are all of a piece; the vehicle windscreen to perform as a moving proscenium within which the changing composition is constantly framed".

The project originated with the Highways Agency in 1997 and has been funded to the tune of £11,000,000 by the Arts Council lottery fund, Transport for London, and a mix of public and private sponsors. It extends beyond the immediate route of the A13 to embrace projects in local housing estates, parks and other spaces. The strategy aims to make practical improvements to the environment around the A13 – to footpaths, cycle routes, underpasses and lighting, for example – as well as introducing an element of delight.

Among realized *Artscape* projects are the Charlton Crescent subway by Anu Patel, landscaping and lighting at Farr Avenue by Jason Cornish and Phil Power,

and Thomas Heatherwick's twin round-abouts at the Goresbrook Interchange.

There is nothing timid about de Paor's approach – the 70-metre-long *Holding Pattern* light sculpture can be clearly seen from passing aircraft – and his work on the A13 corridor has fuelled efforts to improve Barking town centre, where Tim Foster's Broadway theatre, Allford Hall Monaghan Morris's new library and a public square by Muf are new landmarks, and an extensive public art programme is planned as part of the regeneration campaign.

The Pump House at Movers Lane Junction exemplifies the thinking behind *Artscape*. Just 4.2 metres square and 6.4 metres high, the building is a functional piece of equipment, housing flood-pump control systems for an adjacent six-lane underpass on the A13. But it has also been conceived as a work of art. Constructed of pre-cast concrete panels, acid-etched, polished and sealed with anti-graffiti coating, the Pump House incorporates 456 acrylic rods cast end-on into the panels. Controlled by a computer and constantly changing colour with the passage of the day and the seasons, the rods read as voids within the mass of the building. By night, the building appears to be pumping out colour.

Above
A stretch of the A13 is being improved and humanized by various projects under the *Artscape* banner (top). Essentially functional, the building has been conceived as a work of art, a tough object that forms a marker for the passing traveller (bottom).

THE ROUNDHOUSE, CHALK FARM ROAD CAMDEN, NW1

JOHN MCASLAN + PARTNERS, 1997–2006

John McAslan + Partners has a reputation for reviving the fortunes of neglected historic buildings: the restoration of the De La Warr Pavilion at Bexhill-on-Sea, East Sussex, for example, was a landmark project for the practice. It faced a real challenge, however, when commissioned by philanthropist Torquil Norman to convert the crumbling Roundhouse in north London into a state-of-the-art performance venue.

Built as an engine shed in 1846, and housing a turntable, the Roundhouse quickly became redundant and was used as a gin warehouse for nearly a century before its reincarnation as a focus of the 1960s rock and fringe theatre scene. Facilities were, however, primitive, and by the 1980s alternative uses for the decaying building were being canvassed – one abortive proposal was its conversion into a store for the Royal Institute of British Architects' drawings collection. Torquil Norman bought the Grade II*-listed building in 1996 with the aim of turning it into a performing-arts centre targeted at young people. Norman's project, subsequently given additional funding by the National Lottery, had the enormous advantage of retaining intact, and restoring, the great internal space and its magnificent iron-and-timber roof structure. A new steel roof has been ingeniously constructed above and around the existing structure, providing acoustic insulation and provision for lighting and sound systems. The central glazed oculus, long obscured, has been opened up and fitted with triple glazing and black-out facilities. A new gallery level has been inserted to provide additional accommodation for audiences of up to 3300 people, and WCs and a bar have been slotted in below.

The basement level, originally containing nothing more than ash pits for steam locomotives, has been radically reconfigured beneath a new concrete floor slab, with rehearsal and recording studios around a central performance space seating two hundred. From the start of the project it was obvious that not all the facilities required could be accommodated within the historic envelope without compromising its character. A new wing was therefore constructed, wrapping around a section of the drum and facing Chalk Farm Road. It contains stairs and lifts, a café/bar, the box office and administrative spaces set off a top-lit galleria, which functions as an enjoyable, dynamic social hub. The new architecture is polite and well-detailed, in a straightforward contemporary manner. It is the restored Victorian drum that is the star of the show, externally little changed but internally transformed in a way that highlights the quality of its structure. The main performance space is highly flexible, with no fixed seating or stage.

Some feared that the familiar ethos of the Roundhouse would be lost in the process of repair and conversion, but miraculously it has survived the transformation. This is one of the best examples of adaptive reuse in recent years, and a model for what might be achieved elsewhere. The total cost of the project, excluding technical fit-out, was £19,000,000, which seems exceptional value for money.

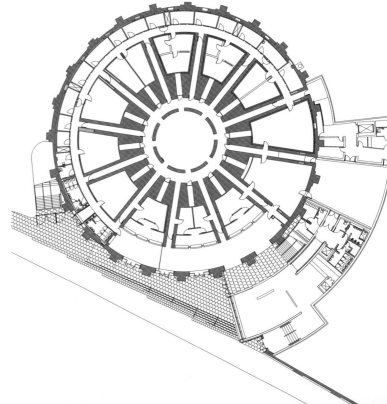

ROYAL GEOGRAPHICAL SOCIETY EXTENSION
EXHIBITION ROAD, SOUTH KENSINGTON, SW7

STUDIO DOWNIE, 1998–2004

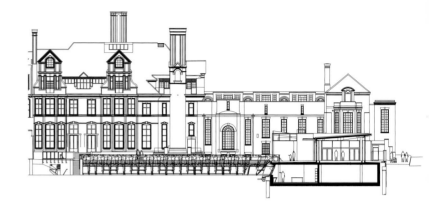

Craig Downie's discreet pavilion at the northern end of Exhibition Road is a short walk up the street from the more forceful intervention of Foster + Partners at Imperial College. Housing a new exhibition space, public reading room and reception area for the Royal Geographical Society (RGS), the pavilion is a modest but elegant addition to the townscape of 'Albertopolis', the collection of museums conceived by Prince Albert at South Kensington in the nineteenth century.

The new building is just one part of an overhaul of the society's premises to a masterplan by Studio Downie dating from 1997. The RGS, founded in 1830, came to Lowther Lodge, its splendid headquarters on Kensington Gore, in 1913. The building, designed by Richard Norman Shaw, had been completed forty years earlier as a private house. In 1930 a new wing was added on the corner of Exhibition Road, incorporating a 750-seat lecture theatre, to designs by Kennedy & Nightingale, which showed sympathy for Shaw's work. An upgrade of the heavily used theatre was an important element in the overall development plan. This also involved refurbishing the Shaw building to provide new educational facilities and greatly improved storage and study spaces for the society's huge archive, including 500,000 historic maps.

Creating a new building within the garden as the public face of the RGS was

more of a challenge, particularly in Kensington & Chelsea, a borough not renowned for its sympathy for new architecture. Yet the new pavilion is both uncompromisingly modern in its vocabulary and uncommonly sensitive to its surroundings. By excavating part of the garden, Downie was able to secure space for the reading room and book stacks, and archives storage at lower-ground-floor level – much of the new storage space is set beneath an extended garden terrace that is an excellent place in which to hold summer parties. Angled glazing, inspired by Ahrends Burton Koralek's now iconic 1970s additions to Keble College, Oxford, provides controlled natural light for the reading room. The ground-floor exhibition space and reception area – the only parts of the £7,000,000 development visible from the street – are housed in a lightweight glazed pavilion of steel, glass and concrete, with a silvered copper roof. This structure has beautiful detailing, with warm red brick used to tie it visually to its Victorian neighbour. A helical stair connects the two levels. A 20-metre-long glass balustrade facing the street incorporates etched glass panels by artist Eleanor Long. This element is a delightful feature of a genteel, academic neighbourhood into which Downie has introduced, to quote the *Architectural Review*, "an object lesson in modern urban etiquette".

Right, top and bottom
The project included the remodelling of the garden, which has been partly excavated to provide additional study and storage spaces. A basement reading room is accessed via a spiral staircase.

Right, middle
The building is screened from Exhibition Road by a wall of etched glass.

Opposite
The new Study Centre is contained in a lightweight pavilion attached to the historic Lowther Lodge.

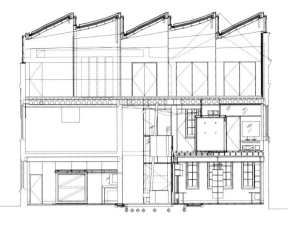

SIOBHAN DAVIES STUDIOS, ST GEORGE'S ROAD, ELEPHANT AND CASTLE, SE1

SARAH WIGGLESWORTH ARCHITECTS, 2006

Siobhan Davies is one of the leading figures on the British dance scene and heads Britain's foremost independent dance company, as well as being heavily involved in professional training and broader educational initiatives. From its foundation eighteen years ago her company existed without a permanent home, but in the spring of 2006 it moved into its new base in Elephant and Castle in south London.

The project involved the conversion and extension of a redundant, three-storey school building of 1898 on St George's Road – other buildings on the site remain in use by the Charlotte Sharman Primary School. The brief was to provide rehearsal spaces, changing and therapy rooms, offices and meeting rooms plus a main studio that could accommodate up to sixty people for public performances. Sarah Wigglesworth (who won the commission in competitive interview) had the advantage of an association with the company that extended over a decade – she understood and sympathized with its culture and responded strongly to its special needs.

The solid, decent but unremarkable old school building offered plenty of scope for continued use but equally for fairly radical adaptation. The decision was made to remove the staircase slot that connected the two classroom blocks and to insert a new double-height space, the natural focus of the building, that connects all the internal spaces. These include the offices and changing-rooms in the western block, and meeting rooms and the smaller rehearsal studio in the wing to the east. A "sofa in space" – a balcony complete with oversized sofa – overhanging the void at first-floor level is an engaging place in which dancers can relax between rehearsals. Stairs, lifts, WCs and plant are located in a new extension to the rear of the building facing the school playground. It is a lightweight, partly glazed structure, suspended on steel beams, that contrasts agreeably with the solidity of Victorian brick. A smaller extension contains an escape stair at the side of the building.

The principal space, the main rehearsal and performance studio, sits on top of the building, replacing the existing second-floor rooms – a matter of "making something of the roof", says Wigglesworth. Though modest in scale, it is a memorable and dramatic space where walls and ceiling, in a radical reinterpretation of the gothic tradition, are one. The studio can be blacked out, or opened up to give dancers views over London. An all-timber structure, using monocoque construction, was considered, but was ruled out on the grounds of cost in favour of a composite of timber and steel. Elements of the old rooms were retained, so that their memory has been preserved in the new space. Externally, the billowing roof structure, designed with engineers Price & Myers, reads as a tent or a boat, a new landmark on the busy road. The architect considers its overlapping shells to be "gravity-defying forms that seem to swell above the plane the dancers work on".

Sarah Wigglesworth is best known for the extraordinary Straw Bale House, completed in 2001 alongside the railway tracks out of King's Cross in north London, a challenging new-build project almost too complex with ideas. This very different project, costing a modest £4,200,000, is an assured performance and an object lesson in the creative marriage of old and new.

Opposite

Internally, the studio has an almost gothic quality, with controlled natural light providing an intense, enclosed but naturally lit space that responds to the needs of dancers.

Far left

The services are accommodated in a new block next to the playground of the former school.

Above and left

The main rehearsal and performance studio is placed on top of the converted school, and has a dramatic roofscape, which is a landmark on the approach to Elephant and Castle.

UNICORN THEATRE FOR CHILDREN
TOOLEY STREET, SOUTHWARK, SE1

KEITH WILLIAMS ARCHITECTS, 2000–05

Opened in time for the Christmas season of 2005, the Unicorn Theatre is one of only three new theatres built in London in the last thirty years. It is an outstandingly confident, competent and visually delightful work that firmly establishes Keith Williams (who won the job in competition in 2000) as a contender for other major cultural projects in Britain and beyond: in 2006 he was working on a new opera house for Wexford, Ireland.

The Unicorn Theatre was founded in 1947 by Caryl Jenner, who used former Army trucks to bring performances by professional actors to children around London. Twenty years later, it settled at the Arts Theatre in Covent Garden, where it remained until 1999, but always had aspirations for a home of its own. The Tooley Street site, a short walk from London Bridge station, emerged as a possible location as a direct consequence of Norman Foster's masterplan for More London, the large riverside development on the south bank of the Thames that includes City Hall. Providing space for an established cultural institution such as the Unicorn bolstered the credibility of More London as a genuine mixed-use urban quarter, not simply an office ghetto. The £13,700,000 project was also in tune with Southwark Council's regeneration agenda and it received generous support from the Arts Council lottery fund and other sources of public money.

The Unicorn's artistic director, Tony Graham, wanted a building that would be "rough yet beautiful" and that did not patronize its youthful audience: "children grow up, not down", he commented. The input of Graham and his colleagues, and also of local schoolchildren, was a significant influence on the development of Williams's proposals.

The building contains a main theatre (the Weston), which seats up to 340, a smaller studio theatre (the Clore), and a rehearsal studio, plus a foyer, a café, education and meeting spaces, and the usual backstage facilities. The Unicorn has a powerful impact on its surroundings, its contrasting transparent and solid elevations reflecting, Williams says, not just the public and the private, backstage components of the building, but equally ideas about "a dynamic future as well as the architectural precedent of this part of London, the narrow streets and warehouses that once occupied the site". Working with engineers from Arup to make optimum use of a tight site, the architects devised a structural solution that places the main auditorium, free of columns, above the open, glazed ground-floor, double-height foyer and the studio theatre set behind it. The staircase to the auditorium is contained within a corner tower, cantilevered over the foyer.

Externally, the solid box of the auditorium is clad in pre-weathered copper panels; elsewhere, brick, terracotta and stucco are used as facing materials. Projecting the theatre box out over the narrow historic street – coincidentally named Unicorn Lane – that lies to the west of the building provides extra space in the auditorium. (The plan's skew was intended to relate the building to an adjacent new office development, but the designs for the latter changed, so the two structures remain out of alignment.) A projecting glass box slotted in below the raked auditorium seating punctuates the copper cladding; behind is a multi-purpose space that serves variously as boardroom, function area or simply as a place where school groups can consume their packed lunches.

On the Tooley Street elevation the green room, traditionally an enclosed and often claustrophobic retreat, breaks through as a second glazed extrusion, allowing actors to see out and be seen.

There is nothing in the building that 'talks down' to its users or, it must be said, much evidence of the "roughness" that the client envisaged. Details, at least those front of house, are remarkably refined, with nothing extraneous or wilful. The use of stone floors, walnut joinery and high-quality concrete gives no hint of the relatively tight budget for the project. The main auditorium is carefully scaled to the needs of its primary users, with a semicircular form that positively encourages a sense of intimacy.

The success of this building, for audiences, performers and for the public who merely enjoy it as an incident in the cityscape, derives from the way in which Williams and his team conceived it as a series of dynamic interlocking volumes. These allow the Unicorn not only to enthral audiences but also to hold its own in a potentially overbearing context of commercial development.

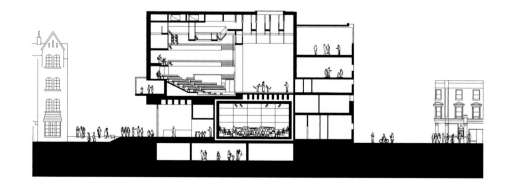

VICTORIA AND ALBERT MUSEUM OF CHILDHOOD, CAMBRIDGE HEATH ROAD BETHNAL GREEN, E2

CARUSO ST JOHN, 2002–06

The Victoria and Albert Museum of Childhood in Bethnal Green began its existence as an institution dedicated purely to the local area. In 1865, a group of benefactors bought the iron sheds (nicknamed the 'Brompton boilers') that had temporarily housed the South Kensington Museum – later the Victoria and Albert Museum (V&A) – and re-erected them as a museum at Bethnal Green. It later became a branch of the V&A and in 1974 was relaunched as the Museum of Childhood, housing the V&A's collection of toys.

Externally, the building is extremely sober, the rich decoration planned by architect James Wild having been omitted on grounds of cost. Inside, however, the iron structure is of exceptional quality, exhilarating in its lightness and grace. An architectural competition held in 2002 resulted in Caruso St John, best known for the New Art Gallery Walsall in the West Midlands, being appointed to draw up a development strategy to remedy the building's shortcomings, principally an acute lack of space for storage, offices and visitor facilities. In addition, it was proposed to restore the historic interior and strip away the clutter accumulated over more than a century. Phase I of the project, with a modest £1,500,000 budget, was completed in 2003. It included the provision of new furniture – chunky but not inappropriate – and lighting, and the refurbishment of the existing structure and the surviving Victorian display cabinets. A shop, reception area and café were installed on the ground floor. A new colour scheme – as opposed to a reinstatement of the original polychromatic designs – was developed by the architects in collaboration with artist Simon Moretti. As a temporary measure, a new entrance ramp and steps were built of timber, pending the construction of Phase II.

The second phase of the project, which required the museum to be closed for a year, was completed in late 2006. It provides a new entrance area, WCs and additional gallery space in a two-level pavilion attached to the front of the museum. A new learning centre, doubling the museum's capacity for school groups, was part of the project. The forecourt was completely remodelled to form a gently sloping approach, accessible to all.

Caruso St John has been experimenting in a number of recent projects with the revival of architectural decoration. At Bethnal Green, the façade of the new addition is clad with polished marble and granite panels incorporating intricate patterns inspired by the work of Victorian designers, notably Owen Jones. It is this aspect of the project, finally realizing something of James Wild's vision for the building, that gives it special interest, hinting at the potential for an architecture of richness and referentiality that avoids the historicist clichés of the worst of Post-modernism.

WHITECHAPEL ART GALLERY EXPANSION
WHITECHAPEL HIGH STREET, WHITECHAPEL, E1

ROBBRECHT EN DAEM ARCHITECTEN, 2004–08

The Whitechapel Art Gallery, completed in 1901, was described by Nikolaus Pevsner as "wonderfully original and quite an epoch-making building". One of three striking London buildings designed by C. Harrison Townsend – the others are the Bishopsgate Institute in the City and the Horniman Museum in Forest Hill – the gallery was founded by social reformer Henrietta Barnett and largely funded by the progressive philanthropist J. Passmore Edwards. Despite the completion of an extension (by Colquhoun Miller) in the 1980s, this internationally acclaimed centre for the display of contemporary and modern art has remained desperately short of space. When a new exhibition is installed, the gallery has to close as there is no storage space. Visitor facilities are poor and educational programmes are heavily oversubscribed. The building has ceased to meet the needs of the community it was intended to serve.

The decision by the borough of Tower Hamlets to vacate the public library adjacent to the gallery – and to replace this facility with a new Idea Store (see pp. 52–53) – provided an obvious site for expansion. The 1890s library by Potts, Son & Henning (also funded by Passmore Edwards) is not of the calibre of its neighbour but it is a listed building of some charm that could not be demolished. An international competition in 2004 for its reuse was won by Ghent-based Robbrecht en Daem Architecten, whose portfolio includes a number of arts projects in Belgium and The Netherlands. The £10,000,000 project was developed with artist Rachel Whiteread as consultant and will be carried out with the young London practice Witherford Watson

Mann as associates, with a view to reopening the gallery in 2008.

Externally, the library will remain unchanged, apart from the street façade being cleaned. Two new galleries will be formed in existing spaces: the commission gallery in the former ground-floor reading room, and the collections gallery in the fine top-lit first-floor space. Overall, display space at the Whitechapel will be increased by nearly eighty per cent. There will also be a new space for the storage and study of

the gallery's extensive archive. The education and research tower behind the street frontage will accommodate a research centre, greatly increased education space, and galleries intended for use by schools and community groups. The project is rooted in a renewed sense of commitment to the East End, in line with the aims of the Whitechapel's founders a century ago, but equally will ensure the gallery's future as an international centre of artistic excellence.

Above and opposite, top left
The former public library adjacent to the Whitechapel Art Gallery is being converted to house new display, storage and study spaces.

Opposite, top right and bottom
Two new gallery spaces are provided in the former library, at ground- and first-floor levels (top right and bottom right), while a new education space (bottom left) is housed in the block facing the street.

YOUNG VIC, THE CUT, SOUTHWARK, SE1

HAWORTH TOMPKINS, 2006

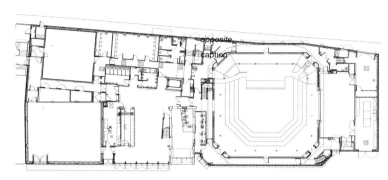

Located 150 metres to the west of the famous Old Vic Theatre, the Young Vic was founded by Frank Dunlop in 1970 as an off-shoot of the National Theatre, but is now an independent institution. On a wartime bomb site, within a shell constructed of raw concrete blocks, architect Bill Howell of Howell, Killick, Partridge & Amis provided a new auditorium with 450 seats, a studio and a café. An existing shop was converted to house the foyer. Intended as a temporary facility, Howell's building became a permanent fixture and was extended over the years in an *ad-hoc* fashion. The theatre faced closure under increasingly stringent health and safety regulations if no improvements were made, and in 2003 a major reconstruction was commissioned.

Haworth Tompkins, founded in 1991, is a youthful practice with a strongly urban agenda, reflected in its Coin Street housing (not far from the Young Vic). Past projects include a major reconstruction of the Royal Court Theatre in Sloane Square, the Open-Air Theatre, Regent's Park, and two incarnations of the Temporary Almeida. At the Young Vic, as at the Royal Court, the challenge was to preserve the essential character of a well-loved institution ("light-footed, critically engaged and classless") while equipping it with the facilities it badly needed: a more spacious foyer, an improved café and bar, enhanced

technical provision, and expanded rehearsal and storage spaces as part of a complete back-of-house rebuild. Specialist theatre-design practice Studio Todd Lecat collaborated with the architects on the design of the performance and rehearsal spaces.

Haworth Tompkins's £12,500,000 scheme, completed in the autumn of 2006, has retained the Howell auditorium largely as it was, raising its roof to provide space for a new technical walkway. The entrance through a former butcher's shop is also almost unchanged, though there is now an additional double-height foyer space with café and bar on two levels. To the west of the main auditorium are two new studios containing rehearsal space that can also be used for performances, with seats for up to 210 people. Adequate office space for the theatre's management has finally been provided.

The most obvious change has been to the exterior of the theatre. A new elevation to The Cut was hand-painted by artist Clem Crosby and encased behind industrial mesh. By night, it is lit from below, giving the Young Vic a new street presence.

Haworth Tompkins has a particular skill for working with old – often quite ordinary – buildings and responding to their spatial and material qualities. It is a talent that emerges powerfully in this project.

Above and opposite, bottom
The first-floor bar overlooks the new double-height foyer at the heart of the theatre complex.

Opposite, top
The updated frontage is an eye-catching addition to the street, especially at night, when the mesh façade of the auditorium is dramatically lit.

LEISURE

ASPREY STORE
FOSTER + PARTNERS

CITY INN WESTMINSTER
BENNETTS ASSOCIATES ARCHITECTS

EMIRATES STADIUM
HOK SPORT ARCHITECTURE

INN THE PARK
HOPKINS ARCHITECTS

OLYMPIC AQUATIC CENTRE
ZAHA HADID ARCHITECTS

ROAST RESTAURANT AND BOROUGH MARKET
GREIG + STEPHENSON

ST MARY'S GARDEN HALL
TERRY PAWSON ARCHITECTS

WEMBLEY STADIUM
FOSTER + PARTNERS/HOK SPORT ARCHITECTURE

THE ZETTER
CHETWOODS

ASPREY STORE, NEW BOND STREET, W1

FOSTER + PARTNERS, 2001–04

Norman Foster's store for fashion retailer Joseph in Sloane Street (completed in 1979), with shelving based on the famous 'book wall' at Chareau and Bijvoet's Maison de Verre in Paris, is one of many stylish but ephemeral shops fitted out by prestigious architects that have long been gutted or spoiled. Foster's store for jewellers Asprey in New Bond Street will, it is hoped, endure longer. The practice was commissioned by the new owners of the company to create stores in London and in the Trump Tower, on Fifth Avenue, New York, that expressed "the timelessness, values and craftsmanship associated with Asprey's goods through contemporary design".

Asprey has had a presence on New Bond Street since 1846 and, although no longer owned by the Asprey family, still occupies its original premises, which expanded into adjoining properties in the second half of the nineteenth century. The splendid Victorian cast-iron-framed frontage is a virtually unique feature, and was applied to a row of five houses dating from the 1770s. Behind the façade, however, the store was a rather confused accretion of spaces, while the rear of the block was an unseen backland, with the original fabric bearing the scars of a series of additions and alterations.

Foster's approach to recasting the block marries careful restoration and radical intervention, and was also adopted with great success at the Royal Academy of Arts in the early 1990s, and later at the British Museum Great Court. The rear elevations of the listed Georgian houses were faithfully repaired, with later accretions removed. The 'backland' has become a covered court, enclosed by a lightweight steel-and-glass roof and containing a thrillingly unsupported spiral stair connecting all levels of the complex. Inside the original buildings, new custom-made showcases, the renewal of lighting and other services, the rationalization of internal spaces, and the retention of significant historical features (such as the 'boat house' office used by the original Mr Asprey) have transformed the Asprey retail experience. The use of a limited palette of fine materials – plaster, stone, hardwood and leather – is in tune with the image of the company as a luxury brand.

Above and below

The store focuses on an internal court that has been elegantly glazed over – a smaller version of Foster's Great Court at the British Museum. A sinuous stair connects all levels of the building. The project also includes the restoration of a group of Georgian houses occupied by the firm for more than 150 years. The cast-iron frontage is a notable feature of New Bond Street (below, left).

CITY INN WESTMINSTER
JOHN ISLIP STREET, SW1

BENNETTS ASSOCIATES ARCHITECTS, 1999–2003

New and highly individual 'designer' and 'boutique' hotels – the Sanderson and the Zetter (see pp. 94–95), for example, both conversions of existing buildings – are transforming what was for too long a staid scene in London. The four-star City Inn is targeted firmly at the business traveller and the upper end of the tourist market: it wears its style lightly but sets a new benchmark for new-build chain hotels. City Inn is a rapidly expanding newcomer to the hotel business, already successfully taking on the established names and regarding high-quality design as a vital ingredient in its formula. It has opened, or plans to open, hotels in every major British city.

This City Inn – with 450 rooms, claiming to be the largest new hotel opened in London in thirty years – is in the rather dowdy hinterland of historic Westminster, close to the river and Tate Britain. The site, behind Millbank, is closely hemmed in by office and apartment buildings, and had remained empty for many years because of the perceived difficulties of developing it. Bennetts Associates is a large practice with much experience in the commercial field but none of hotel design. The rationale for commissioning this firm, however, is clear when the ingenuity of the plan is considered, and, at £35,000,000, the cost

of the 22,000-square-metre project is claimed to be thirty per cent less than that of comparable developments elsewhere.

If buildability was fundamental to the project, the resulting building is far from formulaic. The fully glazed façade to John Islip Street is an elegant *tour-de-force* that sets the tone for what lies behind. It fronts a twenty-four-storey block linked by a two-storey podium to a second block extending through to Thorney Street. A lift tower resolves the acute angle between the two blocks. A new pedestrian route has been created from John Islip Street into Thorney Street and on to Millbank, providing a valuable point of entry to the hotel from the Embankment. The 80-metre-long covered passageway is adorned with artwork by Susannah Heron, commissioned in association with the Tate, and in the summer forms an al-fresco extension to the hotel's ground-floor restaurant and café. The high-quality interior fit-out by Proof Consulting, culminating in the impressive top-floor Sky Lounge, is in tune with the overall aspirations of the project, which combines hard-headed business sense with a sincere ambition to position good design as a key selling point in the competitive hotel market.

Left
The City Inn's glazed façade sets the building apart from its somewhat mundane context. Its lower floors, which link the two higher blocks, are an ingenious solution to its awkward, hemmed-in site. The pedestrian route into the building includes an artwork by Susannah Heron.

EMIRATES STADIUM, ISLINGTON, N1

HOK SPORT ARCHITECTURE, 1999–2006

In the late 1990s Arsenal Football Club's decision to quit its historic ground at Avenell Road in Highbury, north London, was controversial. There was even the possibility that the club would move to another area of London – in fact, it had been founded in Woolwich, across the River Thames – but Islington Council was anxious to see it remain within the borough. Highbury Stadium is itself extraordinary, with two splendid Art Deco stands (dating from the 1930s) incorporating such facilities as bars and restaurants of a standard not found at any other British football ground. Now listed buildings, the east and west stands have been converted to housing as part of a sensitive redevelopment of Highbury by Allies and Morrison.

The new Emirates Stadium, located 500 metres from the old ground on former industrial land adjacent to the east-coast railway line, reflects the huge ambitions of one of London's 'super-clubs'. It was intended to be a landmark structure, with greatly increased capacity (seating 60,000) and state-of-the-art spectator facilities, including ample provision of private boxes. HOK Sport Architecture won the commission in 1999. On the basis of the designs, Arsenal was able to secure £100,000,000 from the Dubai-based Emirates airline in return for putting the latter's name on the stadium for up to fifteen years.

HOK Sport Architecture's Rod Sheard argues that sport is "the world's first truly global culture … . Consequently, the stadium will become the most important building any community can own … ." The project, costing a total of £170,000,000, is linked to a regeneration campaign for the surrounding Lower Holloway Road area, which includes the construction of 2000 new homes, healthcare and nursery facilities, and a waste-recycling depot. The stadium is surrounded by a new urban park, a valuable amenity.

The roof structure of the elliptical stadium is conceived as a 'floating' dish, seamless in appearance, suspended over the 'saddle' of the seating bowl and supported on two huge steel trusses, each 220 metres long. The slick glazed cladding of the landmark stadium bowl gives it the look more of an airport terminal than of the traditional football ground. Impressive claims are also made for the low-energy credentials of the project.

Right

A cutaway diagram shows the levels of seating up to the canopy.

Opposite

Seating up to 60,000 people, the stadium sets a new standard for club grounds in Britain. An important agenda for the project is the advocacy of sport as a regenerative force in the city.

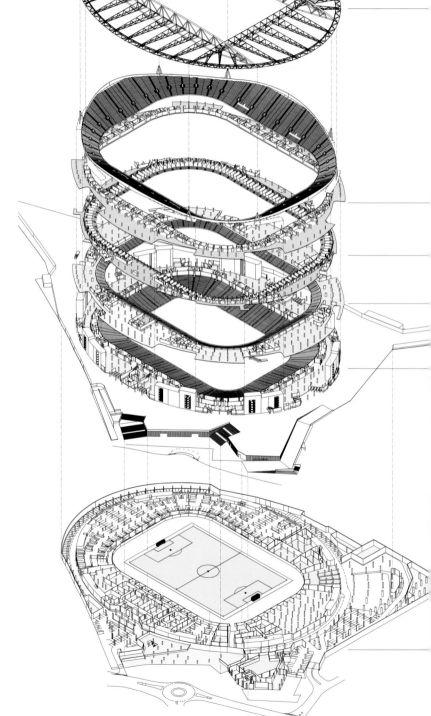

INN THE PARK, ST JAMES'S PARK, SW1

HOPKINS ARCHITECTS, 2004

Below and opposite
Clad in and partly constructed from timber, Hopkins's Inn the Park is essentially a picturesque landscape pavilion. From the covered terrace there are fine views of the lake and beyond to the London Eye.

Inn the Park exemplifies a type of project at which Hopkins Architects excels: building in sensitive contexts using a broad palette of materials in an entirely modern but understated manner. The building, which accommodates an informal café and a stylish restaurant run by entrepreneur Oliver Peyton, replaced the 'Cakehouse', an undistinguished pavilion-like circular structure of concrete and glass housing facilities that provided less ambitious fare.

Commissioned by Royal Parks (the agency that manages the eight such spaces across London), the building is designed to merge with the green landscape of St James's Park and is located at a key point, close to the lake and at the inter-section of two pedestrian routes. Hopkins, responding to a landscape strategy drawn up for the park by landscape designer Hal Moggridge, conceived it as "a grotto rather than a temple, a part of the landscape rather than an object on display". The building is indeed part of the landscape, as it is sunk into a grassy hillock so that

visitors can walk on its roof and enjoy fine views of the lake and the skyline of Whitehall beyond. A curving, covered, elevated terrace, set out with tables and with a long bench at ground level, sweeps out to provide al-fresco seating for up to 120 people close to the lake. (The use of a colonnaded elevation is in the best tradition of the English Picturesque.) Set behind, at the centre of the irregularly planned building – the form is that of a teardrop – is the 100-cover restaurant, with sliding glazed doors that can be opened in fine weather. Kitchens and other service spaces are placed to the rear, buried within the hillock.

The structure of the building is a mix of mass concrete, for the buried areas, and timber frame, for the external terrace. The palette of materials is in tune with the location, with plentiful use of timber inside and out, but there is nothing sentimental or folksy about a building that is precisely detailed in the usual Hopkins manner. The internal fit-out is by leading British designer Tom Dixon.

OLYMPIC AQUATIC CENTRE, STRATFORD, E15

ZAHA HADID ARCHITECTS, 2005–11

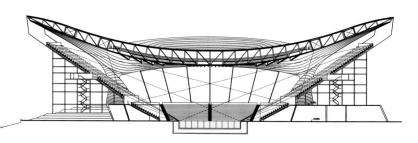

In July 2005 London was confirmed as the venue for the Olympic and Paralympic Games in 2012. Britain's success – Paris had been widely tipped to win the Games – was underpinned by a comprehensive masterplan, developed by a team including Edaw, Allies and Morrison, Foreign Office Architects and HOK Sport Architecture. The masterplan was for the Lower Lea Valley, an area of east London patently in need of regeneration and renewal. In February 2005 the commission for the first of the buildings in the Olympic Park, the Aquatic Centre, had been won by Zaha Hadid. Like other leading British architects, including Norman Foster and Richard Rogers, the Iraqi-born, London-based Hadid had established her success with projects outside Britain. The Olympic commission is one of a number of Hadid projects now under construction or in development in Britain, including the Architecture Foundation building in Southwark (see pp. 40–41) and a transport museum in Glasgow.

Since the rapturous summer days of 2005, doubts have crept in about the architectural and urban consequences of the Games. Such figures as David McKay – who was heavily involved in Barcelona's impressive Olympic bid of 1992 – and architect David Chipperfield have criticized the masterplan. There have also been disputes with the private sector about the interface between the Olympic site and the huge Stratford City development near by, and suggestions that future building projects will be tightly constrained in terms of procurement and cost. Indeed, the original plan for the building was amended in November 2006 to a smaller building in order to reduce costs, although the

capacity remained unchanged. The future of the Olympic site now rests with the Olympic Delivery Authority, an agency established to oversee its completion.

The Aquatic Centre has a key role in the masterplan for the entire Olympic site, as it is the first building that visitors will encounter en route from the new Eurostar rail station at Stratford City, from where trains will shuttle spectators to St Pancras station. A new bridge will sweep across the building to provide access to the main Olympic concourse and the stadium. Two smaller bridges lead into the Aquatic Centre, which lies at the lowest level of the site.

The design of Hadid's building is inspired by "the fluid geometry of water in motion", in tune with its location by the banks of the (somewhat sluggish) River Lea. Its undulating metal-clad roof, designed in consultation with Arup, stirs memories of the expressive architecture of Felix Candela and Eero Saarinen in the middle of the twentieth century: the 'double wave' covers the two pools, for swimming and diving, with the entrance lobby in between. The complex geometry of the roof, with its double curvature, could hardly have been achieved without state-of-the-art computer design technology. Inside the building, the form of the roof rises and swoops, following the lines of the spectator seating.

Designed to seat 20,000 spectators during the Games, the centre will normally accommodate no more than 3500 people when it functions as a sports facility for Londoners after 2012. If the Olympics produces little else of lasting architectural value, this building by a world-renowned architect will be remembered long after 2012.

Above

The first of the buildings for the 2012 Olympics to be commissioned, the Aquatic Centre is a focal point of the plans for the Lower Lea Valley. The site's main entrance walkway runs past it (middle).

Opposite

The building sits beneath a dramatic double-wave roof. Hadid's poetic use of concrete recalls the work of such classic Modernists as Candela and Saarinen.

ROAST RESTAURANT AND BOROUGH MARKET
STONEY STREET, SOUTHWARK, SE1

GREIG + STEPHENSON, 1997–2005

Below

Since the 1990s, Borough Market has been undergoing a process of regeneration as a source of high-quality food for Londoners and tourists, with the historic market structure progressively restored.

Bottom and opposite

Housed in part of the former Floral Hall, removed from Covent Garden, Roast has a strikingly modern aesthetic, contrasting with its Victorian context.

London's historic markets have had a mixed fate. Covent Garden in the West End was a pioneering exercise in reuse but serves a largely tourist clientele. Spitalfields in east London has been half-demolished to make way for an office development (see pp. 218–19). There are continued doubts about the long-term future of Smithfield in the City, as commercial development is encroaching on the fringes of the site.

Borough Market in Southwark, in the circumstances, offers an encouraging story of renewal and reinvigoration. Until quite recently it was a slowly declining wholesale market, operating in a huddle of buildings. Ranging in date from the 1850s to the 1930s, these buildings were threaded around and under the railway tracks that carry trains into Charing Cross and Cannon Street stations. Since its success in a competition of 1995 for a strategy to renew the market, Greig + Stephenson, a locally based practice, has been steadily refurbishing the buildings. At the same time, the market has been transformed through the development of a strong retail trade specializing in high-quality fresh food, in particular organic produce. In seven years the number of stalls has grown from six to more than one hundred. The revitalized market is a key feature of the area around London Bridge and Bankside, the flagship of Southwark's recent regeneration programme.

The incorporation of the portico of the old Floral Hall from the historic Covent Garden market buildings into the restored Borough Market was a brilliant move, allowing the demolition of a dull building from the 1950s that sat at the centre of the market complex on Stoney Street. Covent Garden's Floral Hall was largely restored and extended by architects Dixon Jones as part of the reconstruction of the Royal Opera House. The portico, however, could not be reused and so was dismantled and stored outside London pending the emergence of a suitable new use for it.

Even before its removal from Covent Garden, the portico had been much mutilated and had lost its distinctive barrel-vaulted roof. Greig + Stephenson reconstructed this key feature of the building, which had been acquired by Borough Market's Trustees for a nominal £1. The restored iron structure – a number of missing elements had to be specially fabricated – has been painted silver to distinguish it from the green-painted market buildings around it. It houses the Roast restaurant, opened in 2005. A substantial new extension (comprising eighty per cent of the total restaurant building) is conceived as a straightforward, wedge-shaped modern structure of concrete and glass that makes no attempt to ape the style of the Floral Hall portico.

Borough Market is a booming success, not only because of the quality and variety of its produce, but also because it is a memorable place that is enjoyable to visit, part of a richly textured city quarter that includes Southwark Cathedral, Clink Street and the rebuilt Globe Theatre. It is hardly surprising that in 2005 the market was formally twinned with Barcelona's famous Boqueria Market. There is a touch of European vitality and sophistication to Borough Market now entirely missing in the tourist tat of Covent Garden.

ST MARY'S GARDEN HALL, ST MARY'S ROAD
WIMBLEDON, SW19

TERRY PAWSON ARCHITECTS, 2003

Given the Church of England's role as the custodian of a major part of the nation's architectural heritage, its record in recent decades as a patron of new architecture has been disappointing, to say the least. Too many fine historic churches have been disfigured by banal additions containing social spaces, offices and WCs, most of them designed as feeble historical pastiche.

Terry Pawson's Garden Hall in Wimbledon gives a new significance to the term 'church hall' (so often associated with a draughty Scout hut with a trestle table and tea urn). The hall stands south-west of St Mary's parish church, an imposing structure medieval in origin but largely rebuilt in the nineteenth century. Located in a conservation area, the site was a garden, adjoining the churchyard, which had been partly turned over to parking. The new building is placed on one side of the site, leaving space for a pleasant lawned garden.

Viewed from Arthur Road, the hall appears as a plain rectangle of smooth ashlar, punctuated by a large window of opaque glass that rests on a wall of roughly coursed masonry. The site was excavated

to achieve a generous internal height of 4 metres in the hall (which can be partitioned to provide two spaces) and to respect the scale of the existing buildings in the area. A simple steel cross is the only explicitly Christian element in the composition. The building opens up to the garden, with a fully glazed elevation and sliding doors to embrace the external space. Rooflights provide additional controlled daylight, and a narrow slit of glazing provides views into a small garden area to the west. Internal finishes are simple but good quality, the aesthetic being one of white walls and wooden floors and doors. The servery, toilets and other subsidiary spaces are placed against the garden wall that backs on to the churchyard.

This modest and understated but extremely elegant building, just down the road from a fine private house that Pawson completed in 2002, serves the needs not only of the parish but also of the wider local community and is heavily used all year. It is a marker for both new design in historic areas and a more enlightened commissioning approach on the part of the Church.

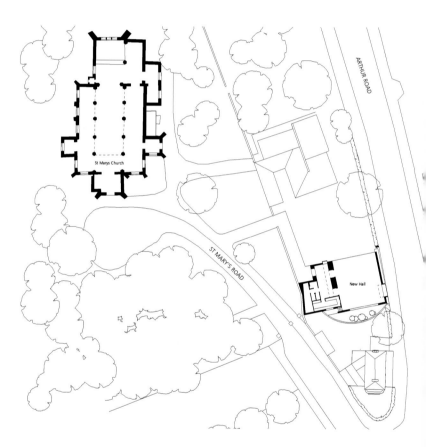

Above

The new Garden Hall is set discreetly apart from the historic church of St Mary.

Opposite

Concealed behind a garden wall, the building opens up to a generous garden and peers over a boundary wall to the road beyond.

WEMBLEY STADIUM, WEMBLEY, HA9

FOSTER + PARTNERS/HOK SPORT ARCHITECTURE, 1996–2007

Wembley, home of British football, has been described as "the most advanced stadium in the world, a benchmark for future stadium construction", and, in the hands of Foster + Partners and HOK Sport Architecture, the completed stadium can hardly fail to be anything but world class. Early in 2006, however, the National Lottery-funded project was getting publicity of the worst sort, as the FA Cup Final, due to be held there in May, had to be moved to Cardiff. A series of construction delays and technical problems had put back completion of the new stadium, though this was confidently promised for the latter part of the year. It has since been confirmed that the Cup Final will be held at Wembley in 2007.

Not so long ago, Foster + Partners' Millennium Bridge across the River Thames was the subject of popular mirth, as a technical fault caused it to be temporarily closed shortly after its opening. Today, however, it is used and enjoyed by millions, and has become a much-admired London landmark. The same is likely to happen in the case of the new Wembley. The original stadium on the site, built for the British Empire Exhibition in 1924 and used for the Olympics in 1948, was widely loved – the World Cup Final of 1966 was one of the most inspirational events held there. But the demolition of its 'twin towers' was surprisingly uncontroversial: it was generally realized that the building had had its day, could not provide facilities to international

standard and was outclassed by the venues being constructed in Britain by such football teams as Arsenal (see pp. 82–83).

The new stadium seats 90,000 – nearly a third more than its predecessor – and has vastly increased circulation space, escalator links to the upper tiers, and 2600 toilets (more than any other stadium in the world, it is claimed). Steeply raked seating provides unobstructed views for all spectators. There is full access for disabled visitors, including three hundred viewing positions for wheelchair users. Catering facilities will be far superior to those in the old stadium. Football is the focus of the new Wembley, but the stadium is also designed to cater for athletics, with reduced seating and an elevated running

track and field that can be installed above the football pitch. This operation, using a modular prefabricated steel system, will take ten weeks to complete, but is planned to take place only twice or three times in the stadium's lifetime.

The key feature of the new stadium is its partly retractable roof, which can be closed to provide cover for all seats. The roof is supported on the great arch, visible from many parts of London, that will replace the twin towers as the symbol of British football. Some 133 metres high, spanning 315 metres and weighing 1750 tonnes, the arch was hoisted into position in the summer of 2004. By the summer of 2007 the stadium should have taken its place as one of the great sporting venues of the world.

Left
The practical rationale of the arch is to support the partially retractable roof.

Opposite
The 315-metre span of the great arch, dramatically illuminated by night, provides a marker for the stadium across north London (top left and right). Closer at hand (bottom) it forms an impressive point of entry to the 90,000-seat stadium.

THE ZETTER, ST JOHN'S SQUARE
CLERKENWELL, EC1

CHETWOODS, 2001–04

Located in Clerkenwell, an area transformed in the last decade or so from a neglected to an extremely fashionable part of London, the Zetter (opened in 2004) is a classic boutique hotel with a degree of style that would not be out of place in Manhattan. In contrast to other such hotels, which appear to depend on fit-out and furniture for effect, the Zetter reflects the input of an architectural practice with a deft approach to reusing old buildings and a serious interest in environmental issues.

The raw material was of good quality: a tough, five-storey, Grade II-listed, late Victorian warehouse long used as the headquarters of the Zetter's football pools company, consisting of timber floors carried on cast-iron columns and beams. The aim was to maintain its integrity, retain all significant features and leave its exterior essentially unaltered, while adding a lightweight, set-back top floor, on a horseshoe plan, that does not impact on views from the street. New windows and shutters were specially made to match those existing. The ground-floor reception area and restaurant retain their original form, with restored cast-iron columns and an up-to-date industrial aesthetic in tune with the tastes of clients – Clerkenwell is heavily populated (and visited) by architects, designers and media professionals.

Central to the £5,000,000 project was the creation of a five-storey semi-elliptical atrium at the heart of the deep-plan building, reached from the main staircase and lifts, around which walkways provide access to all fifty-nine guest rooms. Sophisticated fire engineering was required to remove the need for a secondary escape stair, which would have taken up precious space. A bar occupies the centre of the ground floor, which is day-lit from above. Daylight also pervades the guest rooms, which have opening windows, and glazed panels filter light into bathrooms, usually artificially lit in hotels. It is this use of natural light and the manipulation of space that create the calm atmosphere that is such a feature of the building, setting it apart from the general run of London hotels. The building responds to the context of the ancient St John's Square, which is bisected by the Victorian Clerkenwell Road but forms an attractive space to the north, where the hotel restaurant spills out on to the pavement.

An unusual facility, in line with the project's serious environmental aspirations, is the extraction of water from an aquifer 150 metres below the street. It is used as 'grey' water for flushing WCs and cooling the air-conditioning system, and, filtered and carbonated, for the bottled water supplied to guests.

The clients asked for design flair and for a building that was "intensely practical, comfortable, serviceable, hardwearing, on budget, and on time". The architects have delivered on every count.

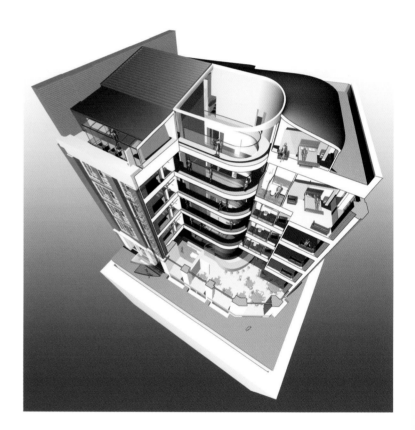

Above and opposite
The full-height atrium is the heart of the reconstructed Victorian block housing the Zetter. Internally, the emphasis is on high style; some rooms have access to external terraces.

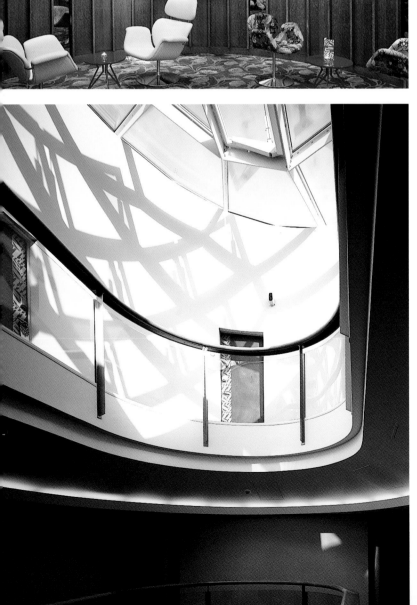

EDUCATION

BEN PIMLOTT BUILDING, GOLDSMITHS, UNIVERSITY OF LONDON
SMC ALSOP

CENTRAL SCHOOL OF SPEECH AND DRAMA
JESTICO + WHILES

CHELSEA COLLEGE OF ART & DESIGN
ALLIES AND MORRISON

CLAPHAM MANOR PRIMARY SCHOOL EXTENSION
DE RIJKE MARSH MORGAN ARCHITECTS

CLAPTON PORTICO LEARNING CENTRE
BRADY MALLALIEU ARCHITECTS

ENFIELD COLLEGE
VAN HEYNINGEN AND HAWARD ARCHITECTS

FAWOOD CHILDREN'S CENTRE
SMC ALSOP

GRADUATE CENTRE, LONDON METROPOLITAN UNIVERSITY
DANIEL LIBESKIND

HALLFIELD SCHOOL
CARUSO ST JOHN

IMPERIAL COLLEGE FACULTY BUILDING
FOSTER + PARTNERS

INSTITUTE FOR CULTURAL HERITAGE, UNIVERSITY COLLEGE LONDON
DIXON JONES

INSTITUTE OF CELL AND MOLECULAR SCIENCE, BLIZARD BUILDING, QUEEN MARY, UNIVERSITY OF LONDON
SMC ALSOP

JOHN PERRY NURSERY
DSDHA

LAW DEPARTMENT, LONDON METROPOLITAN UNIVERSITY
WRIGHT AND WRIGHT ARCHITECTS

LOCK-KEEPER'S COTTAGE GRADUATE CENTRE, HUMANITIES DEPT, QUEEN MARY, UNIVERSITY OF LONDON
SURFACE ARCHITECTS

NDNA LONDON REGIONAL CENTRE
COTTRELL + VERMEULEN

NEW ACADEMIC BUILDING, LONDON SCHOOL OF ECONOMICS
GRIMSHAW

SCHOOL OF SLAVONIC AND EAST EUROPEAN STUDIES UNIVERSITY COLLEGE LONDON
SHORT AND ASSOCIATES

SURE START CENTRAL BRENT CENTRE
GREENHILL JENNER

SURE START KILBURN
MEADOWCROFT GRIFFIN ARCHITECTS

SURE START LAVENDER
JOHN MCASLAN + PARTNERS

WESTFIELD STUDENT VILLAGE QUEEN MARY, UNIVERSITY OF LONDON
FEILDEN CLEGG BRADLEY ARCHITECTS

WESTMINSTER ACADEMY
ALLFORD HALL MONAGHAN MORRIS

WORLD CLASSROOMS
FUTURE SYSTEMS

BEN PIMLOTT BUILDING
GOLDSMITHS, UNIVERSITY OF LONDON
LEWISHAM WAY, NEW CROSS, SE14

SMC ALSOP, 2002–05

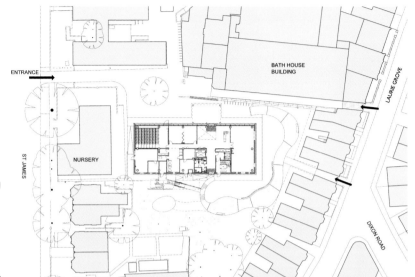

Surprisingly simple in appearance compared with Alsop's other recent work – the rooftop sculptural feature notwithstanding – the Ben Pimlott Building attracted some negative critical comment on its completion. Ellis Woodman of *Building Design* complained about its "shed-like gaucheness" and "distinctly anaemic façades", and disliked the "scribble" sculpture (Will Alsop's own creation).

Alsop was appointed in January 2002, following a high-profile competition, to design a two-phase development for Goldsmiths. The Ben Pimlott Building, named after a distinguished warden of the college who died suddenly in 2004, is the first phase of the project; another building housing further facilities for the college will be constructed next to it once funding has been secured. The Ben Pimlott Building contains four floors of visual-arts studios above lecture and conference rooms (on the ground floor), laboratories and offices for the department of psychology (on the first floor), and digital media laboratories, including film-editing and sound-recording studios (on the second floor). The mix of activities reflects the range of teaching and research at Goldsmiths, which is well known as the breeding ground of a new generation of British artists.

Located in a relatively obscure part of south London, Goldsmiths wanted to make a splash with its new buildings. Its core is the former Royal Naval School of the 1850s, from which it has expanded over

the last century into a variety of converted premises, including the former Deptford Town Hall. A new library by Allies and Morrison, completed in 1997, is its only recent purpose-built facility.

Alsop's building occupies a gateway site, giving Goldsmiths a serious presence on the street and a connection to the local community. Its elevated site makes it a prominent feature of the local skyline, but it eschews the colourful display of the practice's Peckham Library in favour of a purposeful industrial aesthetic not inappropriate to the activities contained within. Three elevations are clad in aluminium, with relatively minimal fenestration; the south elevation is animated by a dramatic escape stair. The north elevation, in contrast, is entirely glazed, enabling daylight to flood the interior and spaces inside to be opened up to public view. The interiors are highly flexible, with tough finishes and the potential for reconfiguration in line with users' needs. At the top of the building a two-storey section is cut away to provide a terrace for outdoor displays.

Costing less than £7,000,000, the building seems to be good value for money, and the use of a design-and-build contract does not appear to have undermined the architect's intentions. This is not one of Alsop's greatest works, perhaps, but it is a highly serviceable and discreetly glamorous building that responds strongly to the client brief on many levels.

Right and opposite

With its sculpture elements, and elevated above the surrounding houses, although set back from the street (right, top), the new building is a striking

addition to the skyline of south-east London. Alsop's creation of twisted metal enlivens the cut-away terrace (right, middle).

CENTRAL SCHOOL OF SPEECH AND DRAMA
ETON AVENUE, SWISS COTTAGE, NW3

JESTICO + WHILES, 2004–05

In terms of urban design, Swiss Cottage is something of a mess: it is an extended roundabout funnelling traffic into the noisy canyon of Finchley Road, with the building from which the area takes its name (originally of the 1840s, but rebuilt many times) lost among later development. The borough of Hampstead planned an ambitious new civic centre here in the 1960s, but only the public library and swimming pool, both designed by Sir Basil Spence, were built before the borough was merged with that of Camden and the plans axed. The library survives and has been sensitively refurbished by John McAslan, but the pool was razed in favour of a new leisure centre by Terry Farrell, part of his masterplan for the civic centre site, which includes housing.

The restored library and the Hampstead Theatre, designed by Bennetts Associates and completed in 2003, have brought a new sense of place and purpose to Swiss Cottage, further reinforced by Jestico + Whiles's new building for the Central School of Speech and Drama. The school was founded in 1906 and in the 1950s moved to Swiss Cottage, where it has long had to operate in cramped and substandard premises – some of which must remain until the second phase of the Jestico + Whiles project is funded and built.

Expansion of student numbers made a new building (the west block) vital. Housing nine new rehearsal studios, it is an extraordinarily straightforward structure, clearly designed to give the school street cred and to respond to the challenge of Bennetts Associates' theatre opposite. In urban terms the building has to mediate between the bland commercialism of Finchley Road and the edge of the Belsize Park Conservation Area, to which it forms a protective barrier. The site is irregular and the new block had to connect to existing buildings – the junction, with the second phase unbuilt, remains awkward.

A mix of acrylic render, zinc cladding and glazing – the usual contemporary materials – is used on the exterior in a manner that is both bold and stylish. Extensive glazing using transparent, translucent and fritted glass on the main street façades allows glimpses into the building and of the activities inside. The zinc cladding provides a visual link to the flytower of the Hampstead Theatre, and a new public square provides a practical link between the two institutions. Boxes containing teaching, rehearsal and production spaces are expressed in render. Internally, the plan is rational and comprehensible: the staircase and lift core comprising the 'knuckle' of the building form a natural social focus. The completion of Phase II of the project will see the rationale of the building revealed.

CHELSEA COLLEGE OF ART & DESIGN
MILLBANK, WESTMINSTER, SW1

ALLIES AND MORRISON, 2001–05

The new home of Chelsea College of Art & Design (now part of the University of the Arts, London) formerly housed the Royal Army Medical College. The attractive buildings in a neo-baroque manner, of red brick and Portland stone, neatly detailed, were constructed between 1898 and 1907. The site, across the road from Tate Britain – the two buildings replaced the notorious Millbank Penitentiary – was vacated by the Army during the 1990s, and was the subject of a number of bids from prospective users. It could easily have

been sold to a developer, with the buildings, now listed, converted to upmarket flats. However, the government, unexpectedly perhaps, resolved to accept Chelsea College's bid.

The buildings, which include barrack and married-quarter blocks and a more formal officers' mess, are arranged around three sides of a central parade ground (latterly used for parking). They were well suited to the college's requirements, offering a range of spaces ideal for adaptation as studios, offices and

workshops. There were proposals to landscape the parade ground as a formal square, with an underground gallery below it – which could possibly be linked to the basement of Tate Britain. This aspect of the scheme has been temporarily shelved on cost grounds, but the central courtyard is often used by students for building large-scale artworks.

Allies and Morrison was an ideal choice for the £37,000,000 project, since the practice has a sympathetic approach to old buildings and is adept at new design

in historic contexts. A number of later accretions were demolished and new structures sensitively slotted in. On John Islip Street brick pavilions have been added to the rear of the married-quarter block, making a new connection to the street. An entrance to the complex was formed between the mess block, which fronts the river, and the adjacent laboratory building. This part of the complex is a light-filled atrium, crossed by walkways and containing a bar, café and shop. A small triangular plot at the end of the atrium has been filled by a new studio/workshop building, with large spaces that could not be carved out of the existing structures (the shape of the site is defined by a surviving fragment of the great wall that enclosed the long-vanished gaol).

The new work is well detailed, robust and elegant throughout, though never at odds with the context. The subtle transformation of this neglected site has reinforced the idea of developing an arts quarter around Tate Britain, which has long been an isolated cultural presence in an otherwise inert quarter of London.

Left

The former Royal Army Medical College on Millbank provided a ready-made campus for the Chelsea College of Art & Design.

Opposite

The development is a mix of refurbishment, conversion and sensitive new build, with a new atrium (right, middle) forming the principal point of entry to the complex. The contrast between old and new is deliberately exploited as a feature of the interiors (top right).

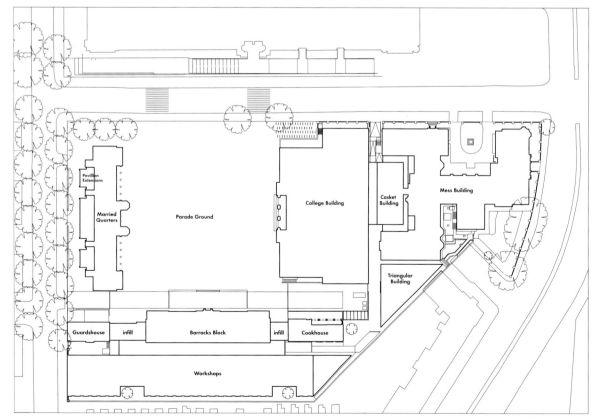

CLAPHAM MANOR PRIMARY SCHOOL EXTENSION
BELMONT ROAD, CLAPHAM, SW4

DE RIJKE MARSH MORGAN ARCHITECTS, 2002–07

De Rijke Marsh Morgan (dRMM) is a young practice with a growing reputation for school design. At Kingsdale School in Dulwich, south London – a building of the 1950s – dRMM added a lightweight roof over the existing playground and a new assembly hall in a lightweight pod. That project was completed in 2004. For Clapham Manor Primary School, originally built in the nineteenth century, the brief from Lambeth Council was to replace an extension dating from the 1960s and the caretaker's house with new accommodation in line with the school's enhanced status as a Department for Education and Skills 'beacon'. The school is located within a conservation area and has the Grade II-listed Odd Fellows' Hall as its neighbour. The new four-storey building, providing a relocated main entrance, offices and classrooms with full access for the disabled, is scheduled for completion in 2007. The project involves the remodelling of spaces within the existing school building to accommodate present-day educational practice, including provision of enlarged classrooms.

The new, £2,000,000 building relates in scale to the existing school, but stands free of its brick façades; a glazed stairwell and double-aspect lift connect the two. It makes no concessions to the style of the older one but is clad in polychromatic, patterned glazing over a curtain-wall system, "a graduated loop of colour that shifts as it moves around the building, picking up the vernacular hues of its neighbours … and the greens of the soft landscape towards the rear," according to the architects.

The detailed treatment of the elevations was developed in close consultation with the school community and local residents. Clear, translucent and solid panels are used as an overlay on the façade to allow daylight to penetrate the interior while controlling solar heat gain. Their arrangement appears to be random but is a response to the internal organization, maximizing light, fresh air (through opening windows) and views where needed. The colourful box is elevated on a recessed plinth of butt-jointed glazing, providing the requisite transparency for the main entrance area and school offices. With its brilliant reworking of the traditional curtain wall, this project inserts a contemporary, jewel-like object into an austere Victorian townscape, offering local children a new and highly stimulating learning environment.

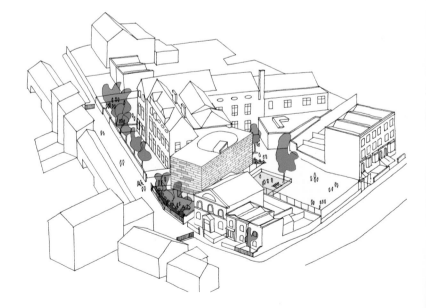

Opposite, right and below

Contrasting stylistically and in materials with its Victorian neighbour, dRMM's addition to Clapham Manor Primary School in fact provides an infusion of sensitive modern design in a conservation area, with strong use of colour to lift the spirits of both users and passers-by.

CLAPTON PORTICO LEARNING CENTRE
LINSCOTT ROAD, CLAPTON, E5

BRADY MALLALIEU ARCHITECTS, 2002–05

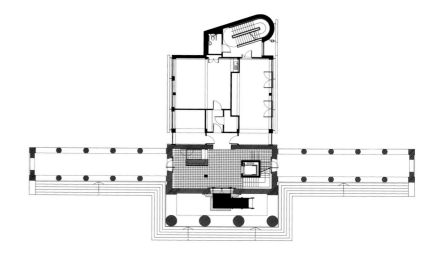

The Clapton Portico is one of those local landmarks that help give identity and a sense of place to even the most ordinary quarters of London. In fact, it is a rather pathetic survival of lost grandeur. It was formerly the central feature of the London Orphan Asylum, built in 1823–25 to designs by W.S. Inman in a bold Greek Revival manner and on a grand scale. The portico fronted the central chapel of this institution, which moved to Watford in the 1870s. The buildings were sold to the Salvation Army, which constructed a 4700-seat auditorium behind Inman's portico. They fell victim to the clearance policies of the 1960s, when everything except the portico and flanking colonnade was torn down by the local authority to provide space for the expansion of the adjacent school.

Brady Mallalieu's project has finally given this Grade II-listed survival an assured future and a use. The aim was to preserve the dignity and enigmatic quality of the building in a scheme to incorporate it into a new city learning centre. In line with current orthodoxy, the new-build element of

the scheme is as far as possible detached, in physical and stylistic terms, from its historic neighbour, which was the subject of a careful repair operation funded by grant aid from English Heritage. The design strategy was to retain the open character of the colonnade, by placing all the new accommodation in a block immediately behind the portico, which itself offered little scope for conversion. A new staircase and lift were inserted within the listed structure.

The new building, with a steel-clad roof extending over the retained portico, is toughly but elegantly detailed, with an external screen of aluminium louvres. It contains classrooms and staff offices on four levels, with WCs and an additional stair in an elliptical projection to the rear. It is to be hoped that funding for landscaping can be obtained, so that a more satisfactory setting for the building can be provided. This is an exemplary project combining new and old that has contributed positively to the regeneration of a relatively underprivileged area of London.

Right, top
A staircase and WCs are housed in a curved projection at the back of the building, leaving the main block free for well-proportioned classrooms and offices.

Right, middle and bottom
The striking portico and colonnade is enhanced by the new block, which is clad in aluminium louvres and sits behind the existing structure.

ENFIELD COLLEGE, HERTFORD ROAD ENFIELD, EN3

VAN HEYNINGEN AND HAWARD ARCHITECTS, 2003–05

Enfield College was an unremarkable complex of buildings in a London borough that has little architecture of quality and interest. The decision in 2001 by the college's governors to overhaul its buildings and, radically, demolish those that were no longer of practical use, was therefore to be welcomed. A budget of just over £5,000,000 was set aside for this programme of renewal and a design competition organized. Van Heyningen and Haward was appointed early in 2002 to produce a masterplan and design the first phase of the development. It was a sound choice, as the practice has a proven record in the field of educational architecture and an imaginative approach to extending and refurbishing existing buildings, as well as a design flair that is driven by a real feeling for the appropriate use of materials.

The masterplan aims to improve the overall environment of the college and to provide it with a social focus in the form of a central square, approached via a new entrance sequence from Hertford Road. The first new building on the site, Kingfisher House, designed by Van Heyningen and Haward, was constructed between 2003 and 2005. It encloses the new College Square to the south. The brief for the building called for twenty-four teaching spaces with a new reception area that serves the entire campus.

The new two-storey building is a model of practical, rational and – necessarily in the context of a tight budget – economical design. Its elegant presence also meets the client's need for a new 'gateway' to the site that provides the college with an attractive public face. Teaching spaces are arranged along an east–west spine and are generously day-lit, with large sun-shaded windows on the south side and translucent cladding on the north elevation. Circulation spaces on the first floor are top-lit. Heavy concrete construction, with external surfaces simply rendered, and opening windows providing natural ventilation, ensure comfortable conditions in hot weather. The double-height reception area acts as the college's 'shop window'. This practical but stylish design does much to lift the spirits in a mundane corner of the London suburbs.

Above

Elevational drawings reflect the essentially modular, highly rational concept behind Van Heyningen and Haward's design.

Below

Enfield College is an exemplar of calm and rational design, with an emphasis on practicality rather than high style that responds to changing demands in the field of education.

FAWOOD CHILDREN'S CENTRE, FAWOOD AVENUE, STONEBRIDGE PARK, NW10

SMC ALSOP 2001–04

In common with educational projects by DSDHA, Greenhill Jenner, John McAslan + Partners and others, Will Alsop's Fawood Children's Centre represents a new approach to nursery-school design that responds to the real needs of children and their parents. Such buildings have been underwritten by a government commitment to funding new nursery schools in disadvantaged areas of Britain.

The Stonebridge Estate in north London certainly falls into that category. It was developed during the inter-war years, initially with two-storey houses, which gave way in the 1960s to brutally ugly slabs of local-authority flats. By the 1990s it had become a typical 'sink' estate, plagued by unemployment, poverty and rising crime. The transfer of the estate's management to a Housing Action Trust (HAT), however,

signalled the start of a campaign to regenerate the area physically and socially, with much of the existing housing scheduled for clearance.

An existing nursery built in the 1960s, the Evan Davies School, had provided good facilities in difficult circumstances, but, after consultation with local residents, it was decided to create a new nursery on a new site on the north side of the estate. Alsop was appointed by the Stonebridge HAT in 2001 to develop proposals. The new centre was to be larger than its predecessor, open for longer hours – thus catering for working parents – serve an extended age range (six months to four years) and offer dedicated facilities for children with autism or special needs. The client wanted a building that was a symbol of regeneration as well as a practical resource for the

community. In SMC Alsop it chose the ideal architect to realize that vision.

Instead of a compartmentalized building in the traditional mould, Alsop gave Stonebridge a huge, flexible, economical space. The building is a light-filled portal-frame shed, with a partly translucent pitched roof, containing a series of smaller freestanding structures – a design approach he pioneered at Peckham Library in south London (located in another underprivileged area of the capital). The detailed brief for the building evolved gradually in discussion with the client and the future users. The internal landscape – essentially an 'inside/outside' space – contains a sand pit, water garden, cycle track and other delights for children. Freestanding pavilions are formed from recycled shipping containers (a commodity

of which there is a permanent glut) piled up to three storeys high. There are no extraneous trimmings, and the industrial character of the building is mitigated only by the free use of vivid colour. Externally, the centre is clad in stainless-steel mesh with brightly coloured lozenges at the upper level. It feels reassuringly secure but never defensive or intimidating.

The centre was shortlisted for the Stirling Prize in 2005, the judges being initially "bemused" but ultimately "having been won over by its sheer bravado, carrying away with them an impression of amusement and delight". This is surely one of Alsop's best buildings to date – as well as one of his cheapest, at a cost of £2,400,000 – and a classic instance of a happy marriage of architect and users, who seem to love the place.

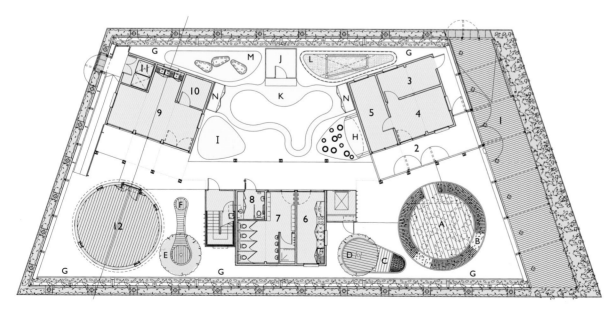

Left

Services, such as toilets, private offices and the kitchen, are contained in heated units (coloured orange). Play areas include a water garden and cycle track (M and K), and a yurt (12). The entrance deck is on the right-hand side of the plan.

Opposite, top left

Internally, recycled shipping containers are used to form rooms in the open space.

Opposite, top middle, top right and bottom

Cheap and cheerful but a visible symbol of regeneration, SMC Alsop's Fawood Children's Centre is part of the ongoing renewal of the Stonebridge Estate in north-west London. The use of vivid colour is an important part of the project.

GRADUATE CENTRE, LONDON METROPOLITAN UNIVERSITY, HOLLOWAY ROAD, HOLLOWAY, N7

DANIEL LIBESKIND, 2001–04

Below and opposite

The Graduate Centre has many of the characteristics familiar from Libeskind's earlier works, with dramatic form to the fore, but on this occasion crammed on to a small site and with little apparent relevance to the practical brief.

One of only two buildings in Britain by Daniel Libeskind – the other is the Imperial War Museum North in Salford, near Manchester – this is a disappointing performance by an architect of global stature. Libeskind won the 1000-square-metre, £2,500,000 project in a competition in 2001, beating, among others, Future Systems and Hodder Associates. The client (then the University of North London) clearly aimed to create a landmark 'iconic' structure on the Holloway Road, where the university occupies a rather mundane collection of buildings. The centre had to be integrated with an adjacent block from the 1960s, thus linking into the existing circulation system of the campus.

Libeskind, whose love of (sometimes extraneous) symbolism is legendary, christened the project 'Orion' after the constellation, though the night sky on the Holloway Road is upstaged by street lights. He envisaged the building as "a guiding light for developing a unique icon … [and] a landmark attracting visitors to the cultural programme within by its articulated forms".

The building consists of three intersecting blocks, dramatically angled in the usual Libeskind manner and clad in a smooth skin of 316 embossed stainless-steel panels, out of which windows are jaggedly sliced. The internal spaces (two seminar rooms and a lecture theatre) could be called 'interesting' but are essentially functional and free of frills, since this was a low-budget project. Walking up the staircase, with its leaning walls, is a somewhat disorientating experience.

It is hard to resent the presence of this laboured but distinctive building on one of north London's less engaging thoroughfares, but its tortuous symbolism seems entirely arbitrary. Berlin's Jewish Museum, which cemented Libeskind's reputation, was a wonderful fusion of form, narrative and emotion. Here, the form seems to say nothing and emotion is entirely lacking. But the building is already an interesting period piece. Oddly, Surface Architects, a young practice, pursued similar ideas with greater success in their graduate centre for Queen Mary, University of London (see pp. 124–25).

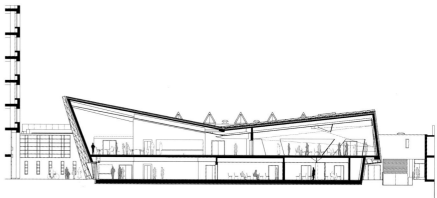

HALLFIELD SCHOOL, HALLFIELD ESTATE BAYSWATER, W2

CARUSO ST JOHN, 2001–05

The Hallfield Estate was the first major work by Denys Lasdun (in collaboration with Lindsay Drake) after the disbandment of Tecton, the partnership founded in the 1930s by Berthold Lubetkin, of which Lasdun was a member. The housing is very much in the Tecton tradition, but the school, completed in 1955 and now listed Grade II*, is unmistakably a Lasdun building. It anticipates, on a small scale, the drama of his later works (such as the Royal National Theatre) and certainly reflects the influence of Le Corbusier, in particular the Pavilion Suisse.

A competition in the late 1990s for an extension to the school, with Lasdun as one of the judges, resulted in a victory for Future Systems. The practice's flowing, organic approach to design was both sympathetic to the existing building and yet emphatically of a new era. Funding was, however, not forthcoming and the scheme was abandoned. In 2001 Caruso St John was appointed to develop fresh proposals. By this time the need for additional accommodation was becoming urgent, as the school had been using temporary huts spread across part of the playground for nearly twenty-five years. The brief to the architects provided for six new classrooms for juniors and three for infants. The new buildings were completed and occupied in 2005.

Even for a practice as thoughtful and history-conscious as Caruso St John, the challenge of building in the context of a Modern Movement icon was considerable. The scheme was subjected to intense scrutiny by planners in the borough of Westminster, English Heritage and other heritage groups. Caruso St John's initial idea of constructing the new buildings in hard black engineering brick was vetoed, depriving the additions of a subversive element of drama. (Lasdun used black brick for the infants' classrooms, but regrettably they were painted off-white in the 1970s.) Instead, a light-cream brick, not far removed in hue from London Stock, was used.

The other key planning issue, apart from materials, was the position of the new buildings in relation to the existing school. Lasdun's composition, with its sweeping contours and profusion of mature trees that survived wartime bombing and subsequent redevelopment, is an essentially romantic response to the site, in the mould of Le Corbusier. The two new blocks read as a natural extension of the earlier school, echoing Lasdun's engagement with the site and taking advantage of a variety of views – classrooms are at the corners of the blocks with views out in two directions. In Peter St John's words, they read "as if they are the last pieces of a complicated jigsaw". Inside, exposed red-brick walls and black floors provide a powerful contrast to the more neutral internal palette of the original building. This project has all the subtlety and controlled drama expected of Caruso St John: it respects the icon to which it forms an addition but is not unduly reverential.

Above and opposite, bottom
The two new blocks are set either side of the original buildings, and surrounded by trees, which provide an attractive and calming setting from inside and outside.

Opposite, top
The school is pleasantly small in scale in comparison with the surrounding blocks of the Hallfield Estate.

IMPERIAL COLLEGE FACULTY BUILDING
EXHIBITION ROAD, SOUTH KENSINGTON, SW7

FOSTER + PARTNERS, 2001–04

For all its academic excellence, Imperial College had, until quite recently, a poor record of architectural patronage. Apart from its residential blocks by Sheppard Robson – recently demolished to make way for new blocks by Kohn Pedersen Fox – the college's rapid expansion during the 1960s produced nothing beyond the routinely functional. At that time, some fine Victorian buildings on the South Kensington site, including Thomas Collcutt's magnificent Imperial Institute, were flattened to facilitate the expansion.

The four buildings completed during the 1990s by Foster + Partners for Imperial College, along with several commissions to other practices, have helped to remedy the situation. The excellent Flowers Building (1994–98), housing medical research and teaching accommodation, was the first, and the unashamedly showy Tanaka Business School, incorporating a new main entrance to the college on Exhibition Road, the largest and most prominent. The Faculty Building is located immediately to the rear of the Business School, in Dalby Court, an internal square that contains, at lower level, the college's massive heat and power plant – a facility that could not be moved. The building forms part of Foster + Partners' wider masterplan to improve Dalby Court

and pedestrian routes across the campus. By constructing a deck across the court, with a ramped route that cuts through the Faculty Building, Foster formed a new link between Exhibition Road and Queen's Lawn, the formal heart of the college. Basement levels provide a small parking area for cars plus space for 600 bicycles.

The rationale behind the building reflects the agenda of the college's Rector, who sought to apply the lessons of the commercial sector to its administration. All heads of department, plus key managerial staff, have offices in the building, and there is plenty of space for meetings and other 'interaction'. The fit-out of the interior is elegant and practical, and the building is designed for low-energy operation. What makes the Faculty Building distinctive is its external cladding, featuring solid panels in three shades of blue, selected by Danish designer and perennial Foster collaborator Per Arnoldi. Forming a pattern on the glazed façade, the panels appear to be randomly placed but are in fact calculated to shade offices from solar gain. Columns painted deep orange, set along the edge of the ramp and visible through the façade, provide another element of strong colour; the days when Foster's palette was confined to grey and silver have gone.

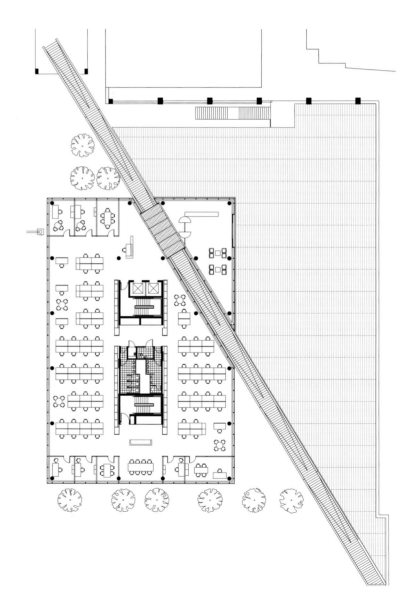

Right

The plan shows the way in which a new route across the campus cuts through the Faculty Building. Storage space for bicycles is provided at basement level.

Opposite, top

The strong use of colour is an important element of the scheme, with solid panels on the glazed façade additionally helping to baffle solar gain.

Opposite, bottom

The Faculty Building sits in a previously sterile internal court containing the college's main power plant, which had to be accommodated in the scheme.

INSTITUTE FOR CULTURAL HERITAGE
UNIVERSITY COLLEGE LONDON
GORDON STREET, WC1

DIXON JONES, 2002–

Won by Dixon Jones in competition in 2002, the Institute for Cultural Heritage project has secured funding and looks set to be realized. The new building fills a gap site on Gordon Street that has remained empty since the destruction by wartime bombs of the great hall of University College London (UCL), which stood there. The site is framed by the Bloomsbury Theatre (dating from the 1960s) and a handsome nineteenth-century terrace occupied by the college.

The project has more than one agenda. The first is the provision of a new home for the college's manuscripts and rare books, and for the remarkable Petrie Collection of more than 80,000 Egyptian antiquities, few of which are currently on display. Secondly, the building gives UCL a second 'front door', on the eastern side of its campus, which currently has a distinctly 'back of house' ethos compared to the handsome Greek Revival front quadrangle on Gower Street. Lecture theatres, a gallery for temporary exhibitions and a cafeteria are also included in a scheme that makes optimum use of the site.

Addressing a confused context, the new building takes its cue in terms of scale from the Bloomsbury Theatre, mediating between the bold, even arrogant form of the theatre and the decorum of the adjacent terrace. The street façade is mostly devoid of windows, reflecting the practical needs of the museum areas on floors one to three. The library spaces on the upper floors are set back, while the double-height reception area features a fully glazed elevation to the street, with a projecting canopy above the entrance. The reception area is a dignified space, marking the point where academia meets the city: it is a social as much as a circulation space. The Petrie Collection is accessed by escalator, recalling Dixon Jones's use of these devices at the Royal Opera House and National Portrait Gallery. Lifts serve the upper-floor library spaces. (Book stacks are provided on two basement levels and served by dedicated lifts.) The reception area forms part of a new level route across the college from Gordon Street to Gower Street.

Building in a modern way in historic contexts is something that Dixon Jones does with great skill. This building, though less ambitious in scale than the practice's major cultural projects in London, does a lot more than fill a gap.

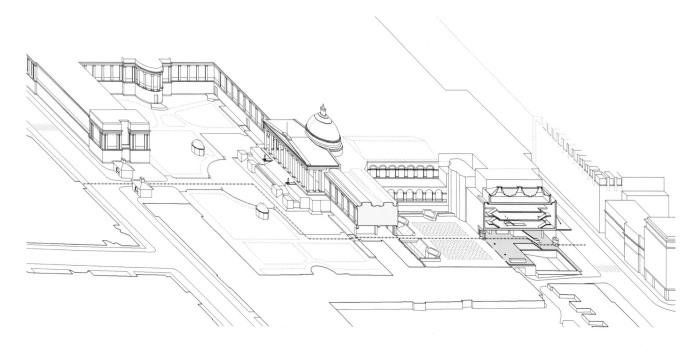

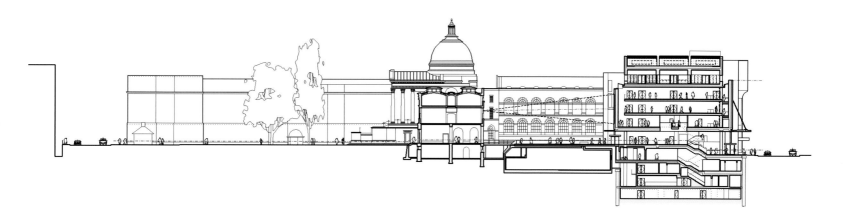

INSTITUTE OF CELL AND MOLECULAR
SCIENCE, BLIZARD BUILDING
QUEEN MARY, UNIVERSITY OF LONDON
TURNER STREET, WHITECHAPEL, E1

SMC ALSOP, 2001–05

Will Alsop's Peckham Library, winner of the Stirling Prize in 2000, remains one of the new architectural landmarks of London, a popular, colourful building that makes a strong case for iconic structures – as long as they are in the right place. His £45,000,000 medical school for Queen Mary, the subject of a prestigious competition in 2001, is in an equally unfashionable corner of London, tucked away behind the decaying Victorian blocks of the Royal London Hospital, to which the school is attached. (The hospital is soon to be comprehensively rebuilt, under a private finance initiative project, to plans by HOK – see pp. 152–53.) In this instance Alsop's taste for the expressive, colourful and even outrageous was tempered by a highly practical brief. The result is a building that is hugely stimulating as a place to work and study, and which makes a strong contribution to the public realm.

The brief provided for laboratory and research space for four hundred people, lecture and seminar rooms, a lecture theatre seating four hundred, and a cafeteria. In addition, a highly novel feature is a public exhibition space intended to foster interest in science and medicine among young people. Above ground, on either side of a central paved plaza, the building is divided into two parts, which are connected by a glazed link bridge at first-floor level. The

lecture theatre and cafeteria are in the smaller of the two blocks and are connected to an existing medical school building. The long spine of this building forms the point of entry for members of the public.

The laboratories extend across the site at basement level. Upper floors of the main block contain offices, areas for writing up experiments and meeting rooms around a central atrium that extends down to the basement, providing the laboratories with natural light. (They are also lit by roof lights set in the plaza.) Within the atrium three sculptural pods – a familiar feature of Alsop's buildings – accommodate seminar and meeting spaces accessed at ground-, first- and second-floor levels. A fourth, bright-red, two-storey pod, known as the Centre of the Cell, contains 195 square metres of public exhibition space, with controlled views into the laboratories, and is entered via the bridge.

The most remarkable feature of this building, however, is its transparency, as the public square provides intriguing views into and through it. (The glazed façade of the main block is punctuated by painted glass artworks by Bruce McLean, a regular collaborator of Alsop.) Medical schools were traditionally private, secure places. Alsop's building seeks to demystify the process of medical education, to open up spaces, where practical, in order to engage the public in what goes on inside.

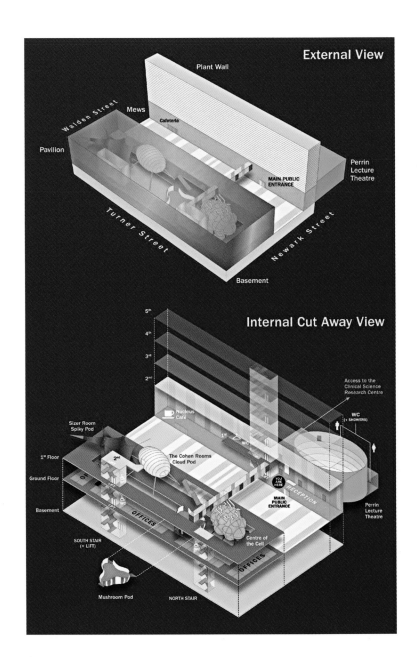

JOHN PERRY NURSERY, CHARLES ROAD DAGENHAM, RM10

DSDHA, 2002–04

This precise and elegant but highly practical little building, constructed in ten months and costing less than £500,000, is one of a number of 'neighbourhood nurseries' – some new, others adaptations of existing buildings – opened as part of a pioneering initiative by the borough of Barking and Dagenham. This project focuses on the more deprived areas of the borough, which generally is far from affluent, although it is a crucial part of the Thames Gateway. Three projects have been commissioned from DSDHA, the practice formed by Deborah Saunt and David Hills in 1998. At the time of the commission, DSDHA had yet to complete a freestanding building, though it had won a CABE-sponsored competition for nursery school design.

The brief in this instance was initially for a building accommodating twenty-six children within the curtilage of the existing John Perry Primary School. (As Phase 2 of the project, a fifty-place daycare facility was constructed on adjacent land.) The architects conceived the new building as 'a studio for children', closing one end of a courtyard surrounded by low-rise school buildings dating from the 1950s. One of their inspirations was the idyllic studio and garden created by Barbara Hepworth in St Ives. Instead of a conventional enclosed environment, the client wanted open, light spaces that connect with the outside world (the typical family home in this part of London is a local-authority flat). The use of polycarbonate sheet, a cheap but tough material, to form the western elevation of the building, facing the existing courtyard, was a response to this requirement. Aluminium-framed windows are set at child height. This elevation incorporates the most dramatic feature of the building, a boldly projecting canopy, cantilevering out 10 metres over the courtyard. Elsewhere, walls are constructed of insulated timber stud clad in brick – a hard Dutch engineering brick with an iridescent surface – with bands of clear glazing at high level, offering a defensive look to the outside world.

Inside the building, and in the revamped courtyard, the idea of a landscape for children has been realized with joy and imagination in spaces that are colourful and stimulating but never contrived or condescending. This is a building that invites discovery. It embodies DSDHA's quest for architecture that is comfortable but inspirational, both complex and simple, and strongly rooted in an exploration of the possibilities of materials. The firm is one of a number of young practices forging a new London vernacular.

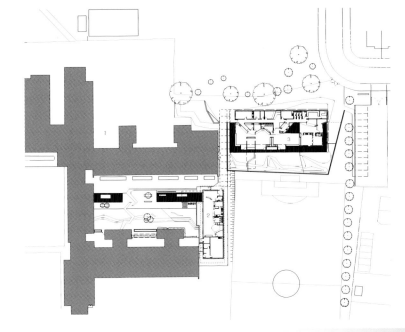

Opposite, right and below

DSDHA's additions to the John Perry Nursery include
an extension to the existing school with a revamped
internal landscaped courtyard (opposite), and
a freestanding daycare facility clad in Dutch
engineering brick (below).

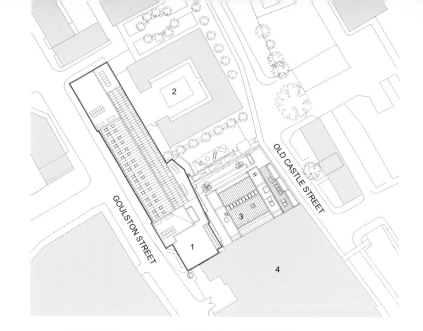

LAW DEPARTMENT, LONDON METROPOLITAN UNIVERSITY, HOLLOWAY ROAD, HOLLOWAY, N7
WRIGHT AND WRIGHT ARCHITECTS, 1995–2003

The new Law Department at London Guildhall University stands adjacent to Wright and Wright's Women's Library for the university, completed in 2002. Since its completion, London Guildhall University has merged with the University of North London to form the new London Metropolitan University, with its principal campuses at Whitechapel, on the edge of the City, and at Holloway Road in north London. The two buildings share an architectural vocabulary that is rational and pragmatic, responds strongly to practical issues and eschews empty gestures. The use of red brick clearly defers to the adjacent Calcutta House, a converted tea warehouse now used by the university.

The site for the Law Department on Goulston Street was created by the demolition of a redundant swimming baths, although the basements from this building were reused. Commissioned as long ago as 1995 but constructed in 2001–03, the building contains a conventional mix of lecture and seminar rooms and cellular offices for staff, all arranged on a longitudinal plan that reflects the narrowness of the site. A double-height, top-lit atrium extends the length of the building at the rear. All the main seminar rooms open off this space – though there

is a large lecture theatre at basement level – which functions as much more than a corridor and acts as a place for social and academic discourse. Externally, the rear of the building has a largely blank elevation, since it faces a block of inter-war flats built by London County Council ; this is, in every sense, a diverse quarter of London.

The building looks solid and immoveable, sober and dignified. It is faced in masonry and constructed on a concrete frame that is left exposed at various points inside the building. There is, however, a strong element of flexibility in the project: the seminar rooms can be reconfigured by means of moveable partitions, and the cellular offices could readily be stripped out if another spatial arrangement were needed. An unusual planning requirement was the provision of a barrow store for nearby Petticoat Lane Market.

The project uses ordinary, robust materials in a tough but polite manner – no gimmicks here, just a building that is thoroughly considered and well detailed. Oak furniture designed by the architects adds to the quality of the interior. This is a building that is easily ignored, but deserves respect for its response to the urban context and close attention to the needs of users.

Right
Located within a stone's throw of the City, Wright and Wright's Law Department, like the practice's earlier Women's Library, defers to the urban context in its use of severe red brick.

Opposite
Internally, the building provides a variety of dignified and enjoyable spaces, including the double-height, top-lit atrium.

LOCK-KEEPER'S COTTAGE GRADUATE CENTRE, HUMANITIES DEPT
QUEEN MARY, UNIVERSITY OF LONDON
MILE END LOCK, MILE END, E1

SURFACE ARCHITECTS, 2003–05

Not so long ago, Queen Mary, of all the major colleges of the University of London, seemed to have the most disadvantages in terms of its site, which is a long way down the Mile End Road in east London, next to Regent's Canal. Today, with the East End newly fashionable, Queen Mary is capitalizing on the huge potential of its locale and commissioning some high-quality buildings for its expanding campus: MacCormac Jamieson Prichard, Hawkins Brown, Sheppard Robson and Feilden Clegg Bradley (see pp. 136–37) have all built there in recent years, and SMC Alsop's Institute of Cell and Molecular Science, next to the site of the Royal London Hospital, is already an icon of east London (see pp. 118–19).

Led by two former assistants of Will Alsop, Andy McFee and Richard Scott, Surface Architects is one of the more off-beat young practices in London, eschewing the deadpan objectivity of such architects as Caruso St John and Sergison Bates in favour of determinedly expressive and colourful design. An earlier project by Surface for Queen Mary was the insertion of toilets and a lift for the disabled into the library, in a strikingly sculptural intervention that made a virtue of necessity.

The £650,000 graduate centre provides workspaces, seminar rooms and a common room for postgraduate students in the arts and social sciences. The new block, a series of interlocking forms in the best Deconstructivist mould, wraps around the north and west sides of a converted early nineteenth-century lock-keeper's cottage that had long been derelict. A boldly projecting extrusion on the canalside incorporates a huge picture window for the common room. To the rear, the building is clad in smooth aluminium. A double-height foyer space connecting old and new buildings contains a stair and bridge link (facilitating full access for the disabled) that the architects describe as a "tendril". Strong colour is used freely inside. Is this project an example of 1980s revival (as one critic implied) or the forward-looking work proclaimed by the architects? Such a question may be irrelevant, as the building is an enjoyable addition to the campus, and a pleasant place in which to work.

Below and opposite, bottom left
The new Graduate Centre includes both a converted lock-keeper's cottage and the new extension by Surface Architects, linked by a double-height foyer. With its vivid colour and strong form, the building is a stimulating addition to an essentially nineteenth-century context.

Opposite, top
The form of the Graduate Centre was developed with reference to pedestrian routes leading around the cottage and from a proposed new square behind the building to the canal.

Opposite, bottom right
Seminar rooms offer intriguing views over Regent's Canal.

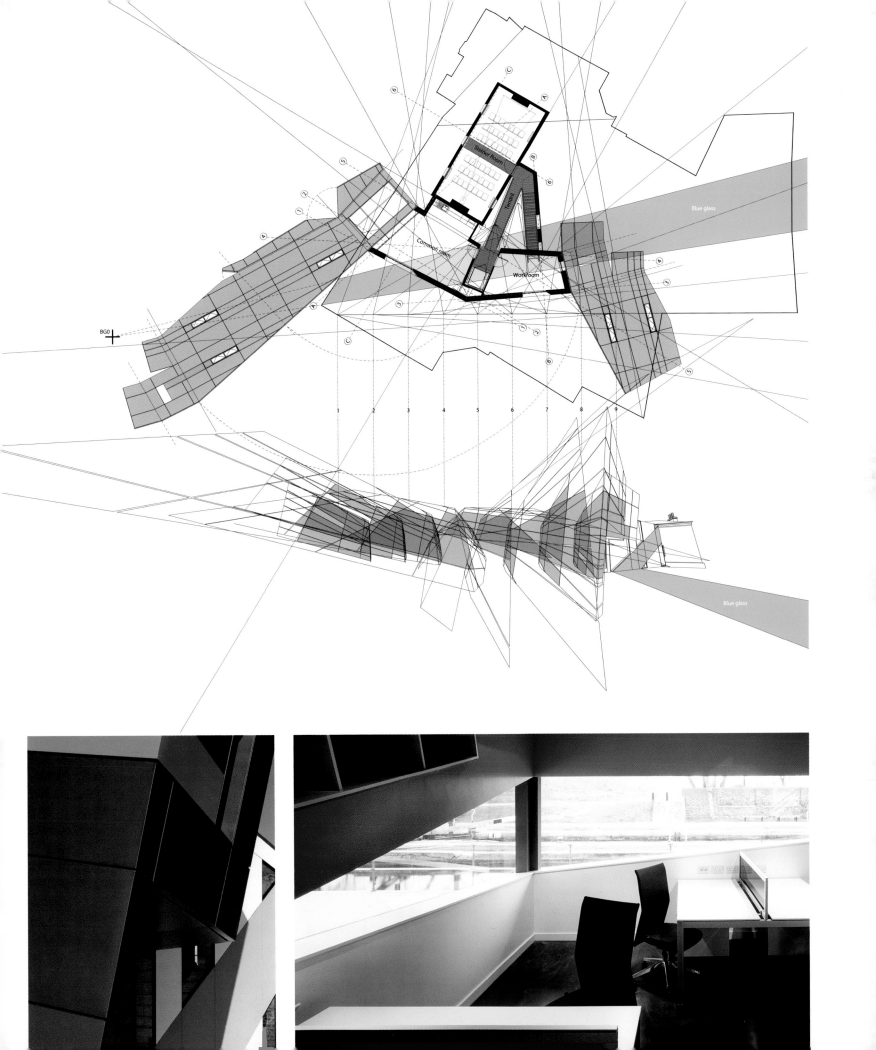

NDNA LONDON REGIONAL CENTRE
THORNCLIFFE ROAD, HOUNSLOW, UB2

COTTRELL + VERMEULEN, 2002–04

Cottrell + Vermeulen, founded in 1992, has established a reputation for designing schools that are practical and hard-wearing but also enjoyable and inspirational; creating "affordable, child-friendly architecture" is their aim. In 2002 the firm won an invited competition for one of a series of regional centres across Britain developed by the National Day Nurseries Association (NDNA). 'The Nursery on the Green', as this project became known, was seen as a prototype for similar developments elsewhere and a model of good practice in the field. It was to be more than a conventional nursery, potentially offering health care, parent support facilities and training for those working in childcare, in line with the government's Sure Start educational initiative. The project, which won an RIBA Award in 2005, had to be economical – the end cost was £1,000,000 – and capable of being fast-tracked. The designs were conceived with a view to their being replicated on other sites, though in the event this did not occur.

The brief was for a nursery to accommodate ninety-eight children, all aged under five, with scope for future expansion in terms of scale and facilities, on a site adjacent to an existing school. The basic concept is that of a 'tented city', in which the conventional divide between inside and outside is broken down in favour of a free mix of informal, flexible covered spaces under the oversailing roof. Open play areas, one of them a sand-filled 'beach', interconnect with dedicated spaces for the different age groups. Initially the overall covering was to be literally a tent: coated canvas on an aluminium frame. British building regulations, however, prevented this, so GRP (glass-reinforced plastic) on a steel frame was substituted. One important consideration was baffling the noise from aircraft – the site is on a flight path to Heathrow Airport – and from the nearby M4 motorway and A40 road: acoustically insulated ceilings were used and dense external planting has also helped. The project shows a commendable commitment to sustainable design principles, with an effort made to use materials with low embodied energy (involving low-emission manufacturing and transport).

Externally, the building is a simple shed with the appearance of a superior warehouse. Inside, however, it is a delight, thanks to the generous spaces, the even natural light and the use of strong colour. This is a real place for children, stimulating and secure, with delightful gardens on two sides partly covered by the 'big top' roof. It reflects the serious efforts being made to remedy Britain's rather patchy record in the field of pre-school childcare.

Above

The NDNA Centre is essentially a warehouse for children, with a big simple shed containing a series of enclosed and open-plan spaces.

Opposite

Colour is used in an uninhibited way to highlight the structure and animate the interior. Materials made for hard wear include corrugated plastic sheeting.

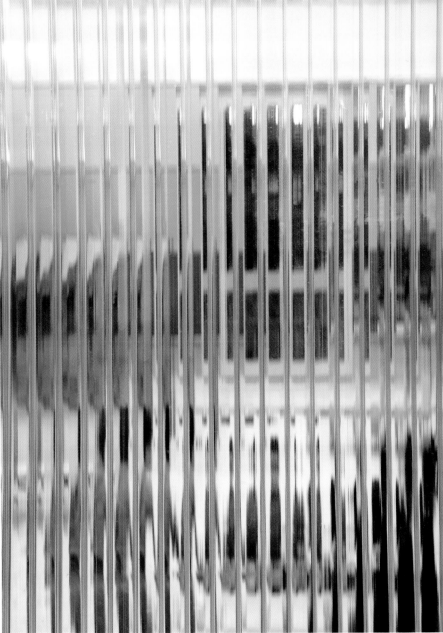

NEW ACADEMIC BUILDING, LONDON SCHOOL OF ECONOMICS, LINCOLN'S INN FIELDS, WC2

GRIMSHAW, 2005–08

The London School of Economics (LSE), for all its internationally renowned academic excellence, has inhabited a lacklustre collection of buildings for the last century. Recent additions to the Aldwych campus in central London, however, include a new library (a radical warehouse conversion by Foster + Partners), a student centre by Kohn Pedersen Fox, and a piazza and coffee bar by MacCormac Jamieson Prichard, as well as the conversion of former commercial buildings on Kingsway.

The new academic building at the LSE is another exercise in reuse, in this instance involving an imposing commercial block, 24 Kingsway. The project, construction of which began in the summer of 2006, will double the LSE's teaching space.

Grimshaw won the £46,000,000 project in a high-profile competition in 2005. It envisages the building as a key urban connector, linking the existing campus to Kingsway and Sardinia Street (on the corner of which it stands), and to Lincoln's Inn Fields, which it faces to the east. The existing forecourt to Lincoln's Inn Fields is recast to form an external amphitheatre to the north and, to the south, a paved terrace, with a café that is open to the public as well as the academic community. By opening up the corner to Sardinia Street and Portsmouth Street, the project is connected visually to the LSE's existing buildings to the south.

An enlarged doorway leads to an internal street running east–west through the building. The focus of the project is the central atrium, a light-filled, triple-height space with gallery levels on all sides, linked by delicate scissor stairs. The lecture and function spaces on the lower ground level are accessed from the atrium. The new glazed roof is extremely lightweight, supported on bowstring trusses to minimize the structure. A roof pavilion accommodates executive meeting rooms and a function suite with splendid views over Lincoln's Inn Fields to the City.

The existing building's environmental failings are addressed by replacing the original windows with new double-glazed units. Natural light and ventilation are maximized and pre-cooled water, extracted from a borehole 100 metres below ground, is used for cooling purposes. Solar collectors and photovoltaic panels are positioned on the roof.

Below
Inside, there is generous provision for everything from large-scale public lectures to private seminars, with ample social space.

Opposite, top
The project includes the creation of a new external social space on Lincoln's Inn Fields.

Opposite, bottom
Actually a conversion of an existing monumental early twentieth-century commercial building, the LSE's new academic building is being radically reconfigured around a central day-lit atrium.

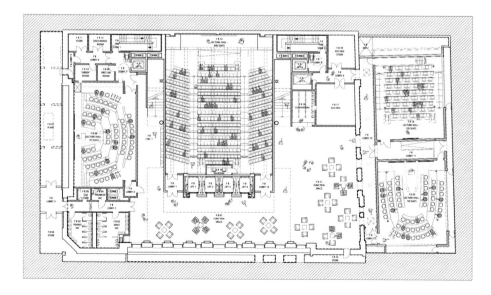

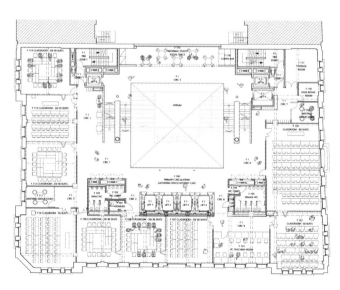

SCHOOL OF SLAVONIC AND EAST EUROPEAN STUDIES, UNIVERSITY COLLEGE LONDON GOWER STREET, WC1

SHORT AND ASSOCIATES, 2003–05

The School of Slavonic and East European Studies (SSEES), now part of University College London (UCL), was founded in 1915 and until recently was housed in a wing of the University of London's Senate House. Its new building, opened in the autumn of 2005, is located a few blocks to the north, close to the main UCL site, on land previously occupied by a delivery yard for the college's chemistry department. Vehicular access for that department had to be provided as part of the scheme and maintained throughout the construction process. Existing foundations, laid for a possible extension of the chemistry block in the 1970s, were reused in the project.

The client brief called for about 3500 square metres of accommodation for 450 students and academic and administrative staff, including space for the outstanding specialist library, the seminar rooms and offices. The seven-storey building is radially planned, with upper floors extending out above the street-level delivery route. Forty years ago the University of London was allowed to demolish large chunks of Georgian Bloomsbury and replace them with new buildings that paid little regard to historic context. In contrast, the street elevation of Short's building is made of load-bearing brick, the basic material of the surrounding terraced streets. It is an extraordinary presence in a side street just off Gordon Square. The architects

refer to it as "a small urban palace", its style making reference to the brick churches of the Baltic. A heftily sculptured parapet supports a steep zinc-clad roof topped by prominent exhaust stacks.

Alan Short has played a pioneering role in the evolution of an environmentally benign, low-energy architecture, of which his engineering block for Leicester's De Montfort University is a striking expression. The SSEES building is naturally ventilated, using passive downdraught cooling for the first time, it is claimed, in a city-centre public building anywhere in the world. The key to the ventilation strategy is the central atrium or light well, which draws air through the interior; a mechanical chiller cools the air in hot weather. One of the challenges of the project was dealing with the implications of this feature in terms of fire safety, as fire officers favour rigidly compartmentalized buildings. In this case, the whole building is treated as one sealed compartment. The street façade is actually an outer screen: the real façade lies behind it, with a dramatic entrance space between the two. The metal- and glass-clad internal structure provides a memorable contrast to the solidity of the street elevation. But the latter is a delight, bucking most current trends to create a highly individual, even eccentric, addition to the variegated public domain of London's central academic quarter.

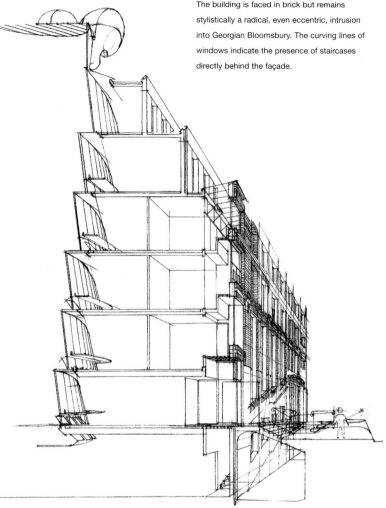

SURE START CENTRAL BRENT CENTRE
BRIDGE ROAD, WILLESDEN, NW10

GREENHILL JENNER, 2005

This project was conceived as part of the government's now abandoned Sure Start programme, targeted at poorer families. This scheme aimed to provide not only nursery care but also a place where parents could obtain advice and practical support on childcare and on such issues as debt and welfare benefits. The Brent Centre is a tough, economical (£1,380,000) but also highly enjoyable building. It incorporates a community hall as well as a nursery for babies and toddlers, crèche and advice centre.

The centre consists of three steel-framed, timber-clad boxes with hipped copper roofs, as well as a nursery contained under a mono-pitch roof at the west end of the site, all disposed around a central spine corridor lit by roof lights. Sheltered play areas extend the usable space outwards in fine weather. Internally, the lofty roofs of the boxes provide flexible light and airy spaces.

The form of the roofs is not arbitrary. The roof lights incorporate louvres that open in response to rising internal temperatures, drawing in fresh air through perimeter windows to cool the space using the stack effect, whereby warm air is exhausted upwards, to be replaced by cooler air.

Everything is simple, direct and economical: this is not a building with the potential longevity of the London board schools of the nineteenth century, but one that takes the issue of social service seriously and adds an element of delight.

Below and right

This Sure Start centre consists of a group of steel-framed pavilions clad in timber with pitched roofs that incorporate louvres to let in fresh air. Play spaces and gardens around the building make it a friendly oasis for children.

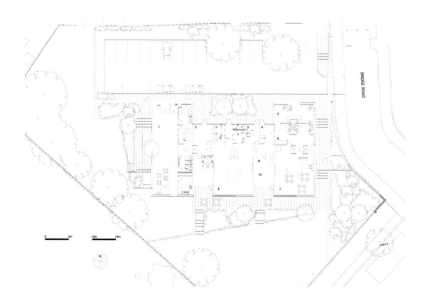

SURE START KILBURN
LINSTEAD STREET, KILBURN, NW6

MEADOWCROFT GRIFFIN ARCHITECTS, 2005–06

This project provides a neighbourhood nursery for thirty-six children and support facilities for parents. The site, close to Kilburn Grange Park in the borough of Camden, was formerly the playground of a Victorian school – now converted to flats – and was given back to Camden Council under an agreement with the developer. (Known as Section 106 agreements, such arrangements involve the release of land to councils for projects that will benefit the community.)

The project is rooted in the architects' conviction that "children need a space of their own in which to thrive and to flourish". In this area of London, the inadequacy of much local housing exacerbates the problems faced by young families, and most children will probably not have space to themselves at home. Meadowcroft Griffin's understated but carefully detailed and well-crafted architecture reflects a long process of research into the needs of the centre's future users. The old playground's enclosing wall was retained and formed a starting point for the design, an initial idea for which was a perimeter brick wall with a garden interior. Another point of reference was the concept of the tree house, beloved of children over the centuries, which is expressed in the first-floor activity rooms with their exposed timber joists, timber-lined window reveals and window seats that allow views into the mature trees around the site. (The constraints of the site meant that part of the building had to have a second storey.) The relationship between external and internal space is crucial, and interior spaces are equipped with big double doors opening up to the courtyard.

Inside the centre, the emphasis is on creating child-scaled areas, including 'secret' spaces they can make their own. The stress is on flexibility, with moveable screens that allow the interior to be reconfigured. Colour is used judiciously: relatively neutral shades inside the building encourage the children to cover the walls in their own paintings and drawings. Natural light infuses the building, and is controlled by the users with louvres, roller blinds and curtains.

This carefully considered building gives new meaning to the oft-abused term 'community architecture'. Designed in consultation with the community, it has real humanity as well as architectural quality rooted in a sure feel for materials, light and space.

Above and left
Sure Start Kilburn sits within the curtilage of a Victorian school (now flats). A broad palette of materials, including exposed concrete, timber and render, embodies the urban contextual ambitions of one of a new generation of architects working on buildings for the community.

SURE START LAVENDER, LAVENDER AVENUE
MERTON, CR4

JOHN MCASLAN + PARTNERS, 2003–05

Another of the centres for children and their parents located in underprivileged city areas under the government's former Sure Start scheme, this project sits on an uninspiring site in open land, bordered by allotments, alongside the busy London Road in the south London borough of Merton. The community centre that formerly stood here was badly vandalized and eventually burned down. The nursery provides space for about ninety children and babies, in a building conceived as a 'pavilion in the park', or rather a series of interconnected pavilions.

The project had to be economical and rapidly constructed, so a modular, 'kit-of-parts' strategy, with components fabricated off-site and applied to a primary steel frame, seemed a logical outcome. The

linear plan is characteristic of McAslan and shows the influence of Louis Kahn that is pervasive in this practice's work. Services and support spaces face the main road, behind a relatively solid eastern elevation, and the activity rooms lie at the rear, with glazed façades opening on to a timber deck and enclosed external play spaces. The 1000-square-metre building also includes a café and training/counselling rooms, which are somewhat redundant since the abandonment of the Sure Start programme.

Colour is used effectively but with restraint, and the use of timber cladding as a rain screen gives the building added texture. The design strategy is highly rational but the outcome is a "simple but inspired building" (as the *RIBA Journal* commented)

that is child-centred and has the straight-forward charm of the best examples of the golden age of school building in the 1950s.

This was a small building by the practice's standards (the total cost was £1,420,000), but justified itself as a research project and test-bed for new ideas, which have been developed in other educational projects. The involvement of Arup as engineers was highly significant in developing "an interdisciplinary approach that recognized and understood the interdependencies between building elements and systems, and how these are layered one on top of the other, reflecting both the order in which construction might take place and the interfaces between contractors".

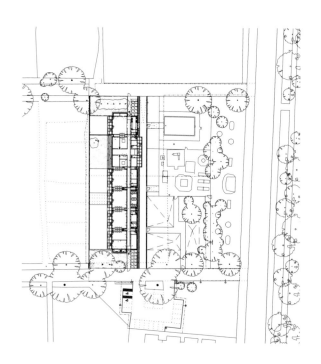

WESTFIELD STUDENT VILLAGE
QUEEN MARY, UNIVERSITY OF LONDON
MILE END ROAD, MILE END, E1

FEILDEN CLEGG BRADLEY ARCHITECTS, 2002–04

The dramatic expansion of higher education in Britain in recent years has had a huge impact on the housing market in a number of cities. In London, students have to cope with an overpriced and highly competitive housing scene, so most institutions have made efforts to increase residential accommodation within easy reach of their campuses. Queen Mary College – or Queen Mary as it is now known – is no exception. The college, part of the University of London, has at its core the late Victorian People's Palace, designed by E.R. Robson (best known for his work as chief architect for the London Schools Board between 1872 and 1889). Post-war buildings include work by Feilden & Mawson, RMJM, Sheppard Robson, Colin St John Wilson and MacCormac Jamieson Prichard.

Feilden Clegg Bradley's £29,500,000 project aims to provide not just housing but also a 'village': a tangible academic community, complete with shop, café/bar and laundry to supplement facilities available on the main campus. The student village occupies a long site, previously derelict, adjoining the Grand Union Canal to the east of the main campus. It provides nearly 1000 bed spaces in flats and maisonettes for students, visiting academics and (that vital element of any higher-education budget) conference use. The new Mile End Park is located across the canal to the east, and the main railway line out of Liverpool Street borders the site to the north.

The scheme includes six buildings, constructed in two phases from 2003 onwards. The first phase, at the core of the site and completed at the end of 2003, consists of three four-storey brick buildings set around landscaped courtyards, essentially inward-looking and secluded, with an appropriately restrained architectural language. In contrast, two more buildings, forming phase two and completed in the autumn of 2004, give the project a potent public presence on the edges of the site. The first is a long eight-storey block, Pooley Hall, at the north end. It screens the village from the railway tracks and is clad in oxidized copper with a series of triangular bays punctuating its long northern façade. The second, Sir Christopher France House, extending along the canalside, is also clad in copper and stands on a timber-clad plinth with a full-height, cut-out section allowing views in and out of the campus. A further phase of the student village is under way.

The scheme is remarkable in many respects. At a time when private developers, catering for a ready market, are providing new student housing of generally banal character, Queen Mary opted for quality. There is nothing institutional or standardized about this housing: it provides no fewer than seventeen different room layouts, for example, and flats for between four and nine students. A great deal of care has been taken to create attractive spaces between buildings. The use of prefabrication (for bathroom pods, for example) and a tunnel-form, in-situ concrete frame allowed the scheme to be constructed in less than two years, under a design-and-build contract that did not sacrifice design quality, thanks to the continuing involvement of the architects at the construction stage. The project contributes to the ongoing renaissance of the East End and reflects Queen Mary's commitment to commissioning excellent new buildings, which also include the Graduate Centre by Surface Architects (pp. 124–25) and the Institute of Cell and Molecular Science by SMC Alsop (pp. 118–19).

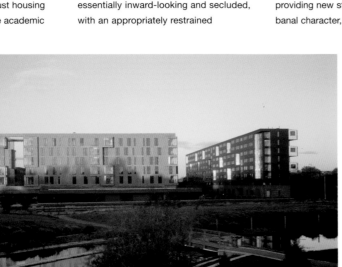

WESTMINSTER ACADEMY
HARROW ROAD, W2

ALLFORD HALL MONAGHAN MORRIS, 2005–07

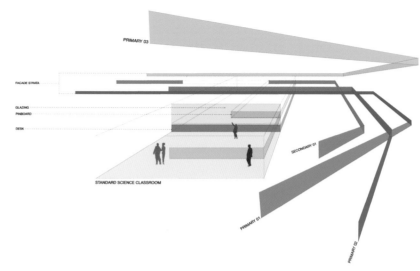

The Westminster Academy caters for nearly 1200 pupils, aged eleven to eighteen, with a special emphasis on business training. It is one of a number of new city academies (specialist secondary schools funded by the private sector) in London designed by prestigious architectural practices, some of them with no previous experience of school design. Allford Hall Monaghan Morris, however, has a track record in educational architecture – for example Great Notley School, Essex, completed in 1999, and the acclaimed Jubilee School in Tulse Hill, south London (2002) – but this £25,000,000 project is its largest school commission to date.

The site, in a far from affluent sector of the City of Westminster, was previously occupied by a local-authority office and health centre. These facilities were relocated elsewhere in the area, along with sports pitches, which have been reconfigured as

part of the academy project. The Westway is a pervasive source of noise and pollution, so it was accepted from the start that the building should be sealed and mechanically ventilated (using underfloor ducts).

At the heart of the school is a four-storey atrium orientated east–west and conceived as a social space, a 'town square' for the school community, as well as a circulation route. Classrooms line the atrium: a single row on the south side, and a double row along the northern edge of the building divided by a central corridor. The rectilinear plan is workmanlike and highly efficient. A separate sports hall, intended for use by the local community as well as by the school, contains indoor sports pitches and a dance studio.

The school is located in an unprepossessing quarter of west London, and the architects sought to create a

colourful and visually appealing new landmark. The exterior is clad in alternating bands of glass and glazed terracotta, ranging in hue from dark green at ground level to yellow at the top. A sleek and smooth effect is obtained by setting the glazing in sheer curtain-wall framing. The sports hall is timber-clad, with large glass walls at each end. Colour is used freely inside the buildings. Internal finishes are tough and durable and require minimal maintenance.

Less of an architectural showpiece than earlier city academies designed by, for instance, Richard Rogers Partnership and Foster + Partners, Westminster Academy offers excellent value for money in a highly practical design that addresses the needs of students and community. It is the twenty-first-century equivalent of the late Victorian London board schools, many of which remain in educational use today.

Above
The façade concept diagram shows the division of the space by colour according to age group.

Below and opposite
Located close to London's Westway, Westminster Academy inevitably has an internal focus, with a four-storey atrium acting as the central community space. Clad in hard-wearing terracotta and glass, the building is sealed against the noise of the busy road.

WORLD CLASSROOMS
GREY COURT SECONDARY SCHOOL
AND MEADLANDS PRIMARY SCHOOL
HAM STREET/BROUGHTON AVENUE, HAM, TW10

FUTURE SYSTEMS, 2003–05

School design is currently as exciting and innovative a sector of the architectural scene as it has been at any time since the 1950s. Future Systems argues that "the qualities of the environment in which you learn and, in particular, light, space, colour and sound, make a real difference to how quickly you learn, and how much you enjoy learning. The classrooms of the future must make children feel comfortable and allow them to learn in their own ways. In order to achieve this, the design must be able to accommodate a number of different learning scenarios."

Future Systems' World Classrooms project, developed with structural engineer Techniker and services engineer BDSP, responds to a Department for Education and Skills initiative to provide portable, reusable classroom buildings that can be quickly installed or removed when needed. Each is designed for thirty pupils and is a self-sufficient, 100-square-metre environment, equipped with its own WCs (contained in a pod) and other services. An external terrace allows the learning area to expand outdoors on fine days. The structure is of moulded glass-reinforced plastic, with pupils' own art work used for external decoration.

The first two units, costing £450,000 each, were installed at Meadlands Primary School and Grey Court Secondary School in Ham, but there is interest from other local authorities and from manufacturers in producing units in quantity, thereby reducing the cost.

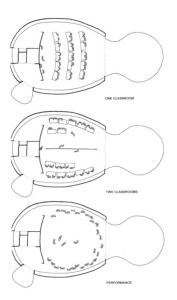

ONE CLASSROOM

TWO CLASSROOMS

PERFORMANCE

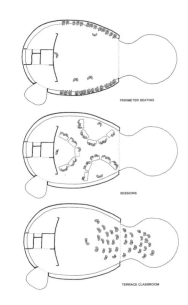

PERIMETER SEATING

SESSIONS

TERRACE CLASSROOM

HEALTH

BREAST CARE CENTRE, BARTS AND THE LONDON NHS TRUST, SMITHFIELD, EC1

GREENHILL JENNER, 2000–04

Below and opposite

While St Bartholomew's Hospital faces comprehensive redevelopment, a number of historic buildings are being retained. The West Wing now houses Greenhill Jenner's Breast Care Centre, demonstrating the potential of old hospital buildings for reuse. While the best features have been retained intact, including the grand staircase (opposite, top left), the upper floors have been subdivided to create diagnostic rooms (opposite, top right), though these are kept back from the edge of the building to allow natural light to permeate.

As the £1,250,000,000 Private Finance Initiative project scheduled to transform Barts and its sister hospital, the Royal London (see pp. 152–53), was shuffled between ministers and civil servants, Greenhill Jenner was commissioned to address the urgent need for an integrated centre for the diagnosis and treatment of breast cancer. Such a centre would build on the hospital's outstanding record in this area of medicine and bring together activities previously scattered across its Smithfield site.

The centre is housed in the hospital's Grade I-listed West Wing, completed in 1752 to designs by James Gibbs. It contained in-patient wards up to the early 1990s and thereafter was left half-empty for nearly a decade, at a time when the very survival of Barts was in doubt. The master-plan for the future development of Barts relegates this building to out-patient use and part of the rationale of the project was to secure a suitable new use for it. In fact, the opportunity to use an outstanding historic building for this purpose, albeit one that had suffered some damaging alterations over the last century or so, provided an opportunity to create a high-quality environment in line with changing ideas of patient care. Not only medical staff but also former patients were involved in the consultation process, which informed the developing design brief from 2000 onwards.

The project is significant in demonstrating how an "obsolete" historic building can be adapted to house state-of-the-art medical facilities. The development of IT (which means, for example, that X-ray images are now stored on computer rather than in banks of filing cabinets) frees up space and makes the operation of the centre more flexible.

As part of the project, two principal ground-floor rooms have been carefully restored as a waiting room/café and conference room respectively, with original features repaired or reinstated. Gibbs's main staircase, which was found to be in poor condition, was dismantled and rebuilt using steel reinforcement. Upstairs, there have been some radical changes, with diagnostic rooms centrally grouped as pods, allowing the edges of the building to be left open and the proportions of the internal spaces to be appreciated. A budget for artworks amounting to three per cent of the total project cost was agreed early on; David Batchelor's neon work on the staircase is the most prominent of these commissioned pieces.

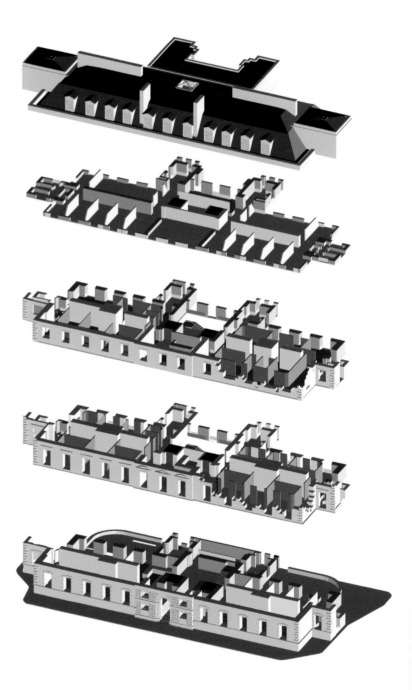

EVELINA CHILDREN'S HOSPITAL
ST THOMAS'S HOSPITAL
LAMBETH PALACE ROAD, LAMBETH, SE1

HOPKINS ARCHITECTS, 1999–2005

Below

The top four floors of wards in the Evelina Children's Hospital are backed by a conservatory with a spectacular glazed and shaded roof.

Bottom and opposite, top right

The wards are welcoming spaces, enlivened by decorated floors and bright colours. Sinuous walkways, rather than the more traditional corridors, lead through them and separate bed areas from nurses' offices and private bedrooms.

Opposite, top left and bottom

The centrepiece is the great conservatory, which sweeps across the multi-storey ward block to enclose an enjoyable day-lit public space, and to provide impressive views out. The building is clad externally in terracotta tiles.

Michael Hopkins's architecture is notable for its extraordinary diversity. London buildings of the last decade by the practice include the rather mannered Portcullis House at Westminster, with the remarkable Jubilee line Underground station beneath it; Haberdashers' Hall at Smithfield in the City and a nearby housing scheme at Charterhouse, both making extensive use of brick; and the sleek steel-and-glass headquarters for the Wellcome Trust on Euston Road. Shortlisted for the Stirling Prize in 2006, the Evelina Children's Hospital, just across the River Thames from the Palace of Westminster, is certainly another outstanding work by Hopkins.

Won in competition in 1999, the project aimed to create "a real children's hospital, not an adult hospital with cartoons on the walls": a light-filled, colourful environment with a distinctly non-institutional ethos. The site is on the south-west corner of the St Thomas's Hospital campus, with the park of Lambeth Palace on the opposite side of Lambeth Palace Road. The 16,000-square-metre, £60,000,000 building, opened late in 2005, accommodates up to 140 in-patients, plus out-patients' departments, operating theatres, consultants' offices, a café, a pharmacy and other facilities, on seven floors.

The field of hospital design is dominated by specialist practices adept at working within the parameters of the Private Finance Initiative (PFI) procurement strategy. Hopkins Architects had never designed a hospital when it embarked on this project, so there was a great deal of learning to be done. This progressive work in many respects provides a vivid contrast to much new hospital architecture developed under PFI; the recent new block for University College Hospital (just across the road from the Wellcome Trust) is a particularly dire example. As the *Architectural Review* commented, much design for the National Health Service too often produces "hospitals resembling rambling horizontal oilrigs rather than places of peace and healing".

The focus of the new Evelina Children's Hospital (a Victorian institution in origin) is the great glazed conservatory, largely naturally ventilated, which rises through the top four floors that accommodate the in-patient wards, a spectacular design in a tradition familiar from other Hopkins projects. The wards are served by snaking routes in place of conventional corridors, another move intended to counter the usual institutional ambience. There are excellent views from the four uppermost levels to the historic heart of Westminster and the Lambeth Palace gardens. Lower floors house out-patients' clinics, operating theatres, and the reception and other support spaces. Externally, terracotta tile cladding is used extensively. The internal aesthetic of the building is one of steel and glass, animated by the use of vivid colour, for example in the bright-red lift towers. Extensive use of artworks is another prominent feature of the building, for instance in the rubber floor coverings.

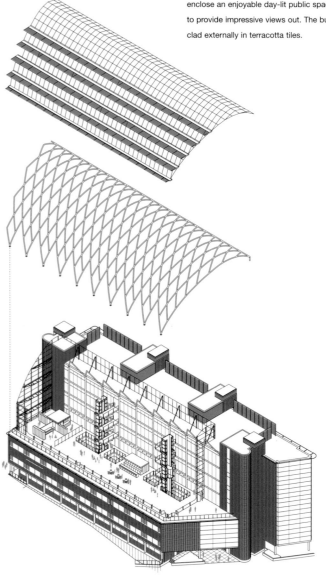

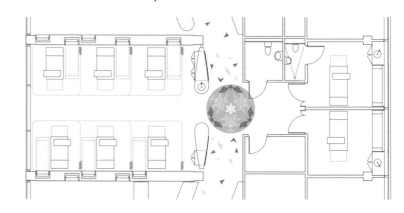

MAGGIE'S CENTRE
CHARING CROSS HOSPITAL
FULHAM PALACE ROAD, HAMMERSMITH, W6

RICHARD ROGERS PARTNERSHIP, 2001–07

Maggie Keswick Jencks, the wife of the architecture critic Charles Jencks, died of cancer in 1995. During her long illness she came to realize the desperate need of cancer sufferers (and their families and friends) for counselling, encouragement and practical support, as well as medical treatment. So the idea of Maggie's Centres emerged, and they are being developed in a number of cities around Britain. Located close to major hospitals, they contain counselling, therapy and meeting rooms and generous social spaces with an ambience unlike that of the hospital itself. The first opened in Edinburgh (reflecting

Maggie Jencks's Scottish roots) in 1996 and subsequent projects in Scotland have involved architects of the stature of Frank Gehry and Zaha Hadid. Each centre is developed as a result of local fundraising so that local communities are involved in the project from the start.

London's Maggie's Centre, attached to Charing Cross Hospital, is being designed, on a non-fee basis, by Richard Rogers Partnership. The site, a short distance from Rogers's riverside offices, is on a prominent corner adjacent to Ralph Tubbs's hospital complex of the 1960s. It is conceived as an 'open house', 370 square

metres in area, and single storey except for a small office area at mezzanine level. A terracotta wall encloses the building, buffering the noise from the street, and the internal spaces, arranged around two open courtyards landscaped by Dan Pearson, are top-lit. The focus is the kitchen and eating area, a place for meeting, socializing and relaxing. In the Rogers tradition, the building has been designed in such a way that it can be adapted in the future, with folding external and internal doors allowing spaces to be reconfigured, and 'plug-in', modular furniture that can be moved freely.

From the street, the building has an elusive presence, as it is wrapped in trees that provide a further buffer against noise and pollution and shade the interior in summer. A lightweight 'floating' roof over the mezzanine floor filters controlled daylight into the heart of the centre. This is a modest project for the practice but one into which a great deal of energy and thought has been channelled. The ethos is essentially domestic – a 'home from home' that contains memories of a series of Rogers houses, from Creek Vean to the architect's own residence in Chelsea.

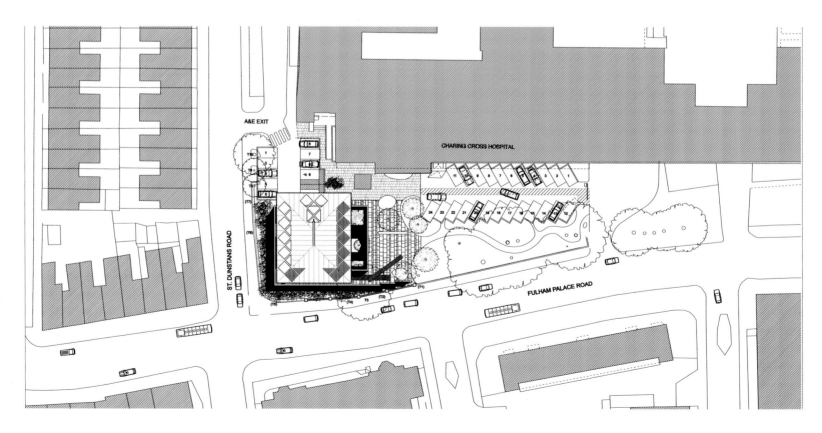

NEW INFIRMARY, CHELSEA ROYAL HOSPITAL
CHELSEA BRIDGE ROAD, CHELSEA, SW3
QUINLAN & FRANCIS TERRY ARCHITECTS, 2005–08

Below and opposite

Quinlan and Francis Terry's Infirmary is a free mix of Classical motifs, and is a controversial addition to Wren's Royal Hospital, although it replaces an unlovable 1960s block. The use of the Tuscan order, seen in Francis Terry's perspective (bottom), recalls the work of Inigo Jones and defers to the pervasive presence of Wren on the site.

Sir Christopher Wren's Chelsea Royal Hospital (built 1682–91) continues to perform the role for which it was founded by Charles II: providing a home for former soldiers in need, known as the Chelsea Pensioners. The seventeenth-century Hôtel des Invalides in Paris provided the model for Charles's foundation, but, constructed in soft-red brick, the buildings have a quiet dignity far removed from the grandiloquence of Louis XIV's France.

The most significant later additions to the hospital were designed by Sir John Soane, including offices and stables. The infirmary on the eastern side of the site, completed in 1961 to designs by government architect Eric Bedford, was rightly described by Nikolaus Pevsner's *Buildings of England* as "harshly functional". At the beginning of the twenty-first century it was judged inadequate for the needs of the many sick and disabled pensioners. A project by the American practice SBA for its replacement did not find favour with planners in the borough of Kensington and Chelsea, and in 2004 Quinlan Terry, the leading British classicist, was invited to develop alternative designs.

Working with SBA and focusing on the external aspects of the building rather than its highly practical interior, Terry (latterly in partnership with his son Francis) followed Soane's example by using London Stock brick, rather than red brick. Publication of Terry's scheme led to intense controversy about whether it was appropriate for the site. However, the scheme secured planning consent in 2005 and the new building is scheduled for completion in 2008.

Quinlan Terry describes his designs as "a mix of Wren and Soane". The use of the Tuscan order – Wren used the Doric on his principal building – is, he says, an act of deference to Britain's most widely revered architect. If there is a non-partisan case against the Terry scheme, it is that the new building is too close in form and scale to Wren's hospital. It aligns with and challenges the dominance of Wren's elevation to Royal Hospital Road. Terry is not, and does not seek to be, an original classicist in the Soane mould. As a rare example of a classicist public building in London, his infirmary may rekindle debate about the relevance of traditionalism.

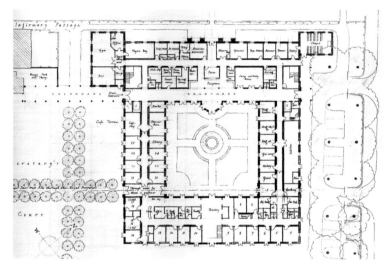

New Infirmary. Royal Hospital Chelsea.

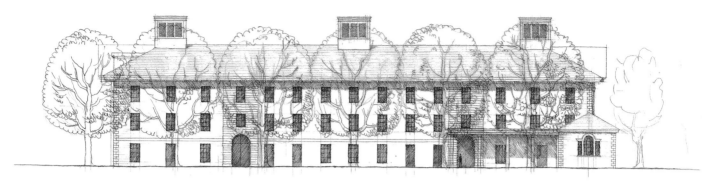

North - East Front
facing Chelsea Bridge Road

Walls   Approved Yellow Stock brickwork laid to Flemish bond
         in lime mortar, flush & lined pointing.
         Rubbed & gauged Yellow Stock brick arches & string course.
         Portland stone (or approved recon) quoins, sills, door surrounds.
         half-engaged pilasters to Tuscan Portico & Colonnade with balustrade.
Windows Hardwood Sashes set in deep reveals, thin glazing bars.
Chimneys Brick & stone as above.

Roof   Penrhyn slate with timber modillion cornice & pediment
Doors   Hardwood.
Rusticated bays   Portland stone (or approved recon)
Dormers Timber, lead cheeks

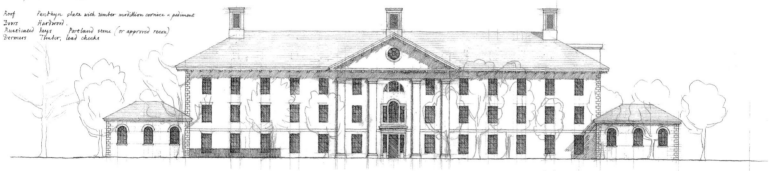

North - West Front
facing Royal Hospital Road

Section looking North - West

1/200 Scale

Quinlan Terry Arch\t
Dedham, Colchester, Essex
August 2004

1219/11 F

Revision D - Dec 04 - Balconies added   Revision A   Oct '04   Chapel windows
Revision E - Jan 05 - Updated for Planning   Rev B   Nov '04   Comments of EH & RBKC
Revision F Apl '05 - Pediment & cupola altered   Rev C   Nov '04   Railings added to area on
                                                                        North-West Front

ST BARTHOLOMEW'S HOSPITAL/
ROYAL LONDON HOSPITAL REDEVELOPMENT
SMITHFIELD, EC1/WHITECHAPEL ROAD, E1

HOK, 2002–16

One of Europe's largest public building projects involves two historic London hospitals, a few miles apart. It is scheduled to extend over more than a decade and to cost around £1,000,000,000.

St Bartholomew's Hospital (known as Barts) was founded in 1123 and until the Reformation was associated with the nearby Augustinian priory, the church of which survives in part as St Bartholomew the Great, Smithfield. Its buildings include the gateway to West Smithfield of 1702 and the early eighteenth-century ranges around the main courtyard, designed by James Gibbs, including the splendid main staircase and great hall, all listed Grade I. The hospital's later additions are of considerably lesser architectural interest. In the 1990s a proposal to close Barts generated intense opposition, and it was eventually decided to retain the site in use as a hospital.

The Royal London Hospital in Whitechapel, east London, was founded in 1740, and the Georgian hospital survives, much altered, on Whitechapel Road. It fronts a large campus with a mix of buildings, a number of them listed, ranging in date from the late Victorian period to the early twenty-first century (for example SMC Alsop's Institute of Cell and Molecular Science; see pp. 118–19). Over several decades indecision about the future of both the Royal London and Barts led to a lack of investment and increasingly unsatisfactory conditions for patients and staff.

In late 2003 the Barts and The London NHS Trust, which runs both sites, appointed Skanska Innisfree as preferred bidder for the redevelopment project embracing the two hospitals, with HOK as architect. Following a period of political indecision, when the entire project seemed threatened by growing doubts on the part of government about the Private Finance Initiative procurement route, work started on site in the summer of 2006. Completion is scheduled for 2016, with major components opening in 2010–12. Up to 1250 in-patient beds will be provided, along with specialist emergency care, and cancer and cardiac treatment facilities.

The Barts/Royal London project comes at a time when the value of the 'super-hospital' is increasingly the subject of debate and attention turns back to devolved, community-based healthcare provision. The architects have sought to address some of the most common criticisms of the large hospitals of the recent past, including the suggestion that such institutions ignore the role of the environment as an agent of healing. On both sites the majority of existing buildings will be demolished – sixty per cent at the Royal London and just over fifty per cent at Barts. Listed buildings will be retained and refurbished. Barts will benefit enormously from the pedestrianization of the central square and its landscaping as the focal point of the hospital. The new hospital building will rise behind the retained façade of the King George V block (from the 1930s) on the south-east corner of the triangular site. Internally, a dramatic atrium forms the heart of the new building. Externally, it is clad in brick and stone; the adjacent, widely admired Merrill Lynch development, completed in 2001, provided a precedent for a contextual approach.

At the Royal London a more adventurous aesthetic was encouraged by planners in the borough of Tower Hamlets and by the Greater London Authority, with major input also from the Commission for Architecture and the Built Environment. Most of the new accommodation is provided in two eighteen-storey towers to the south of the site, complete with roof-top landing pad for Air Ambulance helicopters. These massive new buildings, inevitably dominating the surrounding area, are clad in clear, opaque and translucent glazing in a range of colours, above a brick-clad base. Only twenty-five per cent of the total façade is transparent glazing, and on the south side the buildings are clad in metal filigree (even hospitals are subject to revised building regulation requirements on the control of solar heat gain, although the new buildings are necessarily air-conditioned and sealed). A new civic space is created behind the restored main building dating from the 1750s, with a glazed 'health mall' providing access to all principal departments and giving the hospital a benign public face. Perhaps the last of its kind in London, the Royal London development responds to east Londoners' demands for major investment in local facilities. It remains to be seen whether this investment has been spent to best effect.

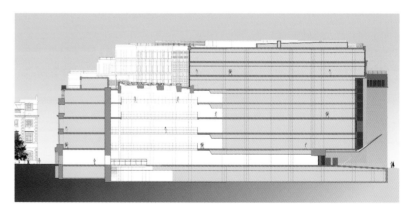

HOUSES AND HOUSING

ABERDEEN LANE
AZMAN OWENS ARCHITECTS

BENNET'S COURTYARD, MERTON ABBEY MILLS
FEILDEN CLEGG BRADLEY ARCHITECTS

BRICK HOUSE
CARUSO ST JOHN

CARGO FLEET
CHANCE DE SILVA ARCHITECTS

CASTLE HOUSE
HAMILTONS ARCHITECTS

DONNYBROOK QUARTER
PETER BARBER ARCHITECTS

GAZZANO HOUSE
AMIN TAHA ARCHITECTS

GREENWOOD ROAD
LYNCH ARCHITECTS

HOUSE AND ARTIST'S STUDIO
DSDHA

HOXTON SQUARE
ZAHA HADID ARCHITECTS

IN-BETWEEN
ANNALIE RICHES, SILVIA ULLMAYER & BARTI GARIBALDO

ISOKON FLATS
AVANTI ARCHITECTS

LOW-COST HOUSING, PEABODY HOUSING ASSOCIATION
ASH SAKULA ARCHITECTS

LOW-COST HOUSING, PEABODY HOUSING ASSOCIATION
NIALL MCLAUGHLIN ARCHITECTS

MILDMAY GROVE
PETER BARBER ARCHITECTS

NEWINGTON GREEN
HAWORTH TOMPKINS

NEWINGTON GREEN HOUSE
PREWETT BIZLEY ARCHITECTS

ONE BLACKFRIARS ROAD
IAN SIMPSON ARCHITECTS

ONE CENTAUR STREET
DE RIJKE MARSH MORGAN ARCHITECTS

OXFORD GARDENS
MICHAELIS BOYD ASSOCIATES

SHOULDHAM STREET
HENNING STUMMEL ARCHITECTS

STEALTH HOUSE
ROBERT DYE ARCHITECTS

STEEDMAN STREET
CZWG

STUDIO HOUSE
SERGISON BATES ARCHITECTS

TOWN-CENTRE HOUSING
SERGISON BATES ARCHITECTS

WRAP HOUSE
ALISON BROOKS ARCHITECTS

YOUNG HOUSE
TONKIN LIU

ABERDEEN LANE, CANONBURY, N5

AZMAN OWENS ARCHITECTS, 2001–03

Aberdeen Lane is a sparse, angular house beautifully cast out of in-situ concrete. Its occupants, a well-known journalist and economist and their four children, had originally intended to commission Ferhan Azman and Joyce Owens of Azman Owens Architects to expand their Victorian town house. When they were shown a piece of scrubby land close to Highbury Fields in north London, however, the idea of an ultra-modern new-build house began to germinate.

The site, formerly a vegetable patch, is hemmed in by a detached house on the west side, terraced mews houses on the east side and a garden wall at the rear. Planning approval had been granted for a house with a north-facing garden, but permission for a reorientated house with a west-facing garden – a much more desirable prospect – was applied for, and granted by the council on condition that the building be of architectural interest.

The north and south walls of the house, which address the lane and the house to the rear, are treated as solid façades with minimal openings, and the house opens inwards to create a courtyard. This maintains a definite edge to the lane and prevents the property from being overlooked. Concrete was an obvious

choice for these fortress-like walls, and its extensive use became the defining feature of the project.

The structure of two interlocking cubes consists of horizontal slabs with double cantilevers, so that the top cube can overhang the bottom one without support. External cavity walls are of reinforced concrete, and were left exposed both externally and internally. The thickness was calculated so that the concrete could be poured and properly compacted using standard materials, to keep costs down. The concrete was poured into birch-faced plywood shutters and the resulting smooth, blemish-free and surprisingly attractive surfaces are testimony to the skill of the contractor and the great care taken over each wall.

In contrast to this solid mass of grey, the west elevation consists entirely of timber-framed glazing. The ground-floor living-room and kitchen both have sliding doors to the courtyard garden, while the windows of the bedrooms above are veiled by vast wooden shutters.

The architects Azman and Owens have gone their separate ways since the project was completed. The clients, however, continue to enjoy their brave and unashamedly modern home.

Opposite and left
The house turns its back on the street to create a west-facing courtyard. All the main living spaces have generous glazed walls, which overlook the exceptionally private outdoor area.

BENNET'S COURTYARD, MERTON ABBEY MILLS MERTON, SW19

FEILDEN CLEGG BRADLEY ARCHITECTS, 2003–04

The Cistercian Merton Abbey (more correctly Priory), founded in 1114, has vanished almost without trace. The site is partly occupied by Merton Abbey Mills, where William Morris established his workshops in 1881 – they have in turn disappeared – and where the Liberty company later built its fabric-printing works. Recently the Mills site, along the River Wandle, has become a thriving centre for small, craft-based businesses, with a regular craft market and associated arts activities a piquant contrast to the nearby superstores and industrial estates. Feilden Clegg Bradley's housing (fifty-two units plus a small area of shops) is a natural extension to the historic site, south of the Mills, and was commissioned by the developer after a previous proposal was refused planning consent.

The scheme is deliberately industrial in appearance, with deep-set windows

puncturing walls of London Stock brick – "a beautiful living environment that extracts the essence of what makes industrial buildings such good spaces for living", as Graham Bizley commented in *Building Design*. Despite the Arts and Crafts context, the architects have eschewed folksiness in favour of a tough, Modernist aesthetic, with echoes of the work of Louis Kahn and Basil Spence. The housing, arranged in three blocks around a south-facing communal garden, is raised above ground-floor parking. The two larger blocks have internal, top-lit, naturally ventilated winter gardens, which contain the circulation decks. These areas form an attractive alternative to enclosed corridors; they were pioneered in 'social' housing schemes, although they are apparently working well in the commercial residential market, providing a welcome sense of

community. Kitchens project into the atria as timber-clad boxes, with small windows allowing residents glimpses of their neighbours' comings and goings.

As is usual with Feilden Clegg Bradley's projects, Bennet's Courtyard has serious environmental aspirations. The installation of good insulation, the use of materials with low embodied energy and a potentially long lifespan, and the careful integration of the new landscape into the ecology of the riverbank are all claimed as progressive moves. Located in one of the less glamorous London boroughs, the scheme provides an innovative model for the low-rise apartment block, a building type too often dominated by stale conventions irrelevant to a new generation of buyers.

Above and below

Bennet's Courtyard forms part of a small industrial estate on the banks of the River Wandle. The communal garden conceals the ground-floor parking below. Extensive glass to both communal and private areas allows residents the benefits of the riverside location.

Opposite

Thoughtful landscaping unites the scheme with the river, while the circulation decks introduce light, air and greenery to the interior.

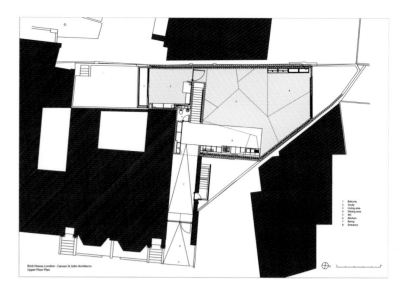

Brick House, London - Caruso St John Architects
Upper Floor Plan

1 Balcony
2 Study
3 Living area
4 Dining area
5 WC
6 Kitchen
7 Ramp
8 Entrance

BRICK HOUSE, WESTBOURNE GROVE BAYSWATER, W2

CARUSO ST JOHN, 2001–05

Brick House is one of the most celebrated houses to have been built in London in the new millennium. This is quite an achievement for architects Caruso St John, since the project is almost invisible from the street. Occupying an awkward site between the backs of three Georgian terraces and the end of a mews in Paddington, west London, its existence is hinted at by a ramp and plain timber door. But beyond this checkpoint the project is marked out as one of the capital's exceptional buildings by its extraordinary manipulation of volume and light, and its honest display of construction materials.

A nondescript ramped hallway leads from the entrance half a storey up to the first floor. The house's magic becomes apparent with the unfurling of a room that covers almost the entire 185-square-metre floor space. It is topped with a 450-millimetre-thick cast-concrete ceiling, elegantly folded like a piece of origami and punctuated with triangular roof lights. The scale and sculptural design are remarkable, and the experience has been likened by the architects to wandering into a Baroque chapel in the midst of the crowded streets of Rome.

The origin of the house's name is immediately apparent: virtually every surface is covered in honey-coloured Cambridge brick. Set with unpigmented lime mortar in an ordinary running bond, the brick wraps around the walls and the floor, even licking up the edges of the bath. The only exception is the kitchen area, where concrete has been introduced. A key

reference was the work of the Swedish architect Sigurd Lewerentz (1885–1975), whose church of St Peter, built between 1963 and 1966 in Klippan, Sweden, uses the same running bond for floors, walls and vaulted ceilings. But while Brick House's austere interior may have monastic undertones, it exudes a definite sense of domesticity at the same time.

The main living space is entirely open-plan, and the ceiling plane, rather than partition walls, defines the kitchen, eating and living zones. Towards the window, for example, the ceiling dives to create a more intimate dining area. A small study and an even smaller bathroom are also tucked in at this level. Downstairs, the space is more private: a labyrinthine hallway leads to four bedrooms, two bathrooms and a utility room.

The site also contains two courtyards, on to which three of the bedrooms open, and a garden overlooked by the master bedroom and the study above. The irregular shapes of these outdoor spaces, which are squeezed between the building and the property wall, are reminders of how ingeniously the architects have shoehorned this house into a difficult site.

Designed from the inside out, Brick House is like a graceful bunker or, as Caruso puts it, "both a cave and a tent, at once enclosing and protective, and open and airy". The house is a unique sanctuary in the busy heart of London, and an outstanding example of what could be done with more of the capital's forgotten yards and alleyways.

Above
Seen in plan and from above, the architects' ingenious manipulation of an uncompromising site becomes clear. The house is rammed between two adjoining properties, with the garden culminating in a jagged point.

Opposite
The main living space provides a masterclass in the brave and honest use of brick and concrete.

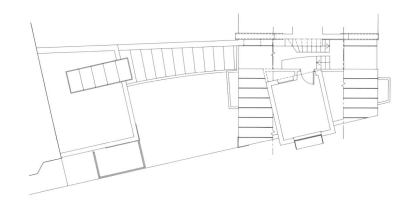

CARGO FLEET, WHISTLER STREET
HIGHBURY, N5

CHANCE DE SILVA ARCHITECTS, 2002–03

Cargo Fleet is an unusual hybrid of industrial materials and domestic architecture. The house takes its name from an abandoned railway station between Redcar and Middlesbrough, where architect Stephen Chance's father and grandfather worked in the steel factories. Chance grew up surrounded by the industrial buildings of northern England, and their geometric shapes and decaying beauty have had a lasting effect on his work. When he and his partner, Wendy de Silva, found a plot in what was then a neglected part of north London, the industrial undertones both of Chance's past and of the site itself inspired this unique residential project.

The difficult wedge-shaped plot lies on the corner of a cobbled road, which forms a loop round a derelict commercial laundry. It marks the end of a terrace of former lace-workers' houses and is hemmed in on one side by a hill and on the other by a railway embankment. Aesthetically, the building is at odds with its surroundings. Inspired by the furnaces, smelting works and signal stations around Redcar, it is a collage of industrial components. The corner windows, for example, resemble signal boxes, while the overhanging timber volume that juts out over the street could be a projecting shed.

The most striking industrial accent, however, is the choice of Cor-ten steel panels as the principal cladding material. This weathering steel, also used by Antony Gormley for the *Angel of the North*, turns first orange and then brown as it weathers and rusts. The architects chose it to reflect the decay and neglect of England's industrial heritage, and to evoke the passing of time. By building with a material that from the beginning signifies its end, they hope to draw attention to the transient nature of any act of creation.

The industrial theme is carried through to the interior, where rough concrete floors and exposed grey plaster contrast with slick wooden panelling and floor-to-ceiling windows. Steel rods connect the freestanding frame to the wall of the neighbouring house, to enable the removal of the full-length buttresses that previously supported it. The gap is now a fully glazed light well, containing the stairs and a dining platform. The buttress scars and bricks of the adjoining house remain exposed.

In contrast to the many references to the past, the layout of the building is in tune with the increasing fluidity of modern life. Two studio houses are linked by a covered ramp, and the building could accommodate a working studio, and a granny annex or flat for an au pair. It could even be split into two separate entities. The house commentates both on the changing nature of England's industrial and built heritage, and on the increasing complexity of people's lives. A bold and challenging statement, it raises as many questions as it answers.

Right, top and middle
Glazed doors shield the concrete ramp and lead to a courtyard sandwiched between the two houses.

Right, bottom
The exterior bricks of the adjoining house are left exposed in a light well containing the staircase.

Opposite
The building confidently addresses its context of Victorian terraces.

CASTLE HOUSE, WALWORTH ROAD
ELEPHANT AND CASTLE, SE1

HAMILTONS ARCHITECTS, 2006–

The reconstruction of Elephant and Castle in south London, scheduled to take place over the next decade, is one of the most ambitious urban regeneration projects in Europe. It will involve the demolition of most of the widely despised post-war housing in the area, along with the drab shopping centre, and the creation of new public spaces and parks. The proposed transformation is likely to cost more than £1,500,000,000 and will include more than 5000 new homes, along with landmark commercial developments. A masterplan for the project was drawn up initially by Foster + Partners, and has been further developed by Make Architects.

Under partner Robin Partington (Foster's project director for the 30 St Mary Axe tower in the City), Hamilton Associates' scheme provides the first of the new landmark towers at Elephant, identified as a suitable location for a cluster of tall buildings. Built for developer Multiplex, it will replace the original Castle House, which dates from the 1960s. The new, forty-three storey, 147-metre-tall apartment building was given planning consent in the spring of 2006. Superficially, it appears to be yet another of the many high-rises built

or planned in London for an affluent urban élite. In fact, the project has some radical aspects. The building's striking profile derives largely from the aspiration to make it a 'green' tower: three large wind turbines, each 9 metres across and mounted at roof level, will power the lighting all year round. The aerodynamic form of the tower is designed to maximize the benefits of wind power. This investment in environmentally friendly energy is a response to recent changes in building regulations, which also dictated the solid shape, cut away where necessary.

The confined nature of the site necessitated a triangular form. Inside the building, in place of cramped corridors and lift lobby spaces, mini atria give a sense of space and light. By installing sprinklers, an unusual feature in a residential building and one that imposes a further cost, the architects have been able to remove internal fire lobbies. The greatest attraction of the tower to prospective residents, apart from its proximity to the City and the West End, is that it offers them spectacular views. One of the most dramatic features of some of the flat will be a direct view of St Paul's Cathedral from the front door.

Opposite, right and below
The striking tower, with its three enormous wind-turbines, will form an important part of the visual identity of the revitalized Elephant and Castle area.

DONNYBROOK QUARTER, PARNELL ROAD/
OLD FORD ROAD, HACKNEY, E3

PETER BARBER ARCHITECTS, 2003–06

Donnybrook Quarter was commissioned in 2003 as a result of 'Innovation in Housing', a competition organized by the Architecture Foundation and Circle 33 Housing Trust. As part of his competition entry, the architect Peter Barber used a quotation from Walter Benjamin's *One Way Street*, in which the literary critic celebrates the theatrical nature of the cityscape of Naples: "Buildings are used as a popular stage. They are all divided into innumerable, simultaneously animated theatres. Balcony, courtyard, window, gateway, staircase, roof are at the same time stages and boxes."

In his design for Donnybrook, which sits on a prominent corner site just south of Victoria Park in Hackney, north-east London, Barber has developed this idea of people activating a streetscape by making shared public space the central element. He describes the project as "a celebration of the public social life of the street". Unusually, Barber first built the streets on

which the new houses would sit. Two tree-lined avenues, an intimate 7.5 metres wide, are laid across the site in a T-shape, with a small square at their intersection. Forty units, ranging from one-bedroom studios to a four-bedroom family house, as well as three live/work units, have been fitted around this plan. Gone are the dark alleys and gloomy stairwells so common in high-density housing schemes, and in their place are the pleasant circulation spaces created by the streets.

The buildings themselves are ingeniously designed to encourage interaction with the public spaces. By developing a new form of housing, the 'notched terrace', the architects have provided every home with direct access to the street, as well as a private outdoor area. Each bay comprises a ground-floor two-bedroom flat with access to a rear courtyard. Above this lies a split-level maisonette, which is reached by a gated external staircase leading through a

courtyard garden at first-floor level. The living area on this level has a fully glazed wall facing south over the courtyard, while the second floor contains two double bedrooms, a bathroom and a balcony overlooking the street. This sectional arrangement satisfies the British planning system's rules concerning overlooking (which dictate minimum back-to-back distances) and makes it possible to achieve the exceptionally high density of four hundred habitable rooms per hectare in a scheme that is only four storeys at its highest.

In a reworking of the Victorian housing type known as the 'back-of-pavement terrace', the notched terraces have no front gardens and present a hard edge to the street. This allows doors, windows and balconies to overlook the public areas, and gives the scheme an impressive sculptural quality. The style references the work of early Modernists, in particular Le Corbusier,

Adolf Loos and J.J.P. Oud, who designed handsome terraces for European cities in the 1920s.

Along the southern edge of the site the gleaming white walls rise to three-and-a-half storeys, and a landmark corner building addresses the junction of Old Ford Road and Parnell Road. Along the eastern edge of the site the terraces elegantly curve along Parnell Road, rising to an impressive four storeys to mark the main entrance to the project.

This is a truly magnificent design both in its logistical planning and in its outward appearance. Best of all, however, are the public spaces around which the buildings have been configured. By creating safe and attractive communal areas, the architects encourage human interaction and provide a groundbreaking example of how urban regeneration can encourage social sustainability in the capital.

Above, left and opposite
Homes in the Donnybrook Quarter are designed to overlook the public street areas, encouraging interaction between neighbours. The buildings take their form from the architecture of the early Modernists.

GAZZANO HOUSE, FARRINGDON ROAD CLERKENWELL, EC1

AMIN TAHA ARCHITECTS, 2003–04

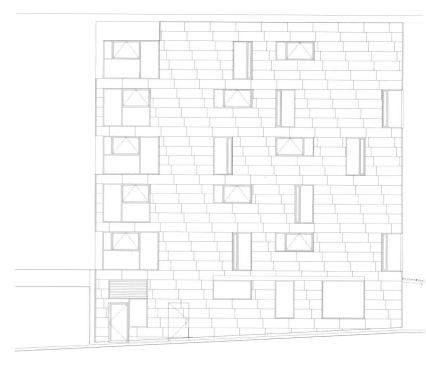

Gazzano House in central London, designed by Amin Taha Architects for developer Solidbau, is an uncompromisingly modern building. Completed in 2004, it has already become an important addition to the Rosebery Avenue Conservation Area, in which it is located. Standing among a series of Grade II*-listed nineteenth-century warehouses and offices, the building has a simple form – a solid block, with bold lines and sharp corners – that allows it to stand its ground, while not overpowering its historically important neighbours. The building consists of ten two-bedroom flats, with an Italian delicatessen on the ground floor. The delicatessen had been trading on the site for more than one hundred years, and the brief stipulated that it should not be uprooted.

A steel frame with pre-cast concrete floor slabs is wrapped in Cor-ten steel, manufactured from recycled metal and among the most durable of cladding materials. As time passes, the Cor-ten will weather to become darker in tone and richer in texture, further integrating the project with its semi-industrial surroundings. The robustness of the cladding and the small windows reflect the gritty, traffic-riddled atmosphere of this traditionally working-class area. Rugged materials continue through to the interior: exposed concrete and plaster finishes are used on the walls and ceilings, and hard-wearing epoxy finishes on the floor. Not only do these help to contextualize the scheme, but they also improve the thermal performance of the building. The same principle lies behind the aluminium-framed, double-glazed windows, designed to use a minimum area of the exterior.

The brief requested a distinctive building, which Amin Taha Architects have certainly achieved. Rather than be overshadowed by its older and more colossal neighbours, Gazzano House stands proudly among them. At a time when high-density living is becoming an increasing priority within London, this scheme provides a brave architectural solution to the use of inner-city spaces.

Right and opposite
Gazzano House provides desirable and contemporary living spaces within a defensive, yet monumental, shell. The scattered windows are a striking feature of the exterior.

GREENWOOD ROAD, HACKNEY, E8

LYNCH ARCHITECTS, 2004–06

Lynch Architects' latest addition to an already impressive portfolio is a new house at the end of a Georgian terrace in Hackney, east London. It was built as a pied-à-terre for a carpenter and a rock journalist who move constantly between London and America. Their children had left home so they required only a small house. Just 100 square metres, it has two modest bedrooms on the first floor, a kitchen and dining-room sunk half a storey below ground level, and a large room for entertaining on the second floor.

The lower level of the house is made from white bricks, with a cantilevered, oak-framed box above. The box forms an inverted blunt pyramid, described by the architects as a bird's nest sitting on an excavated well. The white bricks of the dining-room extend out into the sunken garden, relieving the sense of submersion but also resulting in a feeling of privacy. Inside, a solid staircase wrapped in a plywood skin ascends first into a double-height landing and finally up to the grand L-shaped room on the second floor. Despite the weight and thickness of the oak frame, the interiors maintain a surprising degree of delicacy. White plaster walls fill the shoulder-width gaps between the oak structural members, roof lights introduce shafts of light, and generous swathes of white-glass fenestration at the rear act like Japanese screens, illuminating the interiors.

The timber skin of the house has striated battens on all four sides and subtly projecting elements that give the building depth and variation as the light changes throughout the day. The blank end-of-terrace gable facing on to Dalston Lane is embellished with a balcony that 'peels' away from the façade and reveals the weighty oak structure. Overlooking the street, it replaces the traditional bay window of the house's Georgian neighbours, acknowledging the public character of the room behind it and the main approach to the building. The balcony also breaks the strict geometry of the façade and welcomes views into the interior. It is a characteristic feature of a house that, despite being thoroughly modern both internally and externally, manages to remain a congenial neighbour.

Below and opposite
The solid oak frame informs the appearance of both the interior and the exterior of the building, its contemporary aesthetic challenging preconceptions of oak-framed buildings.

HOUSE AND ARTIST'S STUDIO
HALES STREET, DEPTFORD, E14

DSDHA, 2003–05

The design of the Hales Street house and studio was a collaborative effort between the architects, DSDHA, and the client, photo librarian and art historian Geoffrey Fisher. The building sits on a corner site tucked behind Deptford High Street in south London. Originally lined with Georgian terraces, the street from which the project takes its name was changed beyond recognition by post-war development. A principal aim for both architect and client was that the house would respond to Deptford's mixed architectural style, and in so doing help restore some form of architectural cohesion to Hales Street and its immediate environs. The result is a modern building riddled with ambiguities, acknowledging the past and anticipating the future.

The planning regulations dictated that the site contain a mixed-use development, so the building is split into a residential unit for Fisher and an entirely separate studio space. This is hard to detect from the outside as the units are separated by a partition wall that runs along the crossbar of the H-shaped plan. The only clues to the building's twin purposes are the two entrances leading to Fisher's home from Hales Street and to the studio from New Butt Lane. Both are marked by defensive steel gates, which protect granite-paved courtyards flanked by full-height glazed walls; while the building's brick façade may have a fortress-like feel, passers-by can also peer into both units.

The house contains a kitchen and living area and bathroom on the ground floor and a bedroom upstairs; the studio is entirely open, with a mezzanine level. With the exception of the bathrooms, no spaces are enclosed by partition walls. No attempt has been made to hide either the structure or the services, and exposed pipes, galvanized-steel cabling conduits, and protruding vents and grilles give the building an industrial accent that jars with its domestic duties. But this reflects both Fisher's preference for honest, exposed architecture, and the industrial heritage of the site. To place the building further in context, Fisher salvaged many of the construction materials, including the facing bricks, the floor tiles and the setts in the courtyard, over many years from the Thames foreshore.

Concessions were also made to the surrounding buildings: the pitched roof maximizes the light to the flats to the south and the eaves' height corresponds to that of the former Ragged School across Hales Street. The client is pleased with the effect the project has had on views from Frankham Street, in which a gap has been replaced with a volume that pulls the scene together. Although the building is modern in form it contains a number of historical references, and is both domestic and industrial in character. With one foot planted in the past and another pointing towards the future, it is well equipped to ride the storm of Deptford's continuing redevelopment.

Above

The H-plan of the building is clearly visible from above.

The generous areas of glazing contrast with the inscrutable brick walls at the boundaries of the site.

HOXTON SQUARE, HOXTON, N1

ZAHA HADID ARCHITECTS, 2006–

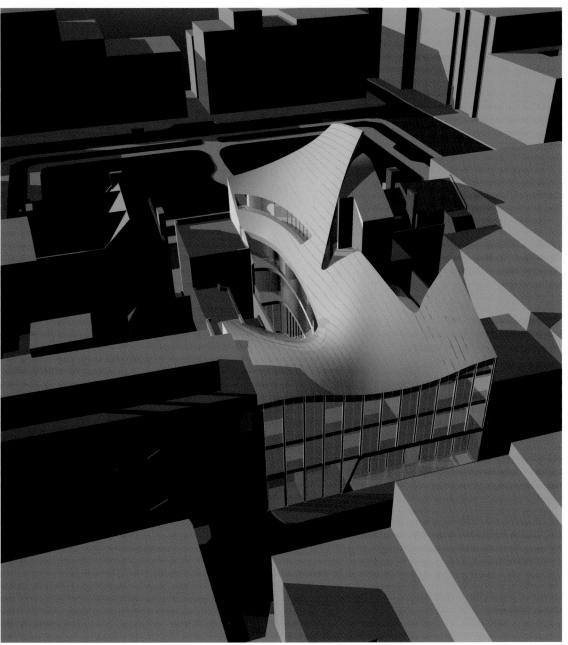

Hoxton Square, laid out in the 1680s, was one of the earliest squares in London, but by the mid-nineteenth century it had become predominantly industrial rather than residential. Its architecture is accordingly diverse in scale and style. With recent interventions – including a gallery and cinema (1997) by Maccreanor Lavington and Buschow Henley's imaginative conversion and extension (2005) of the former St Monica's School, designed by E.W. Pugin, to house business units and flats – the square is once more becoming a fashionable address.

Zaha Hadid's 990-square-metre project, which replaces an undistinguished post-war building, contains a gallery, offices and flats, and extends through to Hoxton Street at the rear. It is conceived as "a single cohesive form that presents the square with an urban sculpture that will bring an elegant element into [its] patchwork character". The curved roof is punctuated by roof lights. Both elevations are glazed right up to the line of the roof, and floor-to-ceiling sliding glass doors provide natural ventilation and a close connection between internal and external space.

Above and left
A lively addition to the varied architectural landscape of Hoxton Square, the building is ingeniously slotted into its site.

IN-BETWEEN, 1 WHATCOTT'S YARD
HACKNEY, N16

ANNALIE RICHES, SILVIA ULLMAYER & BARTI GARIBALDO
2003–04

The international group responsible for In-Between – architect Annalie Riches from England, Silvia Ullmayer, an architect from Germany, and the Italian designer Barti Garibaldo – met on the diploma course at the University of North London (now London Metropolitan University). Priced out of the London housing market and eager to put their design skills to the test, they decided to pool their resources and build together. After a year-long search they found Whatcott's Yard in Hackney, a 360-square-metre storage yard between the backs of two Victorian terraces – hence the name of their project, In-between. Setting up a small self-build mortgage, they each took a year off work to manage subcontractors and work on the construction.

The gated site is accessed through a narrow alley opening on to the yard proper, and is largely invisible from the street. The terrace form was an obvious choice, given the surrounding Victorian terraces and the oblong boundaries of the plot. The building is positioned at the centre of the yard, with the entrances facing north and a strip of gardens extending to the site's southern perimeter, where a wall of the old brick warehouse remains. The sedum roof, tipped into a slight monopitch, notionally extends the neighbours' gardens to the north.

The timber-framed terrace is divided into three identical units, each with a 47-square-metre internal footprint. The south elevation is fully glazed, with timber-framed sliding doors, and casements on the upper levels. The structural frame is made of Parrallam, an engineered timber product more commonly used in roof construction. It offers greater strength and fire performance than unprocessed timber, and can therefore be used in smaller sections (here an elegant 45 mm wide). It also has a distinctive grain, which has here been left exposed. The gables and north elevations of Nos. 1 and 3 are clad in polycarbonate sheet, while the rear of the centre house is fully glazed, breaking up the monolithic surface and providing the terrace with a simple symmetry.

While the collaboratively designed exterior is essentially uniform, the interiors vary enormously and express the designers' own needs and personalities. No. 1 is a house-share with a workspace, No. 2 a two-bedroom house and No. 3 two self-contained flats. The building's structure itself was instrumental in allowing such diversity. The footprint of each house is wider than it is deep, giving a greater ratio of external wall to floor area than is the norm, and increasing the variety of room layouts available. The building is also essentially two storeys high (although each house has an additional gallery level), thus avoiding the stringent fire regulations applicable to taller structures, and allowing the use of staircases without compartmentalization. Finally, the roof spans the 7-metre width of each house without any intermediary support.

The resulting interiors are light and open spaces, with such playful additions as a trapeze for Riches and a double-height bathroom with a skylight above the bath for Ullmayer. The designers have explored the concept of the modest terrace (each house cost just £125,000) and have met their diverse individual needs within a communal framework.

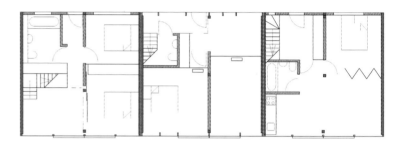

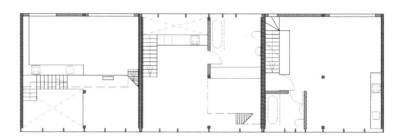

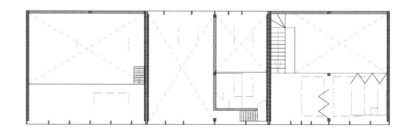

ISOKON FLATS, LAWN ROAD BELSIZE PARK, NW3

AVANTI ARCHITECTS, 2003–04

Below

The south (left) and east (right) elevations. Circulation is concentrated to one side of the building.

Opposite, top left

Flat 16 is a one-bedroom flat. The original sliding door has been restored and the flat has been furnished with contemporary Isokon furniture.

Opposite, top right

The building has been restored to its former glory and now stands as a true beacon of the Modern Movement.

Opposite, bottom

The building's resemblance to an ocean liner is most apparent at night, when the balcony 'decks' are illuminated.

The Isokon Flats in Hampstead, north London, is one of the most important Modern Movement buildings in Britain. Opened in 1934 and known originally as the Lawn Road Flats, the building was the vision of Wells Coates, a Canadian architect, and his clients Jack Pritchard (a furniture designer whose company Isokon lent its name to the building) and his wife, Molly. All three were devotees of Modernism and the Bauhaus, and, having seen the introduction of communal, high-density living in Europe, they hoped to bring the idea to London.

Coates was fascinated by the efficient, all-in-one layout of ships, and his design for Lawn Road followed that of a giant ocean liner. It had thirty-two compact, cabin-like flats, each kitted out with the latest gadgets and such space-saving solutions as hinged tables and sliding doors. There were balcony 'decks', a large sun lounge on the roof, and a restaurant and bar in the basement. The entire building was constructed from smooth concrete and painted pink. Standing among the leafy streets of red-brick Victorian mansion blocks, the Lawn Road Flats proclaimed the Modernist message loud and clear.

During the 1930s the building was a centre for London's bourgeois intelligentsia, with Agatha Christie and Bauhaus founder Walter Gropius among its residents. The Bauhaus teacher Marcel Breuer designed the Isobar (converted into four flats in the 1980s), where sculptors Barbara Hepworth and Henry Moore drank cocktails. After World War II the reputation of the Modern Movement started to suffer and the social pulse of the Lawn Road Flats slowed, so Pritchard sold the block in 1969. By the 1970s it was in the hands of Camden Council and, despite being listed Grade II in 1974, was shamefully neglected. By 2000 it was graffiti-encrusted and uninhabitable.

The Isokon Trust, a campaigning group set up by a local architect, Chris Flannery, and the Notting Hill Housing Trust purchased the block from Camden Council and brought in Britain's foremost expert in restoring Modern Movement icons, John Allan, and his practice, Avanti Architects. Between May 2003 and November 2004 the firm sympathetically restored the fabric of the building, while ensuring that it had a sustainable and secure future. The total cost of the project was £2,300,000. The scheme now provides twenty-five flats for sale under shared ownership, exclusively to keyworkers, with eleven further flats for sale on the open market.

The work included the repair and restoration of the reinforced-concrete envelope of the building; replacement of the asphalt waterproof coverings and upgrading of insulation; and renewal of wall, ceiling and floor finishes, and windows and doors. Light metalwork elements and fitted joinery were refurbished where possible, and replaced to match the original where not. Mechanical and electrical services have been fully re-engineered to comply with current standards, and new communication, signage and security installations have been sympathetically integrated. The immediate environs of the block have been completely rehabilitated, with a carefully detailed scheme of external works and soft landscaping.

As the building was listed Grade I (it had been upgraded from Grade II in 1999), the layout of the rooms could not be altered. Flat 15, Gropius's old abode, has been restored to provide an authentic historical record of the original rooms, while the plywood panelling in Jack Pritchard's penthouse has been refurbished by cabinetry specialist Nick Goldfinger. The remaining flats have been finished with such modern additions as washing machines, fridges and cookers, with the greatest possible respect being accorded to the original design.

The former garage houses a permanent exhibition presenting the history of the building and promoting the understanding of the radical ideas that led to its creation. The Isokon Flats once again stands as a landmark to the Modern Movement, and by providing keyworker housing it supports the social ideals of the Bauhaus movement that inspired its development. In addition, the incredibly well-researched and rigorously executed work of Avanti Architects is an exemplar of how historic buildings can be rehabilitated without their integrity being destroyed. Such impressive work is essential if the architectural heritage of London is to be maintained.

south elevation

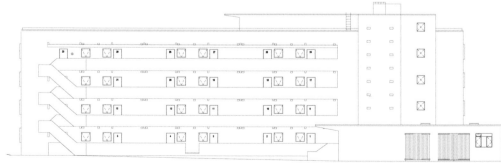

east elevation

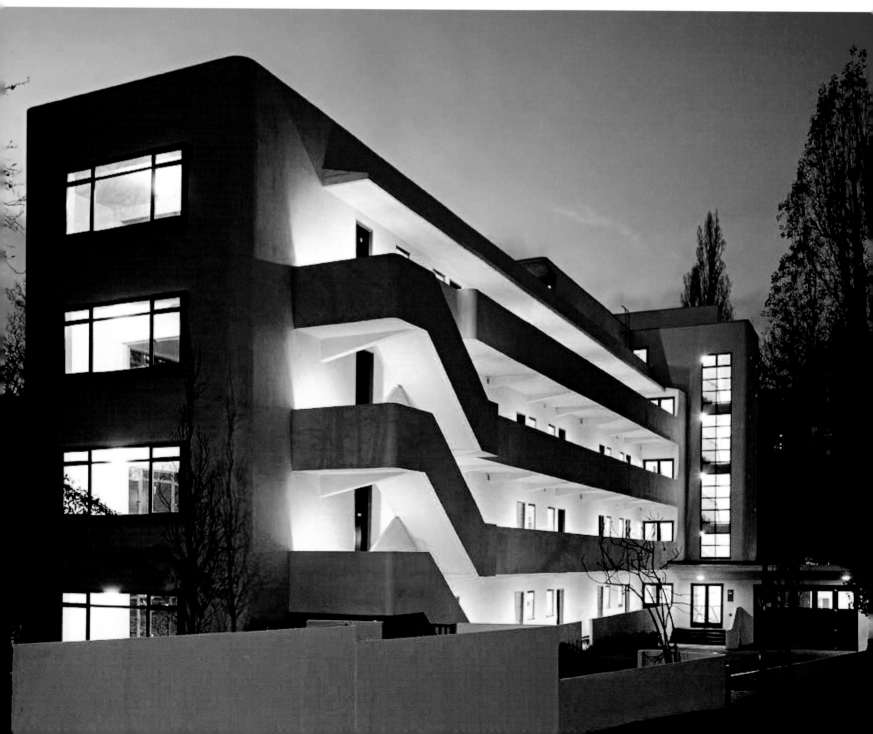

LOW-COST HOUSING
PEABODY HOUSING ASSOCIATION
BOXLEY STREET, SILVERTOWN, E16

ASH SAKULA ARCHITECTS, 2003–04

In December 2002 the Peabody Trust launched a competition, 'Fresh Ideas for Low-Cost Housing', which centred on three sites near London's Royal Victoria Dock in Silvertown, east London. Two outstanding projects have emerged from this contest, one by Niall McLaughlin (see pp. 180–81) and the other by Ash Sakula. The latter's prize was an awkward infill site on Boxley Street, with the tracks of the Docklands Light Railway close by to the north and London City Airport to the east. Here four flats in two adjoining buildings form part of a low-cost shared-ownership scheme.

By far the most eye-catching aspect of the project is the lightweight rainscreen cladding that wraps around both timber-framed buildings. The right-angled walls facing the street are clad in a pale-yellow-tinted reflective breather membrane with translucent profiled glass-reinforced plastic (GRP) laid horizontally over the top. At the rear, where the walls are curved rather than angular, the cladding is silver and the GRP is laid vertically, so that the corrugations run upwards and reach beyond the top of the building. The surfaces glisten as light bounces between the foil wrapping and the outer skin. Ash Sakula worked with the artist Vinita Hassard, who suggested hanging twisted pieces of wire between the two layers to animate the surfaces further. The architects wanted the residents of the project to feel as though they were living in a real-life work of art, rather than a low-cost housing scheme, and their treatment is a striking improvement on traditional cladding materials.

The four flats are near-identical units stacked on top of each other in two pairs.

Challenged with a floor space of just 69 square metres – in which they had to accommodate four people, and provide two bedrooms – the architects rejected both the traditional Victorian template and the open plan (often perceived as a lazy solution). Instead they designed the spaces around a range of modern scenarios. The unusually wide entrance hall doubles as a laundry area or workspace with built-in cupboards and box shelves, and allows natural light to reach the rest of the interior.

The main social space is the kitchen, where all units and appliances are fixed to one wall and the space opposite is free for either a playpen or a table and chairs. The drawing-room can be used as a family room, home office or guest bedroom, while the living-room is less flexible, its built-in perimeter seating inspired by the Ottoman salon and transport cabins. The bedrooms are small and can be used only for sleeping, but the separate WC and bathroom are both large and naturally lit. Outdoor space is provided in the form of an entrance yard or second-floor deck. The only awkward part of the design is the prefabricated deck and staircase structure, its balustrades formed from timber posts and simple chainlink fencing. One feels that a greater elegance here might have been more fitting.

The cladding and internal layout of this scheme subvert traditional expectations of the home, and raise questions about the future of low-cost housing. For a final cost of £1498 per square metre Ash Sakula have replaced a brownfield site with four flexible homes, making a strong architectural statement in the process.

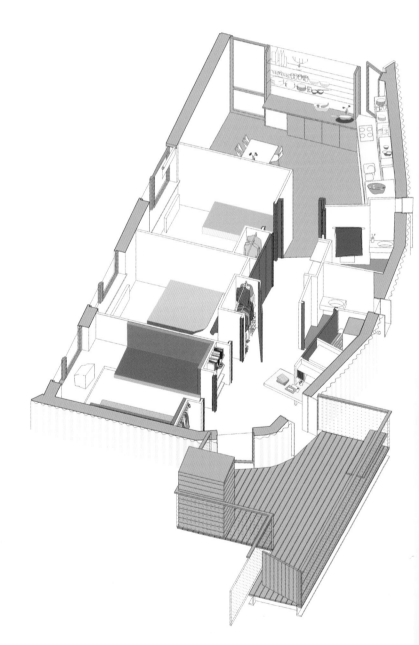

LOW-COST HOUSING
PEABODY HOUSING ASSOCIATION
EVELYN ROAD, SILVERTOWN, E16

NIALL MCLAUGHLIN ARCHITECTS, 2003–04

In December 2002 Niall McLaughlin Architects won the Peabody Trust's 'Fresh Ideas for Low-Cost Housing' competition with a scheme to build twelve flats on Evelyn Road in Silvertown, east London. The project was inspired by the history of the area, which by 1900 was one of the largest industrial complexes in the world, producing such consumer goods as sugar, matches and dye. The site itself was once occupied by the warehouses that stored these commodities, but by the 1990s the area had become wasteland. McLaughlin's scheme plays a key role in the area's regeneration, while also referring to its manufacturing and chemical past.

The building contains four flats on each of three floors. Its prefabricated frame and walls are constructed from timber, with an eye-catching, decorative street frontage that has caused a stir. The architects collaborated with light-artist Martin Richman to develop a system never before used in construction, which employs ribbons of radiant light film to create a 'chemical flare' across the building's façade. Radiant light film, iridescent like

a peacock's feather or petrol on water, is used in the manufacture of packaging, ribbons and shoes. The architects encased the material in modified double-glazing units – one face is cast glass, the other aluminium – and attached strips of film to slats of glass, set alternately to the front and back of the cavity. These varying depths create contrasting reflections, and the screen changes with different light and weather conditions, times of day, and viewpoints.

The interior has unusually high ceilings for low-cost housing, and makes the most of the sun and outlook. Each flat has two bedrooms and a bathroom, with the kitchen, dining and living areas accommodated in one large space on the south side. The flats on the ground floor have a back garden, while those above are provided with a south-facing terrace and corner windows to give views along the street towards the former Millennium Dome and Canary Wharf in the distance. By encouraging collaboration between architect and artist this scheme projects an impressive sense of place while challenging preconceptions of low-cost housing.

Opposite and above

The cladding incorporates radiant light film, enabling natural light to reach the interiors while providing a radical exterior with a constantly changing appearance. The interiors are simple but elegant, a combination not usually found in low-cost housing.

MILDMAY GROVE, ISLINGTON, N1

PETER BARBER ARCHITECTS, 2002–06

Mildmay Grove in north London was in a sense the testing ground for a larger scheme by Peter Barber, Donnybrook Quarter in Hackney (see pp. 166–67). Designed in 2002 for developer Colony and completed in 2006, the scheme features the 'notched terraces' that have proved so successful at the Hackney project. They were developed here in response to a restricted site, accessed through an arch in a Victorian terrace fronting Mildmay Grove. Four courtyard houses and one live/work studio have been cleverly slotted into this plot, which measures approximately 550 square metres.

A walled passageway, on to which the front door of each property opens, runs east–west across the site. Beyond each front door is a private south-facing courtyard garden, which is overlooked by a first-floor roof terrace. The houses themselves have been designed to take full advantage of these adjoining outdoor areas. The ground floor comprises two bedrooms and two bathrooms, with all principal windows facing the courtyard to prevent the adjacent properties from being overlooked. The first-floor open-plan living space has fully glazed sliding doors, which open out on to the roof terrace. At the eastern end of the site, the live/work unit has a roof sloping towards the houses, shielding the entire scheme from the street. Inside, the ground floor has been dropped to semi-basement level to allow for a mezzanine level above. The south-facing wall has a window one-and-a-half storeys high to allow the maximum amount of light into the interior.

In a style similar to that of Donnybrook Quarter, the blockwork has been rendered and painted a dazzling white. Crisp lines and neat geometric forms give the project a proudly modern appearance, which is refreshing in an area of London dominated by Victorian brickwork.

The entire project is a clever exercise in logistical planning. It exploits every scrap of available space to create houses that, despite being close to one other, maintain an impressive degree of privacy. For a total cost of £1800 per square metre, Mildmay Grove demonstrates how odd pockets of land can be transformed into entirely new communities.

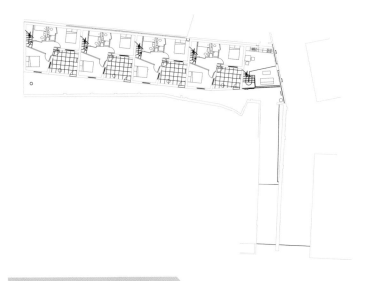

Opposite

The front doors of the terrace houses are reached by a walled passageway along the boundary of the site.

Right

The ground-floor plan shows the 'notched terrace' concept, which allows the construction of flats with private courtyards despite the awkward and restricted site.

Below

The open-plan living spaces receive generous amounts of natural light from a skylight above and glazed doors, which at the far end lead on to the roof terrace.

NEWINGTON GREEN, ISLINGTON, N16

HAWORTH TOMPKINS, 2003–05

Below and opposite

The scheme has a pronounced verticality, and the three service cores of each block are distinguished by their exterior treatment.

The £7,700,000 student-housing scheme designed by Haworth Tompkins for Shaftesbury Student Housing marks a refreshing departure from the stereotypical brick accommodation blocks to which Britain's students have become so accustomed. Located within the Newington Green Conservation Area in Islington, north London, the project provides rooms for two hundred students from City University. Built on a 4800-square-metre site, it consists of two distinct phases. The first was the renovation of the four-storey Edwardian China Inland Mission building fronting Newington Green, and the second the demolition and replacement of Alliance House, a five-storey Victorian building to the rear. The resulting scheme demonstrates how student accommodation can be both architecturally exciting and beneficial to the surrounding community.

The grand façade of the China Inland Mission now provides a double-height covered archway into the site. Alterations have been relatively slight, the only major change being the replacement of two shoddy brick extensions with two small single-storey buildings. These 'bookend'

the retail units on either side and re-establish the symmetrical composition of the main arch. The extension to the south houses a shop and that to the north a restaurant, integrating the scheme with the existing streetscape. The remainder of the building provides eleven maisonettes, accessed via the original stair cores to the front of the building: one core has been altered to provide lift access for disabled occupants and visitors.

The bulky Edwardian building restricts the visual impact of the new scheme on the surrounding area, giving the architects much greater creative freedom than they might otherwise have been granted. They gained permission to demolish the Victorian building by demonstrating that redevelopment could significantly enhance the quality of the environment for residents near by. Whereas the Victorian block extended the full length of the site, leaving only a narrow strip of land along each of the longer elevations and drastically restricting light to and views from the neighbouring houses, Haworth Tompkins's scheme is conceived as free-standing buildings integrated within a garden setting.

Four blocks are irregularly positioned down the plot, giving the neighbouring properties views right across the site and considerably improving the amount of daylight for those immediately to the north.

The design was significantly influenced by fifteen mature trees that punctuate the site. The four blocks are positioned around the trees and reach to a similar height. But the presence of the trees has, most importantly, resulted in a pronounced verticality in the scheme. The cores, housing services, have been expressed as a cluster of three vertical elements: a lift, a stair and kitchens stacked one on top of the other. Each element is treated with a different material. The staircases have been left partly open with a perforated screen of vertical larch boarding to provide protection from the rain. Not only does this save on construction costs and heating bills, but it also encourages a more direct relationship between the occupants and the community. The kitchens are partly embedded in the main blocks, but their core-side exteriors are clad in larch boards. The surface of the lift core is in-situ concrete, the shuttering pattern of which mimics the grain of the

perforated screens. When the untreated larch weathers, the colour of all three core elements will be similar.

In contrast, the accommodation blocks are rendered in a brilliant white polymer, which reflects light around the site, and the windows and spandrel panels are faced in naturally anodized aluminium. The façades are configured as a series of vertical strips: narrow floor-to-ceiling windows alternate with bands of render. According to the architects, this irregularly spaced glazing reflects the way in which the trees meander upwards, although here they are stopped by the butterfly roofs.

Inside, a series of flats leads off from the main core, with either five or seven en suite study rooms sharing a self-contained kitchen and dining area. The windows of the student rooms face east or west around a series of open courtyard gardens. This arrangement further enhances the sense of community, while preventing the neighbours from being overlooked. Beyond the austere entrance arch facing the traffic surging through Newington Green, this is a secret green enclave. There cannot be many better places in London in which to study.

NEWINGTON GREEN HOUSE, ISLINGTON, N5

PREWETT BIZLEY ARCHITECTS, 2001–05

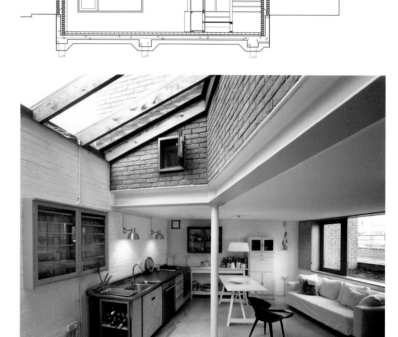

It is difficult to miss Prewett Bizley Architects' first new-build project, a brick oddity with unevenly placed windows. Built by Graham Bizley (as a home for himself and a base for the practice, which he established with Robert Prewett in 2005) over a gruelling six years, the house is attached to the end of a Victorian terrace in the gritty enclave of Newington Green in north-east London, and is progressive yet sympathetic to the traditional brick buildings. Whereas the choice of Ibstock brick was informed by the surrounding buildings and by a desire to keep the costs down, the form of the building was dictated by the irregular 60-square-metre plot. Hemmed in by the road, two properties and a private garden, it presented a challenge in terms of both the physical boundaries and rights of light. The response is a four-storey, turret-topped house that turns its back on its neighbours but embraces the street.

The west façade has no fenestration, with natural light allowed in through a glazed roof, but the street façade is dominated by apparently randomly spaced, exaggerated, plain-glass windows. The most impressive is the strip window to the studio, which wraps around two sides to give views on to the street and down to the green. A window at street level encourages passers-by to peer into the living area, thus severing the barriers between the public and the private, and creating a dialogue between the house and the street. For Bizley this is one of the most important functions of the building.

Throughout the interior, the emphasis is on simplicity and economy, with basic building materials and exposed joints. The ground floor comprises a living, dining and kitchen area; above is the bedroom and bathroom; and stacked on top of these is the office. The fourth-floor tower provides a laundry and shed area leading on to a roof terrace. Connecting these floors, and creating the central spine of the building, is a latticed staircase of plywood and Douglas fir. Such details as this, combined with the functional appearance of the exposed construction, render this an elegant solution to a difficult site, and, by creating such a building for just £212,000, Bizley has proved that the economical brick terrace is still relevant.

Right, top and bottom
The bespoke latticed staircase runs the height of the building and allows light to filter through to all areas.

Right, middle
The glazed roof dissects the exterior brickwork at an angle, allowing for an unexpected interior window, which gives views over the space from the bedroom above.

Opposite
The entire project is a modern take on the quintessentially British building material, brick. An unusual strip window lights the studio from two sides, emphasizing the horizontal proportions of the blocky building, but the boldest element of the house is the pavement-level window, which allows views directly into the living area.

ONE BLACKFRIARS ROAD, SOUTHWARK, SE1

IAN SIMPSON ARCHITECTS, 2004–12

Below
The project transforms a neglected corner site, with affordable housing and public areas as well as a 'five-star-plus' hotel.

Opposite
The tower is a tall but lightweight presence at the southern end of Blackfriars Bridge.

The site of One Blackfriars Road, close to the southern end of Blackfriars Bridge, was the subject of an earlier but now abandoned project by Foster + Partners. Liverpool-based developer Beetham acquired it in 2004 and commissioned Ian Simpson, already working on a major high-rise scheme for the same client on Manchester's Deansgate, to design a mixed-use tower. Though not as tall as the 'Shard' at London Bridge (see pp. 226–27), this tower will be one of London's highest buildings, visible from many parts of the capital (though it does not intrude into any established strategic view corridors). Planning permission for a 226-metre-high tower was originally applied for in 2005, but during the course of 2006 a new planning application was submitted, with the height of the tower amended to 180 metres, consequently reducing the accommodation within it. The scheme is one of a number of medium- to high-rise projects in the Blackfriars Road area, involving practices such as Wilkinson Eyre, Lifschutz Davidson Sandilands and Allford Hall Monaghan Morris. Make Architects has also obtained permission to heighten and reclad King's Reach Tower (which dates from the 1970s) on Stamford Street. The development of a cluster of tall buildings in this part of Southwark is controversial, though broadly in line with Mayor Ken Livingstone's vision of such structures defining the riverside.

One Blackfriars Road, fifty storeys tall in its latest form, will contain a 'five-star-plus' hotel with 261 bedrooms, as well as 64 open-market flats, 32 affordable flats and a publicly accessible sky-deck with unrivalled views over London (at least until the 'Shard' is built). The form of the tower was the subject of intense study, given the prominent nature of the riverside site. It is conceived as a 'bridgehead' for Southwark, so that the axis of the building is north–south. The tower tapers dramatically on the southern side from a very narrow base – to minimize its impact at street level – before changing direction to climb to the sky-deck. The tower's slender shape would not have been possible had it been necessary to accommodate office space, as a comparison with the lower (office) floors of the 'Shard' or those of Foster's 'Gherkin' makes clear.

In this project the architect has developed the double skin seen, for example, in its Number 1 Deansgate project in Manchester. The outer façade is single-glazed, with opening louvres for natural ventilation. The double-glazed inner façade is an environmental layer, thirty per cent opaque with a mixture of fixed and folding screens. Winter gardens are set in the space between the two skins.

Affordable housing is provided in a low-rise block on Rennie Street to the west – an innovative building in its own right. The base of the tower sits in a raised public square, with shops and restaurants, which is also conceived as an open-air art gallery.

The client hopes to have the tower completed and occupied by 2012 – construction will take five years – so that the hotel can accommodate visitors to the Olympic Games that year. A decision from Southwark Council was expected in early 2007 and, with English Heritage certain to raise objections, there is the possibility of a public inquiry that might well make that timescale impractical.

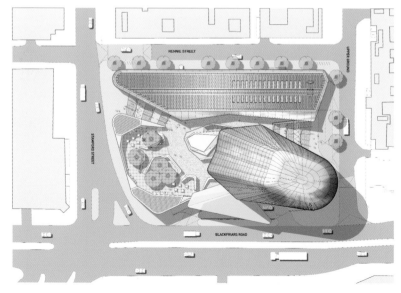

ONE CENTAUR STREET, LAMBETH, SE1

DE RIJKE MARSH MORGAN ARCHITECTS, 2001–03

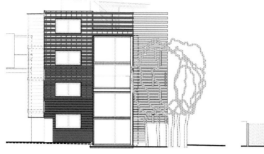
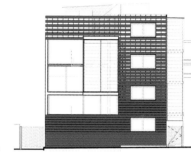

One Centaur Street has transformed an initially unpromising site into a model for future urban housing. Designed by De Rijke Marsh Morgan, in collaboration with the progressive developer Roger Zogolovitch of Solid Space, the building has been slotted into a 368-square-metre gap between a railway viaduct and a row of listed buildings. In order to protect the inhabitants from the noise of the trains, the four-flat building is constructed from in-situ concrete. This also allows for flexibility in the spatial arrangement of the interior: the architects have replaced a standard stacking system with two-storey flats arranged back-to-back on the ground floor, and three-storey flats arranged similarly above. These basic units are designed to extend both horizontally and vertically, and

would allow much greater urban density than conventional housing if the scheme were to be repeated elsewhere.

Externally, the project demonstrates the architects' research into new building solutions, in particular cost-effective prefabricated materials. The concrete frame is clad in a rainscreen of the wood-grained fibrous cement boards most usually seen in North American kit houses. The gaps between these chocolate-brown planks widen as the eye moves up the façade, revealing more of their vertical support structure and the aluminium-faced thermal insulation behind. Toughened glass punctuates these surfaces, generously lighting the living spaces of each flat. A glass stairwell, which provides a communal space and access to all four flats, juts

out from the side of the building to within inches of the brick of the railway arches. This bold addition integrates the old with the new, as the viaduct becomes the visual backdrop of the building's central circulation space.

The interiors of the flats give the impression of great spaciousness and openness, although the fact that they are arranged over different vertical levels creates clearly defined zones. In each a jagged concrete staircase leads to the encapsulated bedrooms and bathrooms, which hang like viewing platforms over the living areas. The north-facing flats have double-height winter gardens and the larger units benefit from an additional room on a third storey. Roof decks sit at the same level as the main railway lines and allow

inhabitants to peer down into the garden below or watch the trains curving out of Waterloo.

One Centaur Street complements its gritty urban setting perfectly, while contributing to the search for a cost-effective solution to London's housing shortage. The project has received a number of awards, including the RIBA London Building of the Year Award in 2003, when the judges commented that "to achieve this sense of special delight in a one-off house would have been commendable; to get it on a tight urban site for speculative private housing is really remarkable." The architects themselves are clearly delighted with the scheme, as they have moved their office into one of the lower units.

OXFORD GARDENS, NOTTING HILL, W10

MICHAELIS BOYD ASSOCIATES, 2004

When Alex Michaelis (the favourite eco-architect of Conservative Party leader David Cameron) bought a plot of land in Notting Hill, west London, he faced an unusual challenge. The site, wedged between two Edwardian terraced houses, was subject to an unusual planning regulation, which stipulated that any building constructed on the site could be no more than 2 metres above the ground. Few architects would relish the thought of designing a house smaller in stature than themselves, but Michaelis had been coveting this spot for fifteen years and refused to be put off.

In place of 1000 cubic metres of London clay, which was removed from the site along with abandoned fridges and other such detritus of illegal fly-tipping, he has built a two-floor, five-bedroom house. The building is completely hidden from the street behind a nondescript brick wall, beyond which a curvaceous ramp leads down into a crisp white concrete cube. The interior gives very little clue that it is below ground level. The open-plan living, dining and kitchen space is generously lit by a vast roof light and glazed doors leading out on to a paved terrace. Smaller skylights built into the patio that surrounds the house provide light for the basement bedrooms. In this way every room, with the exception of the utility room and the bathroom, enjoys at least a glimpse of natural light. The downstairs bedrooms are further illuminated by light reflected from the glass-enclosed swimming pool, around which they are arranged.

The sleek white walls and clean lines of this sophisticated modern home mask the fact that the building has impressive ecological credentials. Michaelis is a staunch believer in reducing energy consumption and investing in renewable energy sources. The house is remarkably well insulated, and windows, doors and roof lights with the same insulation properties as brick were sourced from Denmark. The walls are laced with Kingspan thermal wool insulation, and a sedum roof traps heat while releasing oxygen into the environment. A bank of solar panels above the carport fuels the family's electric car. Another set works a heat pump to bring water up through a borehole that taps into the earth's aquifer 100 metres below the surface. This arrangement provides all the house's hot water – including that for the underfloor heating and the pool – while a filtration system ensures that the tap water is drinkable. The pool also acts as a heat sink, regulating the temperature throughout the house.

As issues of environmental sustainability force their way on to the agenda of the construction industry, Michaelis has proved that helping to preserve the planet's resources does not preclude the creation of a stylish home.

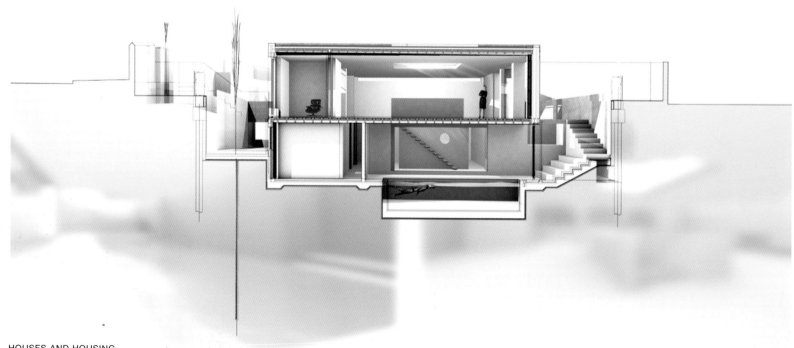

SHOULDHAM STREET, MARYLEBONE, W1

HENNING STUMMEL ARCHITECTS, 2005

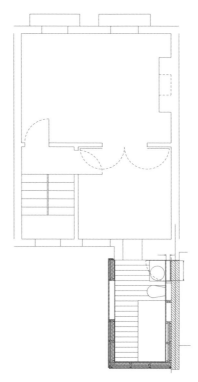

When designing this timber extension to a Georgian town house in central London, architect Henning Stummel was told that any fenestration had to be in keeping with that of the neighbourhood. So instead of compromising his design, he removed the windows, and created a building that proves building regulations in conservation areas can generate, rather than suppress, innovative modern design.

The practicalities of the site – all materials had to be brought in through the front door – made timber the obvious choice for the principal building material. It also offered a compact wall build-up, with good thermal insulation and dry construction (requiring no wet materials, such as concrete). Carpenters were able to undertake most of the building work, thereby reducing the number of subcontractors required and simplifying the construction process. Furthermore, the use of timber means that the extension can be dismantled and removed with relative ease.

The tower has a wooden frame with plywood sheathing inside and out. The plywood gives rigidity to the walls and distributes the downward load of the building. Two bathrooms and a WC/utility room are stacked inside. The rainwater downpipe, water and soil pipes, wiring, WC cisterns, vanity cabinets and mechanical ventilation are all concealed within a 150-millimetre-wide service duct running through all walls parallel to the party wall.

Consequently, two façades are free from services, allowing Stummel to demonstrate an innovative alternative to fenestration. In the place of windows, sanded Perspex boards are placed randomly among the plywood cladding. During the day, the Perspex appears grey and the overall impression is of a monolithic structure, as the plywood boards are painted in different shades of grey. While the Perspex allows natural light into the interiors during the day, at night its role is reversed. When the internal lighting is switched on, the extension comes to life as light beams through the Perspex and out across the garden.

Right
Providing a small but useful addition to each floor, and extending the full height of the house, the extension provides an arresting backdrop to the traditional part of the building.

Opposite
The façade is broken up by randomly spaced Perspex boards. Once night falls, the extension is dramatically illuminated through these 'windows'.

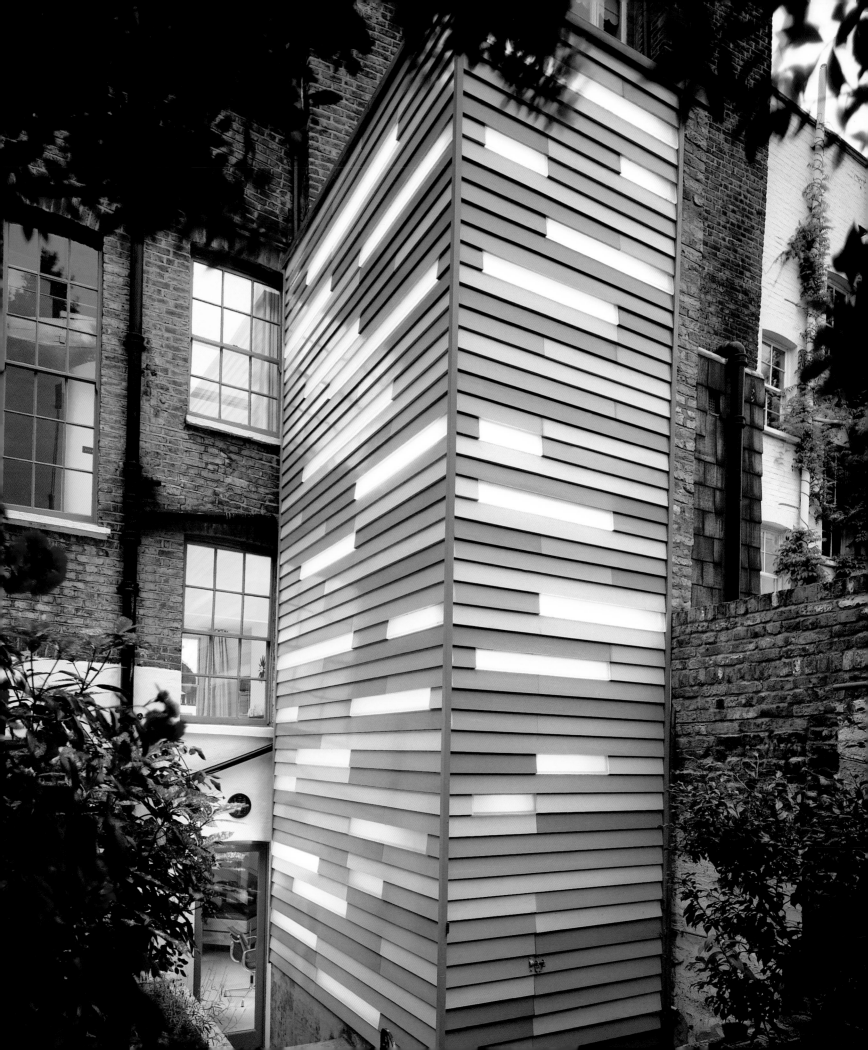

STEALTH HOUSE, GROVE LANE
CAMBERWELL, SE5

ROBERT DYE ARCHITECTS, 2002–04

Stealth House sits between a Modernist detached house dating from the 1960s and an adjoining 1890s Edwardian terrace. The site, bombed during World War II, was formerly occupied by a 1950s building that was abruptly set back from the terrace and that, with its dark engineering bricks and roof of cement tiles, jarred with the rest of the street. In contrast, the new house, designed by Robert Dye for clients Geof Powell and comedian Jenny Eclair, enhances its surroundings. It creates a smooth transition between its disparate neighbours, in particular through being set back in two stages from the street.

This was an architect-assisted self-build project: Dye produced the plans while Powell and his builders undertook the construction work. The house is timber-framed, with stressed plywood panels to allow for the double cantilever at the corners. The black-stained Russian redwood cladding was a contextual response to the black timber balconies on the flats opposite. The cladding is fixed to an inner core, rendered in pale grey K-rend (a traditional Irish building material made of crushed rubble), but there is a slight gap between the two so that the outer skin seems to 'float' over the inner core. The interior walls are plywood, forming a breathable 'skin' for the building.

The roof, made from a grey-green mineralized felt, carries on the line of the brick house to one side. From the street the building looks like a two-storey black house with a grey pitched roof, but the monopitch hides a third storey with a double bedroom and en suite bathroom opening on to a hidden roof terrace, visible only from the rear of the building.

The house, covering an internal area of 200 square metres, makes superb use of a tight site. With a project cost of £260,000, it also represents value for money. But what is really impressive about this project is its contextual sensitivity and the way in which it has re-established a sense of cohesion in the street. Stealth House has received an RIBA Award and the Manser Medal for the best one-off house designed by an architect for a private client. It proves that contextually sympathetic buildings do not have to rely on pastiche.

Right, top
The ground-floor living spaces, which flow into one another, are arranged around a core containing WC and stairs.

Right, middle and bottom
Stealth House acts as a bridge between the distinct architectural styles of its neighbours.

Opposite
The black cladding is especially dramatic at night, when light emanates from the interior.

STEEDMAN STREET,
ELEPHANT AND CASTLE, SE1

CZWG, 2006–

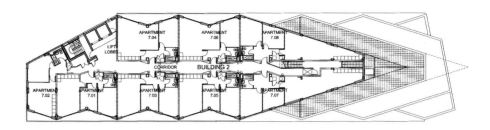

CZWG and especially partner Piers Gough are well-established players in the history of regeneration in Southwark, with a number of projects along the River Thames, between Bankside and Butler's Wharf, completed over the last twenty years. The Steedman Street development is a very different proposition. The site, far from the river and too close for comfort to the 1960s disaster zone of Elephant and Castle, is hemmed in between a busy railway line and the dreary Walworth Road, with rundown warehouse sheds and council housing for neighbours. Elephant, however, is set to be transformed over the next decade. Mass demolition of

failed housing and construction of new mixed-use development are intended to reinstate this pivotal junction, remarkably close to the City and West End, as "the Piccadilly Circus of South London".

CZWG's architecture, once determinedly Post-modernist, seems to have acquired a new cutting edge at Steedman Street. The scheme contains eighty-eight flats for sale, plus ten live/work units, and twenty-five affordable units managed by a housing association. The affordable housing is located in a separate seven-storey block, with the remainder of the flats in a ten-storey block extending along the railway

viaduct. From the upper floors, the views are spectacular, extending to the former Millennium Dome in the east, and to the London Eye and Westminster in the west. The zigzag 'accordion' plan is calculated to capitalize on views, while allowing residents privacy and providing generous balconies. The stepped form of the building produces visual drama, with beak-like canopies on the upper levels, where the flats have spectacular roof terraces.

Piers Gough is a colourful figure who produces consistently colourful buildings. Here purple and green render forms the external cladding of the two blocks, with

metalwork painted a rich red. In places the compromises that resulted from a design-and-build contract are all too obvious, but the architecture is tough enough to survive the process. Over the years CZWG has worked successfully with a number of innovative developers. It now faces stiff competition from younger practices, but on the basis of this project appears to be in lively form. It seems ironic, however, that its architecture has lost the distinctive qualities seen in past projects, such as the housing at China Wharf and the Circle, both in Southwark, at a time when Post-modernism is being favourably re-evaluated.

Right

The flats are ingeniously arranged to give each the best possible views and privacy.

Steedman Street will triumphantly punch the sky with its sharp angular appearance.

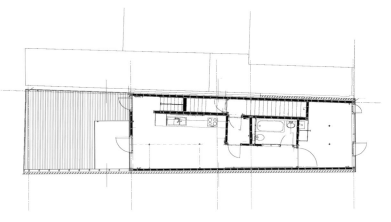

STUDIO HOUSE, BETHNAL GREEN, E2

SERGISON BATES ARCHITECTS, 2000–04

Sergison Bates is known for its reductive approach to architecture, by which the authenticity of construction methods and the nature of the materials are expressed directly and with rigour. Such projects as the Prototype Social Housing in Stevenage (1998–2000) and the Assisted Self-Build Housing in Tilbury, Essex (2001–02), are bold and functional, and display a rare honesty in their use of materials. Studio House, in the previously semi-industrial area of Bethnal Green, east London, is in this vein, and its position (on a piece of derelict land on a street of light industrial buildings and large pre-war housing blocks) reiterates the firm's continuing commitment to regeneration.

In response to a complex brief combining four different programmes – two flats, a studio for an artist, and a space for a joint therapy practice – the architects have used a form that does not immediately announce its purpose. The geometric, 'no-frills' street façade, with its entry porch covered by a mesh screen for security and semi-privacy, can be read as an urban house or a small industrial building. The form was largely generated by two constraints: the extraordinarily narrow site (4.5 × 20 metres), and the planning department's dictates on massing and sightlines. The client asked for a fluid floor plan, with an unorthodox arrangement of

interconnected rooms and changes of level, much like the spatial qualities of Kettle's Yard, the house and gallery in Cambridge.

The timber-framed structure allows both the stacking of a variety of spatial volumes and a compact, elongated form to fit the site. The rooms are arranged around an open courtyard, with staircases placed along one side in long flights. The principal space is the top-floor flat, to which the high-pitched roof lends an attic-like feel. The rear of the building is one storey high with a roof terrace above it at first-floor level. This is a visually complex space: external timber cladding alternates with bands of semi-reflective glass that cover

the solid walls as well as the windows and doors. In contrast, the rest of the building is clad in brick washed over with a mortar slurry. On two of the walls a brick slip system – thinly cut bricks bonded to rebated strips and slotted together in the manner of ship-lap boarding – has been used. This monolithic yet delicate surface adds to the building's contradictory nature, lending it an imperfection that fits well with the fragmented nature of the surrounding streetscape. Studio House may seem nondescript and slightly defensive at first sight, but on closer examination it is intricate in appearance as well as structure, paying homage to its context.

Above
The plan is narrow but well-organized, allowing ample room for the living areas. The first floor (shown here), leads on to a generous terrace.

Far left
The front of the compact building is unfussy in its design.

Left
At the back, wood and remi-reflective glass combine in an attractive but inscrutable façade.

TOWN-CENTRE HOUSING, GARRETT LANE
WANDSWORTH, SW18
SERGISON BATES ARCHITECTS, 1999–2004

Below and opposite, bottom

The six-storey apartment block, which rises at the southern end of the site, follows the undulating form of the original building, and responds to its riverside site with generous green space.

Opposite, top

Randomly scattered windows give an informal feel to the exterior. The covered walkway is entirely clad in larch, with doorways leading to small courtyards.

This impressive transformation of a former paint factory, Wandsworth Workshops, in south-west London, into an elegant mixed-use development demonstrates once again Sergison Bates's dedication to site-sensitive urban regeneration. The project, which cost £4,500,000 and earned the Housing Design Award in 2004, involved the partial demolition, refurbishment and extension of the complex of buildings dating from the 1930s sited on the corner of a busy road and alongside the banks of the River Wandle. The blocks follow the curved boundary line along the street, and this meandering form, combined with the horizontal ribbon glazing, gives them a unique character, which the architects have managed to embrace.

The existing buildings were virtually gutted, with new walls added to form studio/office units of 85–200 square metres and a core of WCs and stairs. A timber-framed single-storey extension, supported on a steel transfer structure, has been added to the existing roof and contains eleven one- and two-bedroom flats. By fitting the extension to the exact footprint of the original building and coating the entire surface in earthy-grey paint, the architects have created a unified façade that successfully integrates old and new.

A covered walkway extends from one end of the building to the other. Its walls, floors and ceilings are clad entirely in larch timber, creating a monolithic surface that dramatizes the light shafts punctuating the ceiling, and frames the views to the west, east and north. Small open-air courtyards lead off the walkway and provide access to each flat. The craftsmanship is noteworthy, with pre-galvanized aluminium sheeting on the openings, canopies and mailboxes of each flat, and doors and window frames of Douglas fir, and the shift from communal to private space is mediated by solid wooden gates. The simple arrangement of each flat centres on a hall connected to the open-air courtyard, with living-rooms and bedrooms opening on to covered balconies.

Additional residential units have been constructed at the southern end of the site, in a six-storey block that accommodates twenty flats (four per floor), with two commercial units on the ground floor. The concrete flat-slab and column structure is faceted in plan, allowing it to follow the site boundary and continue the undulating form of the original building. Such sensitivity to detail is a great strength in the work of Sergison Bates. Here it has allowed the firm to breathe new life into a previously run-down area while preserving the unique industrial character of the existing buildings.

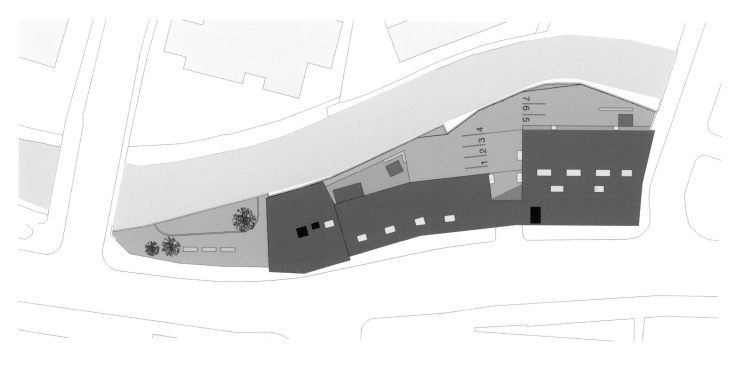

ALISON BROOKS ARCHITECTS, 2004–05

Opposite

The overarching roof provides protection from the elements and the eyes of the neighbours.

Below

The extension dramatically sprawls over the garden, with the large copper-beech tree incorporated into the timber decking.

Viewed from the street, this appears to be an ordinary Chiswick town house, with the stained glass and elaborate detailing characteristic of a Victorian building. Yet the back of this west London home presents a drastically different view. A jagged glass-and-timber structure hovers over the garden, a wooden deck sprawls over the lawn, and the roof extends upwards in numerous directions. Striking, intelligent and completely original, this project by Alison Brooks Architects is one of the most impressive residential extensions recently built in the capital.

The 100-square-metre extension is made predominantly from ipe timber, manipulated into triangular forms. The aggressive angles of the roof mimic the forms of the original Victorian structure. At one end of the building the timber surface swoops down to create a low dining space, with a floor-to-ceiling glass wall framing the outlook over the garden. At the other end, the structure folds upwards to provide more expansive views around and up to a large copper-beech tree, which has been incorporated into the decked exterior.

Light seeps inside through a narrow, glass-encased opening, which runs the entire width of the building, between the original house and the ipe roofing. Despite requesting extensive glazing to maximize light, the clients were concerned about the building overheating in the summer and about being overlooked by a row of houses to the south. The solution was to extend the timber roof beyond the line of the glazed enclosure to connect with the far edge of the deck and create a sculptured outdoor archway. As well as forming a covered outdoor dining portico, this wooden projection protects the interior from both the midday sun and prying eyes.

In the middle of the garden-facing façade the roof folds down to form an internal fireplace. The timber roof and wall surfaces also wrap to form the internal floor and external decking, giving the entire extension a solid sense of cohesion. The complex three-dimensional geometry results from the use of traditional setting techniques, along with strings and lasers, to position the rigorously accurate triangular roof planes and the precise converging lines of the internal ceiling. Throughout the project the traditional has inspired a dramatically modern result.

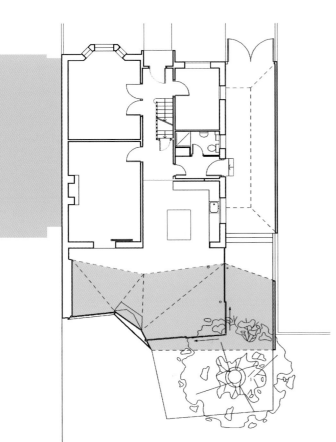

YOUNG HOUSE, POWIS MEWS
NOTTING HILL, W11

TONKIN LIU, 2000–02

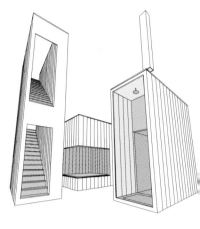

It comes as something of a surprise to see an RIBA plaque nailed to the front of this house in Notting Hill, west London. Seen from the exterior, it appears to be an ordinary mews house, shabbily constructed during the 1980s. But step inside and the building's award-winning credentials become immediately apparent.

When the architects first laid eyes on the mews it was dark, dingy and impractically designed. A garage on the ground floor was so narrow that it was impossible to open a car door inside, and a bulky staircase blocked out most of the natural light. Granted permission by the client to do exactly as they pleased, they gutted the building, even removing the floors. They then constructed three internal towers built from prefabricated medium-density fibreboard and slotted together like a giant Meccano set. The services are contained in one of the towers: on the ground floor is the bathroom, with a dramatic 4-metre-high shower, and above this is the kitchen, with the shower shaft concealed under a worktop. The second storey has been cut away above the kitchen to provide a double-height space lit by a roof light.

The second tower accommodates the sleeping and living areas, with a bedroom on the ground floor and the living area above. Although the living area receives most of the natural light, its floor is made from reinforced glass, through which light can penetrate to the level below. A switch beside the bed activates a horizontal blind to separate the two visually. The third tower provides room for the staircase, storage and a third-floor area where the client keeps his DJ equipment. Cables run from here into every room of the house, creating a sophisticated surround-sound system.

Tonkin Liu is known for its innovative use of light, and the scheme for Young House was inspired by its Q Restaurant in Hong Kong, where lights are used to differentiate between daytime and evening meals. The interior of the London project has no doors and no blinds, so during the day it is incredibly bright. The second floor is painted white, and the first and ground floors darkening shades of blue to create the effect of looking into a pool of water. At night the house is transformed by colour-changing neon lights that illuminate almost every surface. All the lighting elements have at least two settings and each tower is wired separately to allow a bewildering array of colour combinations at any one time. The mews house is a tiny 70 square metres, but Tonkin Liu's inventive layout and use of lighting allow the space to be manipulated to suit a variety of occasions. It may be drab on the outside, but the interiors are far from it.

Top

Notoriously cramped, mews houses are plentiful – and increasingly popular – in London. The Young House is outlined in red on the site plan (left). The three towers (right) replace a badly designed interior arrangement and organize the tight space.

Above

A counter in the kitchen on the first floor hides the 4-metre shaft for the shower below.

Opposite

In contrast to the mews house's day-lit appearance (above), the interior is illuminated at night by an array of vibrant colours.

OFFICES

5 ALDERMANBURY SQUARE
ERIC PARRY ARCHITECTS

198–202 PICCADILLY
ROBERT ADAM ARCHITECTS

ARTIST'S STUDIO
SANEI HOPKINS ARCHITECTS/HUGHES MEYER STUDIO

BANKSIDE 123
ALLIES AND MORRISON

BBC BROADCASTING HOUSE REDEVELOPMENT
MACCORMAC JAMIESON PRICHARD ARCHITECTS/SHEPPARD ROBSON

BISHOP'S SQUARE DEVELOPMENT
FOSTER + PARTNERS

DIFA TOWER
KOHN PEDERSEN FOX

HER MAJESTY'S TREASURY REDEVELOPMENT
FOSTER + PARTNERS

THE HOME OFFICE
FARRELLS

LONDON BRIDGE TOWER/NEW LONDON BRIDGE HOUSE
RENZO PIANO BUILDING WORKSHOP

PALESTRA
SMC ALSOP

PLANTATION PLACE
ARUP ASSOCIATES

SALVATION ARMY HEADQUARTERS
SHEPPARD ROBSON

TRINITY EC3
FOREIGN OFFICE ARCHITECTS

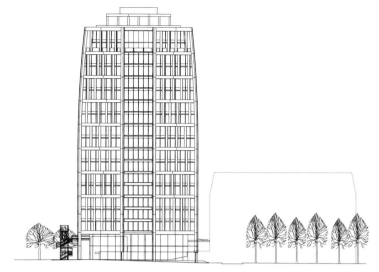

5 ALDERMANBURY SQUARE
WOOD STREET, EC2

ERIC PARRY ARCHITECTS, 2002–06

An earlier office project by Eric Parry, completed in 2002 on the eastern side of Finsbury Square, sought to impart a 'civic' feel to a large commercial block overlooking an important public open space within a conservation area. The office floors behind are standard column-free spaces, but the handsome load-bearing stone elevation reflects Parry's belief (in tune with the preferences of planning officers) that "spaces need weight". In comparison, the stone framing of Foster + Partners' block on the south-western corner of the square looks a rather token gesture.

Due to be completed in early 2007, 5 Aldermanbury Square has similar civic ambitions. Here, however, the steel-framed building is clad in large stainless-steel panels, with the structural frame clearly expressed in front of the glazing, and a second layer of glass allowing natural light to penetrate the office floors while baffling solar gain and glare.

The new nineteen-storey building – two parallel blocks, linked by a central section that includes a triple-height reception area – replaces a tired block dating from the 1960s (Royex House), one of the last of the boxy slabs that once lined London Wall. Since the mid-1980s, Wood Street has been almost totally redeveloped, with buildings by Richard Rogers and Norman Foster and, on London Wall, Terry Farrell's extraordinary Alban Gate prefacing the entrance to the Barbican. Immediately south of Parry's building is the listed police station by McMorran and Whitby – coincidentally, the structural engineer for the new building is Whitbybird, in which George Whitby's son is a partner. The

tower of St Alban's church, all that survived wartime bombing, is the other historic presence in the street, which originally led to Cripplegate, one of the ancient points of access to the City. The gentle tapering (or entasis) of the new building echoes that of McMorran and Whitby's adjacent tower, though its materials form a deliberate contrast with those of the latter. The structure of its façade, with a double-height rhythm above the triple-height ground floor, further reduces its apparent scale. Parry's building also re-establishes the building line on to Wood Street lost in the development of the 1960s, with a triple-height colonnade sheltering the pavement. The project has all the subtlety and attention to context that one expects of Parry, but it also offers an additional benefit in the form of a new public space, Aldermanbury Square. This connects Wood Street to Basinghall Street and links with the upper-level walkways that are a legacy of post-war planning prescriptions and a fundamental ingredient of the Barbican. Trees and other planting, new paving, street furniture and lighting are used to create what the architect envisages as an "enchanted garden", a real oasis of calm in the heart of the City.

Right
The building is clad in stainless-steel panels, with the structural frame in front of the glazing.

Opposite
Set in an extraordinary context of buildings by Richard Rogers, Norman Foster, Terry Farrell and twentieth-century Classicists McMorran and Whitby, 5 Aldermanbury Square, which replaces an undistinguished building dating from the 1960s, is part of the ongoing redevelopment of London Wall.

198–202 PICCADILLY, W1

ROBERT ADAM ARCHITECTS, 2005–07

Twenty years ago, when the Prince of Wales's campaign to revive traditional architecture was in full flood, there seemed every possibility that several major London sites would be redeveloped by a new generation of Classicists. But John Simpson's proposals for "Venice on Thames" (on the site of what is now More London) and his masterplan for Paternoster Square, inspired by Leon Krier and developed with Terry Farrell and a bevy of British and American traditionalists, remained unbuilt, as did the curious designs by Gabriele Tagliaventi for the site in Marsham Street, Westminster, now occupied by Farrell's Home Office complex (see pp. 224–25). Even Quinlan Terry, whose Richmond Riverside scheme of the 1980s seemed to be a harbinger of big things to come, has subsequently built relatively little in London: a set of villas in Regent's Park, a modest office scheme on Baker Street and – forthcoming – the infirmary wing at Chelsea Royal Hospital (see pp. 150–51). John Simpson's Queen's Gallery at Buckingham Palace is perhaps the most conspicuous traditionalist project of recent years in London.

Robert Adam's Piccadilly project is, in the circumstances, a significant expression of what was once called New Classicism. The scheme (nearly 6000 square metres of offices and 2500 square metres of retail space) replaces a dull block dating from the first decade of the twentieth century adjacent to Joseph Emberton's Simpson's building (now occupied by Waterstone's), a listed Modern Movement landmark. Wren's St James's, Piccadilly, is immediately to the west across a narrow pedestrian alley, with the former Midland Bank by Lutyens beyond. Constructed on a steel frame – Adam has no qualms about using modern structural solutions, and the office spaces are of a conventional nature – the building is composed to a Classical formula of base, centre and attics. The double-height base, set behind rusticated pilasters, houses shops. Four storeys of offices are above, with additional accommodation in two set-back attic floors. An octagonal corner tower marks the entrance to the narrow Church Place.

A special feature of the project is the involvement of Scottish sculptor Alexander Stoddart (with whom Adam previously collaborated on a library for the Ashmolean museum in Oxford). Capitals by Stoddart form a prominent element in the Piccadilly elevation, which is shamelessly decorative. The side and rear elevations are altogether less assertive.

Purists of all persuasions will not take to this building. It is shamelessly historicist, with a swagger that is anything but Palladian, and more than a hint of Alexander "Greek" Thomson in its proportions and details. But the piquancy of the contrast it provides to Emberton's horizontality can be enjoyed regardless, and there is none of the air of compromise that seems to characterize much recent commercial development in Westminster.

Above
The principal elevation of 198–202 Piccadilly is unashamedly decorative. With a profusion of sculptured ornament and a showy corner tower, it provides a striking contrast to the simplicity of Joseph Emberton's Simpson's building.

Opposite
The other elevations of the building, addressing St James's Church and Jermyn Street, are less assertive, with a mix of brick and stone cladding.

ARTIST'S STUDIO, ROCHESTER PLACE
KENTISH TOWN, NW1
SANEI HOPKINS ARCHITECTS/HUGHES MEYER STUDIO

2003–05

The private gallery and archive for artist Philip Hughes at the end of a garden in Kentish Town "provided the opportunity to incorporate somewhat conflicting programmes that extended the influence of the garden", according to Francesca Hughes, the client's daughter, whose practice collaborated with Sanei Hopkins on the project. The aim was to create not just a space for reflection "but also the very urban possibility of anonymity to the point of disappearance, of becoming sublimated into context, the brick and buddleia of Kentish Town".

The client acquired the redundant workshop at the bottom of the garden of the Victorian house in which he had lived for some years. The shell was retained, and the building presents a secure, blank face to the lane at the rear. On the garden side, however, there has been a total transformation, with a great wedge-shaped glass enclosure framed by a soffit of mirror glass. The new glass roof extends the line of the existing workshop roof. There are views into the space from the house, with the original brick elevation visible beyond the glass enclosure. The sauna and steam room are contained respectively in a glazed box and a ceramic 'blob' that are freestanding objects within the space. "A very peculiar, but nonetheless charming wonderland in which to escape", commented the *Architectural Review*.

Below, left, and opposite
A tranquil space for reflection, the studio retains a visual link with the house but is separated from it. Large glass doors blur the boundary between the interior and the garden.

Below, right
The studio is subsumed into its context by virtue of an expanse of mirrored glass.

BANKSIDE 123, SOUTHWARK STREET
SOUTHWARK, SE1

ALLIES AND MORRISON, 2000–08

St Christopher House, which formerly occupied the site of Bankside 123, was described by Nikolaus Pevsner as "the largest office block under one roof in Europe" when it was completed in 1959. Long occupied by the civil service, it was certainly one of the largest (and ugliest) buildings of its type in London, and its demolition in 2003 was uncontroversial.

In addition to the blankly utilitarian character of its architecture, St Christopher House was disastrous in terms of urban design: it was a monolithic block providing an impermeable obstacle between

Southwark Street and the river. With the opening of Tate Modern on the riverside, the need for new routes across the site became more pressing. Work began on Allies and Morrison's masterplan in 2000, with Land Securities as client. A key theme was to create these routes, and to mix office use with retailing, restaurants and bars serving the local community and visitors to the area as well as those working on the site.

The three buildings of Bankside 123, providing about 110,000 square metres of space, are conceived as city blocks penetrated by two new pedestrian routes,

with a new square at the eastern end of the site. The architectural language of the scheme contrasts crystal translucency (in Building One), with distinctive aluminium fins to provide shade from the sun, with the more solid aesthetic of the other two blocks. Perhaps more significant than the architecture – which is typical of the better end of early twenty-first-century commercial development – is the quality of the landscape around and between the buildings, where paving, planting, street furniture and artworks reflect a generous budget.

Below

The Bankside 123 development provides new routes from Tate Modern into the heart of Southwark, with public spaces between large commercial buildings.

Opposite

The aesthetic of the scheme – Allies and Morrison's largest project to date – is varied, and includes the use of coloured sun-shading and solid cladding panels. It represents the commercial vernacular of the early twenty-first century.

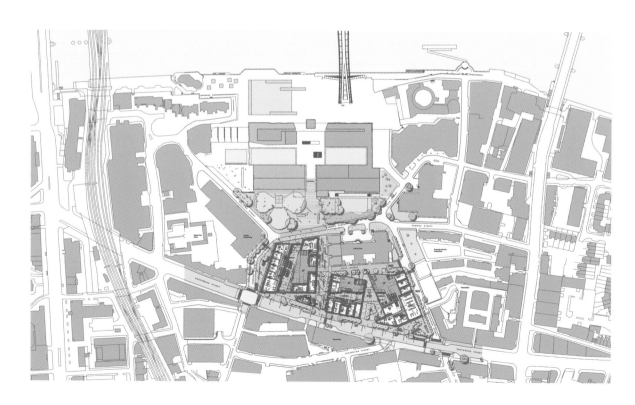

BBC BROADCASTING HOUSE REDEVELOPMENT, REGENT STREET, W1

MACCORMAC JAMIESON PRICHARD ARCHITECTS/
SHEPPARD ROBSON, 2000–09

Below and opposite, top

The first phase of Richard MacCormac's Broadcasting House redevelopment was completed in 2006, and includes a new block to the east of the original Broadcasting House (below), which has itself been internally restored (opposite, top).

Opposite, bottom

The second phase of the MacCormac scheme, which included a spectacular newsroom space, has now been abandoned in favour of alternative designs by Sheppard Robson.

Winning the competition held in 2000 for a comprehensive reconstruction of Broadcasting House in Portland Place (the BBC's historic London flagship) was a landmark victory, even in a career as distinguished as that of Sir Richard MacCormac. Other architects shortlisted included Will Alsop, Stanton Williams and Eric Parry. It was also a landmark for the BBC, which had for a time seemed content to leave imaginative patronage to other broadcasting institutions (ITN had commissioned Norman Foster, for example, and Channel 4 Richard Rogers, to design new headquarters). At the time of writing, however, it remained uncertain how far MacCormac's radical concept for 'BH' would be realized in the completed project.

Broadcasting House, now a Grade II*-listed building, opened in 1932, a striking expression of the BBC's growing status as a national institution. The building, designed by Val Myer, with interiors by Serge Chermayeff, Wells Coates and others

(all now lost), and external sculptural adornment by Eric Gill, was a subtle, Modernistic response to the site, on the bend of Langham Place, opposite John Nash's church of All Souls. The *Architectural Review* described it as nothing less than "a new Tower of London".

Over the next fifty years, with the development of the Television Centre at Shepherd's Bush and subsequently the White City site, both in west London (after the abandonment of Norman Foster's visionary project for a new radio headquarters at Langham Place), the future of Broadcasting House became uncertain. MacCormac's project reinstates it as the base for all BBC radio and music services and news operations, as well as the headquarters of the World Service.

As part of the project, initially developed in partnership with Land Securities and project-managed by Bovis Lend Lease, Myer's building has been restored and updated. The awkward 'catslide' roof Myer

was forced to introduce along its eastern edge (because of rights of light) has been replaced by practical new floorspaces. Phase 1 of the new-build element of the scheme was completed in 2006, to MacCormac's designs, replacing a 1960s block to the east of the original Broadcasting House. The new building is clearly a contextual response to the latter, with Portland stone cladding and a rounded prow addressing the church of All Souls. The development incorporates a generous new public space with cafés and shops. Conscious of the pioneering tradition established by Lord Reith in the 1930s, the BBC commissioned art consultant Vivien Lovell to develop a well-funded public-art strategy for the new building, which is an assured and appropriate addition to the West End scene.

The second phase of MacCormac's project, involving the redevelopment of the 1960s block immediately north of the Myer building, included its most radical

elements. Bovis's decision (approved by the BBC) to appoint Sheppard Robson – admittedly a practice with an excellent design record – to progress this phase involved the deletion of some of the more innovative aspects of the scheme. MacCormac had proposed, for example, a giant (4120-square-metre) newsroom as its focus: a column-free, innovatively engineered space, flooded with daylight and open to view by staff and visitors to the building. In 2006 the BBC, stung by criticisms that its commitment to good design was in doubt, assembled an expert panel to advise on a number of its building projects, including the second phase of Broadcasting House, where there were hopes that MacCormac might be involved in a consultancy role. The saga reflects the fine balance between aspiration and reality typical of many big projects, even when the client is a national institution.

Below

Although controversial, the scheme provides valuable, tree-filled public space for residents, tourists and office workers.

Opposite

The rationale of the Bishop's Square development is the provision of a large area of state-of-the-art office space (top left). The scheme also offers public benefits in terms of new open spaces (right, top to bottom) and an elegant glazed arcade that focuses on the spire of Hawksmoor's Christ Church, itself recently restored (bottom left).

BISHOP'S SQUARE DEVELOPMENT
SPITALFIELDS, E1

FOSTER + PARTNERS, 2001–05

Spitalfields was the scene of a three-decade battle between the development industry and the conservation/community lobby. The Spitalfields Trust (founded in 1977) was responsible for saving dozens of fine early Georgian houses in the area, while a National Lottery-funded project (by architects William Whitfield, succeeded by Purcell Miller Tritton) has rescued Hawksmoor's magnificent Christ Church from utter dereliction. Nothing, however, could save the historic fruit-and-vegetable market, which was founded in the 1680s and finally closed in 1986. The removal of the market opened the way for commercial redevelopment of the site, and schemes by Sir Richard MacCormac, Leon Krier, Quinlan Terry, Swanke Hayden Connell Architects, Benjamin Thompson Associates and Terry Farrell, among others, grappled with the problem of inserting a large complex of modern offices into the fine-grained historic context.

After a long hiatus during the recession of the 1990s, Foster + Partners became involved. The practice's initial scheme proposed two large office buildings on the site of the market buildings (which date from the 1920s), retaining and restoring the original, listed portion of the market, which had been colonized by small businesses. The development, completed in 2005, is radically different in character, but, with 72,000 square metres of offices and 3700 square metres of retail space, marks the absorption of Spitalfields into the City. The East End now starts at Commercial Street, rather than Bishopsgate.

Bishop's Square consists of four long fingers of offices, separated by atria and stepped in form, allowing the creation of

attractive roof gardens on three of the blocks. The architecture of the office buildings is restrained and rational, in contrast to the flamboyance of some of Foster's recent City buildings.

The most positive aspect of the project, however, is its comprehensive approach to the planning of the site. A new landscaped space, complete with gardens and a lily pond, has been created to the west, on what was a lorry park. A second public space, with a steel-and-glass roof, connects the new buildings to the retained Victorian market. Along the southern side of the development a glass-roofed galleria, angled to focus on Hawksmoor's spire, includes shops and cafés. The pavilions of the market on Brushfield Street have been retained, with flats on the upper floors, providing a welcome element of continuity. The generosity of scale and semi-industrial character in the new covered spaces are in tune with the old market beyond, and mitigate the dramatic change wrought by the development, which will house 5000 City workers, half of them employed by a single law firm. A further progressive element is provided by the largest installation of photovoltaic cells in any commercial development in Europe, though these will generate only a tiny fraction of the complex's energy needs.

For some, lawyers' offices, expensive shops and wine bars will never belong in Spitalfields. Yet the character of the area changed for ever when a new breed of affluent residents colonized the restored Georgian houses that form a piquant contrast to the ethnic bustle of Brick Lane. Not even Spitalfields can resist the dynamic of change that is fundamental to London.

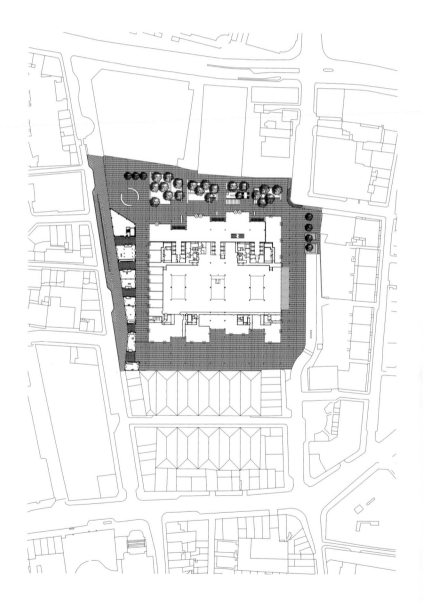

DIFA TOWER, BISHOPSGATE, EC2

KOHN PEDERSEN FOX, 2003–10

Replacing Fitzroy Robinson's Standard Chartered Bank, completed as recently as 1985 and once boasting the most spectacularly planted atrium in London, the DIFA Tower (named after the German firm that commissioned it) will be the tallest building in the City. At 288 metres high, it will provide a dramatic riposte to Renzo Piano's 306-metre-high London Bridge Tower across the River Thames in Southwark (see pp. 226–27). The building is one of several completed or planned towers in this sector of the City, which is not subject to the constraints of planning regulations that protect 'corridors' giving views of the historic London skyline. That group includes Tower 42, Foster + Partners' 30 St Mary Axe (the 'Gherkin'), and the forthcoming Leadenhall Tower (by Richard Rogers Partnership) and Heron Tower, also by Kohn Pedersen Fox (KPF), further up Bishopsgate.

KPF won an invited competition in 2003, and the scheme secured planning consent in the spring of 2006, with construction due to begin in 2007. The building provides 80,000 square metres of office space on floorplates of up to 2380 square metres, as well as three levels of retail and public 'sky-lobbies', with a restaurant at level 43. The striking form of the building is an unashamed exercise in composition (its highly sculptural top floors contain nothing more than plant), a pinnacle to the growing cluster of towers that capitalizes on the increasingly positive public response to tall buildings in London.

At ground level the character of the tower as two interlocking volumes is apparent. Accessed beneath a flowing 18-metre-high canopy, a public route, surrounded by shops and cafés, leads to the long-neglected Crosby Square to the

east, due to be landscaped as part of the project and potentially linked to the recast public domain around the Leadenhall scheme by Rogers. Office areas are entered from first-floor level.

The design of the façade was the subject of intense study, as it was imperative to meet the requirements of stringent building regulations and the Mayor of London's guidelines on sustainability, while maintaining the tower's transparency. The building is wrapped in a ventilated façade, using framed glazing, that reduces solar heat gain and allows natural ventilation. Internal louvres counter direct sunlight, while allowing natural light to illuminate the workspaces. A battery of photovoltaic cells to generate energy from the sun is provided at high level – a token gesture, it might be argued, but at least a step in the right direction.

The DIFA Tower is clearly a product of the 'Gherkin effect': 30 St Mary Axe gave planners and the public a taste for towers of unusual shape. KPF's Heron Tower scheme, designed a few years earlier, was strictly orthogonal, but this product of the same architectural stable has been variously nicknamed the 'helter skelter' and the 'Mexican wrap'.

Right

Meeting the ground in spectacular fashion, the tower will have a highly sculptural form typical of London's new generation of tall buildings.

Opposite

This perspective shows completed and projected City towers, including (from left to right) KPF's Heron Tower, Richard Seifert's Tower 42, DIFA Tower, Foster + Partners' 30 St Mary Axe, and Richard Rogers Partnership's Leadenhall Tower.

HER MAJESTY'S TREASURY
REDEVELOPMENT, WHITEHALL, WC2

FOSTER + PARTNERS, 1996–2002

The Treasury complex (originally occupied by other government departments) was built between 1899 and 1915. It is one of the most prominent buildings in central London, extending along the northern side of Parliament Square and framing the entrance to Whitehall. It is big, bold and confidently neo-Baroque, a key landmark of London in the age of Empire.

By the end of the twentieth century, however, the Treasury building, listed Grade II, was seen as something of an embarrassment, providing poor working conditions for staff, with large areas of under-used space that could potentially accommodate other government departments that were then housed further from the centre of power. Sensibly, the government turned to the commercial development sector for a strategy to rationalize the complex, and a public–private partnership was formed to progress it.

The public face of the building is unchanged. Inside, however, previously unused courts and light wells have been transformed into circulation, social and recreational spaces, with cafés, a library, and, in the larger areas, planting and pools. Some of these spaces are capped by lightweight roofs in the tradition of Foster's

Great Court at the British Museum. Colour is used freely, particularly in large banners by Danish designer Per Arnoldi, a regular Foster collaborator. The great circular court at the heart of the building, long used as a car park, has been landscaped as a pedestrian piazza. Offices have been radically revamped, with an estimated 11 kilometres of partitions stripped out to provide open-plan workspaces. In the process, it was possible to rationalize the Treasury's own accommodation, which now occupies only the western half of the building, leaving the rest for use by other departments.

Sustainability is a key theme of Foster's architecture and one that the government was keen to endorse. The light wells and courts also function as thermal chimneys, with opening vents extracting stale air from the offices. Opening windows have been retained, and upgraded to improve their security. 'Windcatchers' mounted on the roof supplement the natural ventilation system.

The Treasury project is a further example – less conspicuous than the Great Court but in its way just as significant – of Foster's expertise at making new and old work together, a skill first demonstrated in London with the Sackler Wing of the Royal Academy in the early 1990s.

Right and opposite

Massive in scale, the Treasury building has been transformed by Foster + Partners to create new circulation and communal spaces in previously disused courts and light wells, some of them topped by glazed roofs. Office spaces have been reconfigured, with corridors and partitions removed in favour of open-plan space.

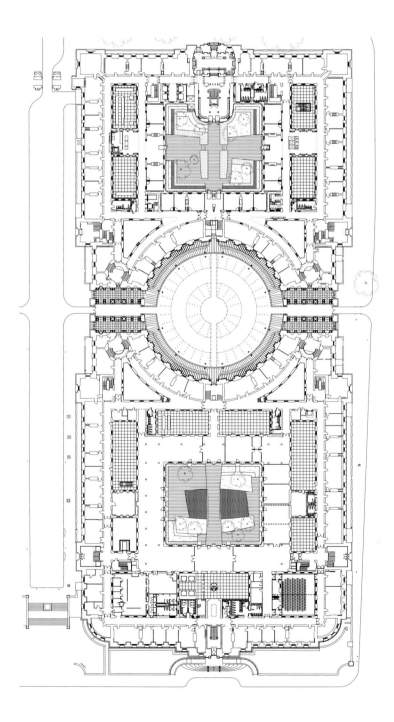

THE HOME OFFICE, MARSHAM STREET, SW1

FARRELLS, 1991–2005

Farrells prepared a masterplan for the redevelopment of the Marsham Street site, occupied by three high-rise office slabs dating from the 1960s, as long ago as 1991, when it was assumed that it would be sold for commercial development. It was not until 1997 that a decision was finally made to demolish the original complex and build the new Home Office there. The Labour government elected that year set aside the results of a competition held in 1996, which had resulted in victory for a cumbrous Classical scheme by Italian architect Gabriele Tagliaventi. Farrells began to develop the present scheme in 1998, and it was incorporated into a Private Finance Initiative (PFI) bid in 2000. The building opened in 2005.

The original towers had been designed by Eric Bedford for the then Department of the Environment and were completed in 1971. At 67 metres tall, they had long been reviled for their adverse impact on distant views of the Palace of Westminster. A maximum height of eight storeys was set for the new 70,000-square-metre development, and allowance was made for increasing accommodation on the site by fifty per cent in the future. The principles of the scheme are essentially those laid down in the masterplan of 1991: the reintegration of the site, permeated by public spaces, into the city fabric, with three buildings conceived as a series of distinct blocks rather than as a megastructure. Residential accommodation is provided in a block to the west, underlining the commitment in the masterplan to mixed-use provision.

The new Home Office draws on the best practice of the commercial office sector to create a working environment for more than 3000 civil servants that is far removed from the drab confines still inhabited by many government departments. Workspaces are largely open plan, and benefit from generous natural light and views out to the 'pocket' parks formed between the buildings. An internal 200-metre-long 'street' running the length of the buildings at first-floor level contains shared resources, including cafés, meeting areas, a print shop and space for the interaction now seen as fundamental to team working. Large atria enhance the sense of connection and communication. Colour is used throughout, and funds for artworks were generous, though the overall budget for the project, which was delivered on time and to cost, was strictly controlled under the PFI scheme. The glass canopy, designed in collaboration with artist Liam Gillick (who also co-ordinated the display of art in the whole building), is the defining feature of the street elevation.

The PFI system has been widely criticized as undermining the quality of design in the public sector. If broader issues of cost and control are left aside, the Home Office is one project where PFI seems to have worked, at least in terms of providing a distinctive and practical building with a benign impact on the public domain.

Below
The Home Office's three buildings are linked on the first floor by an internal walkway. Their relatively low-rise, stepped construction defers to the historic buildings in the area.

Opposite
Artwork is a crucial part of the design of the complex. The street façade, with its striking metal cut-outs, is topped by a glass canopy designed in collaboration with Liam Gillick.

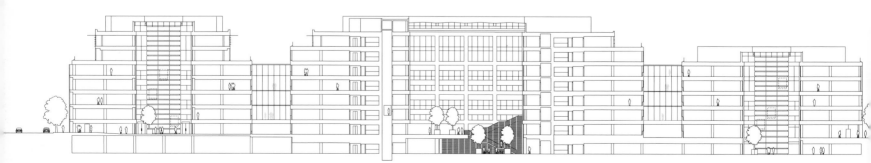

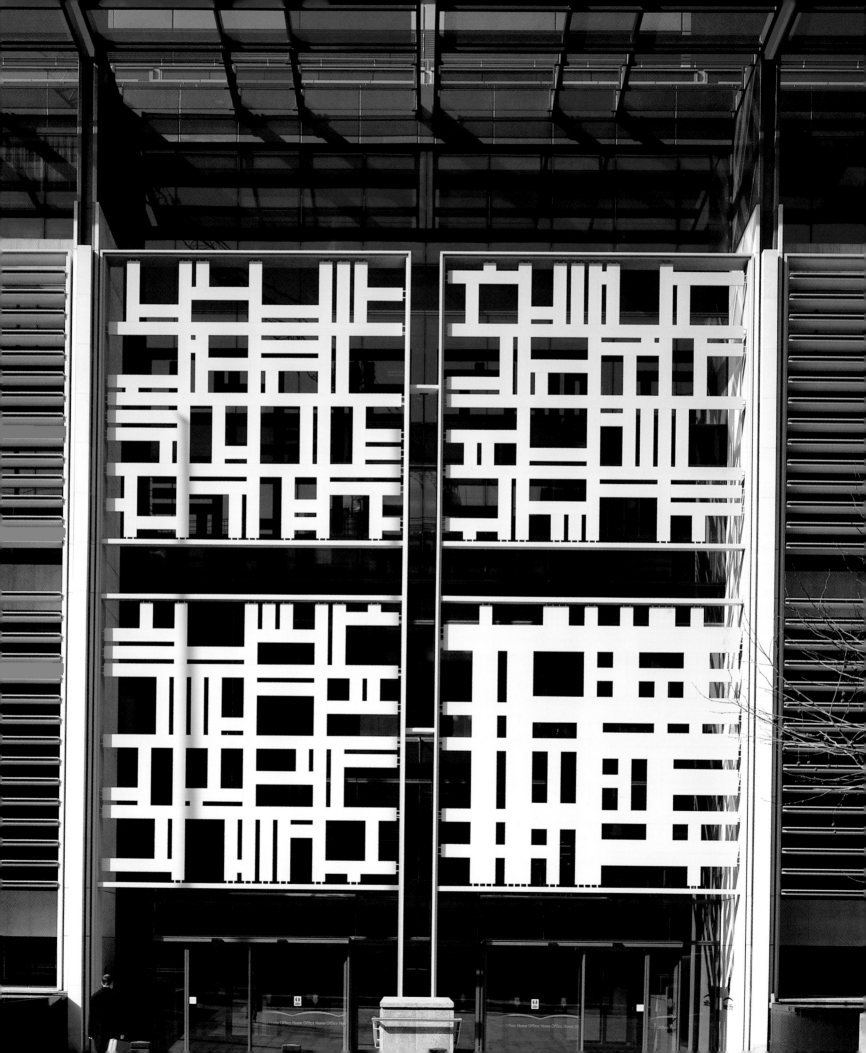

LONDON BRIDGE TOWER
AND NEW LONDON BRIDGE HOUSE
ST THOMAS STREET, SOUTHWARK, SE1

RENZO PIANO BUILDING WORKSHOP, 2000–10

Following on from initial proposals by
Broadway Malyan, Renzo Piano was
brought in by developer Irvine Sellar during
2000 to work on the project for a mixed-
use tower adjacent to London Bridge
station. The "shard of glass", as Piano
named it, finally won planning consent
in November 2003, following a public
inquiry at which English Heritage was a key
objector. (Mayor of London Ken Livingstone
and the Commission for Architecture
and the Built Environment were strong
supporters of the project, which won the
backing of Southwark Council.)

Replacing an undistinguished 1970s
high-rise, the tower was initially conceived
as a structure 420 metres and eighty-seven
storeys high. The actual tower will be 306
metres and sixty-eight storeys high, but it
will still be the tallest building in Europe.
Like Norman Foster's 'Gherkin', it will
certainly become as much a symbol of
London as St Paul's Cathedral or Big Ben.
Demolition of the existing buildings is
scheduled for 2007, with completion
(excluding fit-out) in 2010. The tower will
contain 54,000 square metres of office
space; a two-hundred-bed, five-star hotel
on the top eighteen storeys; and fourteen
storeys of residential accommodation. Some
7000 people will live or work in the building.

'The Shard', as it has been nicknamed,
makes use of advanced glazing technology
to achieve not only exceptional aesthetic
effects – reflections of light and changing
cloud patterns will make the form of the
tower elusive – but also outstanding
environmental performance. The ventilated

double skin of the building, incorporating
extensive shading, reduces heat gain.
Excess hot air from the offices will be used
to heat the flats and hotel. Winter gardens
with opening louvres will provide access
to fresh air and connect with the world
outside (similar examples can be seen in
Piano's Aurora Place tower in Sydney). It
is claimed that the building will consume
thirty per cent less energy than a
conventional structure of comparable size.

One of the project's strongest selling
points, in environmental terms, is its close
proximity to major public transport facilities,
which will be augmented if and when the
Thameslink rail project finally gets the go-
ahead. The Shard contains only forty
parking spaces, but the gains it offers for
rail and Underground users – including a
generous new railway station concourse,
a relocated bus station and an external
public square – are hugely significant.

New London Bridge House (nicknamed
the 'Gem' or 'Baby Shard') won planning
consent in the spring of 2006. Located
west of the Shard, close to Borough High
Street, the building defers to the historic
context of Borough Market and Southwark
Cathedral, and forms almost a foothill to
the Alp-like mass of the Shard. Its faceted
form is partly dictated by the closeness
of the railway viaducts, but Piano has
capitalized on this to produce a structure
of memorably sculptural qualities. He
envisages the building floating "like
the rock of Magritte above the ground,
liberating space and creating a vibrant
public environment".

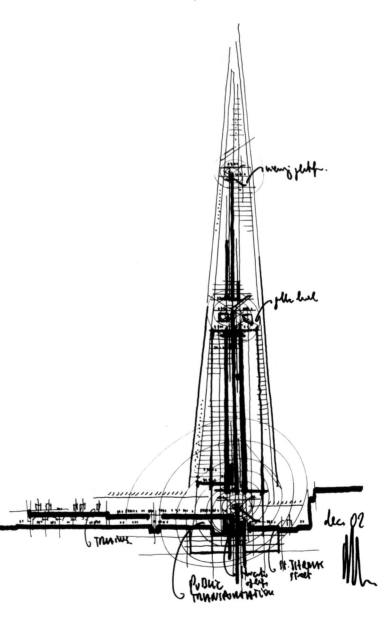

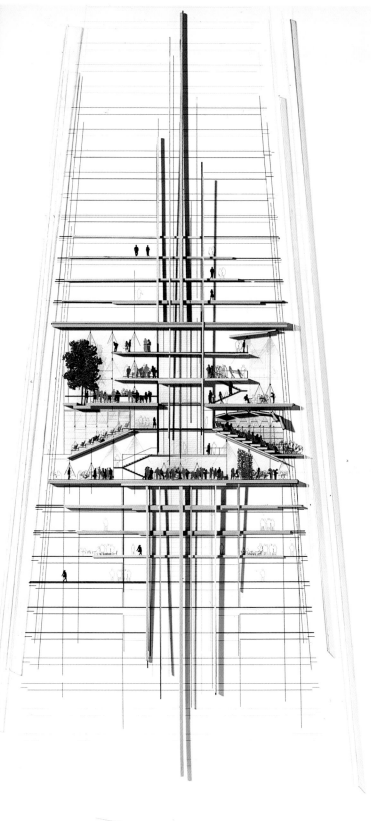

PALESTRA, BLACKFRIARS ROAD
SOUTHWARK, SE1

SMC ALSOP, 1999–2006

Palestra is a heavyweight of a building. The site once contained a renowned boxing ring, but more recently was occupied by Orbit House, an unremarkable block designed in the 1960s by Richard Seifert. The advent of the Jubilee line – MacCormac Jamieson Prichard's Southwark Underground station is just across the road – and Tate Modern made this an attractive locale for new commercial development. The Palestra project launched the idea of Blackfriars Road as part of London's 'South Central' quarter, and has led to the emergence of a number of schemes for sites in the area between Southwark station and the River Thames. A large part of the building has been let to the London Development Agency (LDA), a prestigious tenant, which has its own entrance in an organically shaped pod at ground level.

Alsop first made his mark on Southwark with Peckham Library, a building that became a symbol of the borough's regeneration programme and won the Stirling Prize. Palestra tested his ability to put his stamp on a large (25,000-square-metre) commercial development. He envisaged the building as a series of horizontal planes, the lowest of which is tilted upwards from ground level to provide a covered public space with shops and cafés. Palestra would have had an even more forceful impact had not plans for a top layer of offices, contained within a transparent slab, been removed on the insistence of planners. The application of strong colour, using advanced glazing technology, gives the building a highly distinctive look. Yet it is also a very practical structure, with flexible 30-metre-wide, column-free floors enhanced by double-height cut-outs, mezzanines and terraces.

Palestra is a powerful, even slightly intimidating, addition to the Southwark cityscape and a harbinger of much more to come. It confirms Alsop's ability to transform functional buildings into urban icons – and even into works of art.

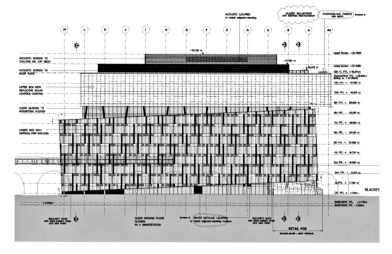

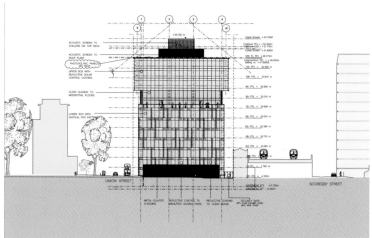

PLANTATION PLACE, FENCHURCH STREET, EC3

ARUP ASSOCIATES, 1996–2004

Plantation Place is one of the largest new office developments in the City and offers considerable benefits for the public realm. It is one of a series of recent office buildings along Fenchurch Street, including Richard Rogers's Lloyd's Register and designs by John McAslan and Kohn Pedersen Fox. A new tower by Rafael Viñoly is set to replace the undistinguished Kleinwort Benson building of the 1960s at 20 Fenchurch Street.

The one-hectare site, bounded by Fenchurch Street, Rood Lane, Mincing Lane and Eastcheap/Great Tower Street, was formerly occupied by Plantation House, a "remarkable, incoherent building" (Nikolaus Pevsner) constructed in phases between 1935 and 1954 to house commodities markets. It was comprehensively refurbished in the early 1990s, but the developer British Land commissioned Arup Associates in 1996 to prepare plans for redevelopment. The complex (not listed) was demolished and replaced by about 100,000 square metres of new office space.

The scheme comprises two buildings: a fifteen-storey block on Fenchurch Street and a ten-storey block to the south, each of which has a distinct character. The northern block is clad in a double skin of glass, while Plantation Place South has a load-bearing stone façade with limited glazing. Stone fins are a feature of both buildings, a response to the planning requirement that the development have a "solid" character at street level. The upper levels of the northern block, in contrast, are a transparent presence on the skyline. Between the two buildings is a new east–west pedestrian route, Plantation Lane, a welcome addition to the City's traditional lanes and alleys.

The project involved complex planning negotiations, and required significant archaeological and historic building issues to be addressed. Sir Christopher Wren's Grade I-listed church of St Margaret Pattens stands at the south-western corner of the site. The modelling of the scheme defers to the rights of neighbours to light and views, with setbacks to reduce its impact on the narrow streets of the City. All in all, it is an ingenious piece of design and a rational retort to the tendency towards 'iconic' structures, with much that is technically innovative, notably the mixed-mode ventilation strategy that reduces dependency on air-conditioning.

As part of the scheme, the client commissioned artist Simon Patterson, well known for *The Great Bear*, a reworking of the London Tube map, to collaborate with Arup Associates on a major work of public art, entitled *Time and Tide*. It consists of a glass screen, 41 metres long and 6 metres tall, forming one side of Plantation Lane. The screen is a giant light box – a painting in light – featuring close-up images of the surface of the Moon in constantly changing colours. Patterson also designed the lettering on the pavement, a "carpet of words" related to the history of the site and the City. This is a bold and effective piece of architectural art, properly integrated into the project and not a pointless addition.

Right and opposite

The two blocks address their contexts, at once sympathetic and iconic in their different ways. Plantation Place South (right) is solid, while the northern block's gleaming volumes (above, right) float above an impressive atrium (opposite).

SALVATION ARMY HEADQUARTERS
99–101 QUEEN VICTORIA STREET, EC4

SHEPPARD ROBSON, 1999–2004

"Modern in design, frugal in operation, evangelical in purpose": this was the client brief for Sheppard Robson's new City building housing the international headquarters of the Salvation Army, an organization known for its religious and charitable activities across the globe but firmly British in origin.

The Salvation Army came to Queen Victoria Street in 1881, three years after its foundation by William Booth. Its first headquarters was destroyed by German bombs in 1941. A replacement building designed by H.M. Lidbetter was eventually completed in 1963, but in 1999 the organization's British operation was relocated to a site near Elephant and Castle in south London, leaving much of the relatively undistinguished Lidbetter block empty and clearly ripe for redevelopment.

Indeed, the Army seriously considered selling the Queen Victoria Street building and moving its international headquarters to its training college in south London. But with the opening in 1999 of the Millennium Bridge, which became a prime tourist route, linking St Paul's Cathedral to Tate Modern, the site (flanking the northern end of this route) acquired a new prominence. The organization's leader at the time, General John Gowans, saw the potential for the building to become 'a window to the world', promoting the Army's message to millions of passers-by.

Advised by space planner Andrew Chadwick, the Army conceived a strategy to redevelop the site, capitalizing on its value for commercial development, and in the process shrewdly providing the organization with a new building of about 3200 square metres, in line with its practical needs, at minimum cost. The Army's new premises occupy the western end of the site, with the remainder redeveloped into speculative offices. Sheppard Robson won the project in a developer/architect competition in 1999 and planning consent was given in 2001, though the events of 11 September that year subsequently put the scheme on hold for a time. The new headquarters finally opened in 2004.

This building exemplifies the best of Sheppard Robson's work: it is purposeful, elegant and immaculately detailed. The architecture is essentially that of the world of business, but then, as Booth insisted, "the devil should not have all the best tunes". The offices that occupy the top three floors of the building are indeed state-of-the-art City workspaces, a vast improvement on those previously occupied by the Army's staff. Offices for the General and other senior staff are at first-floor level, in a series of glazed enclosures flanking the chapel. Services – stairs, lifts and WCs – are pushed to the eastern edge of the building, where they form a natural boundary to the commercial development that lies beyond. But it is the lower levels of the building that form its public face: meeting-rooms, a generous lobby area and an attractive café on the lower ground floor are all clearly visible to passers-by through the glazed façade. William Booth is remembered as a prime exponent of 'muscular Christianity', and this strength is symbolized by the exposed structural steel frame, painted brilliant white, seen throughout the interior and forming a dramatic feature in views from outside.

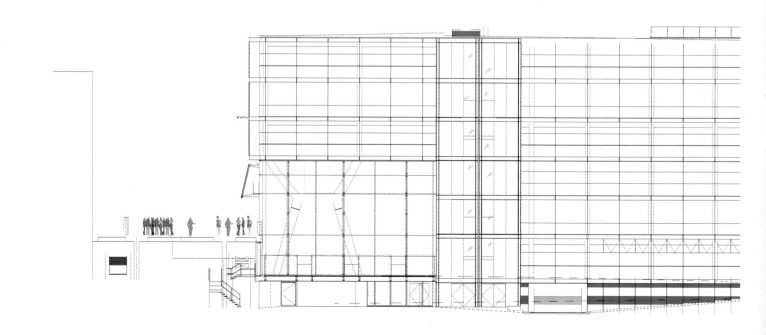

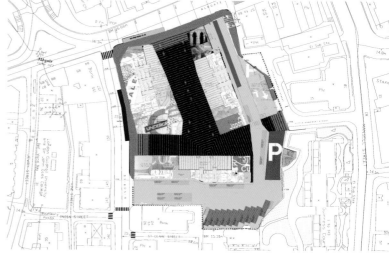

TRINITY EC3, MINORIES/
ALDGATE HIGH STREET, EC3

FOREIGN OFFICE ARCHITECTS, 2004–12

The Aldgate area, on the eastern fringe of the City of London, demonstrates the City's traditional contempt for the East End. The walls and gates are long gone, but the mess of roads and banal buildings around Aldgate High Street forms a daunting barrier between the affluent commercial milieux of Leadenhall Street and Fenchurch Street and the downbeat multicultural mix of Whitechapel and the eastern quarters of Spitalfields.

Foreign Office Architects' Trinity project, commissioned by the Liverpool-based Beetham Organization (who are also behind the One Blackfriars Road project; see pp. 188–89), is an attempt to break down that barrier and to capitalize on the development potential of the lacklustre City fringe. The site literally abuts the borderline between the City and the borough of Tower Hamlets, linking the former to Whitechapel Road, the site for such developments as the Idea Store (pp. 52–53), the expanded Whitechapel Art Gallery (pp. 74–75) and the rebuilt Royal London Hospital (pp. 152–53).

Foreign Office Architects (FOA), which was founded in 1995 by Farshid Moussavi and Alejandro Zaero Polo (who met at Harvard and taught for a time at the Architectural Association), won the scheme in competition in 2004. Along with a 40,000-square-metre retail development currently on site in Leicester, this project has confirmed the practice's elevation from experimental studio to big-league player in the tradition of Foster + Partners and Herzog & de Meuron.

The project provides 136,000 square metres of offices and 2500 square metres of shops and cafés. In contrast to the high-rise projects planned for City sites to the west, including Kohn Pedersen Fox's DIFA Tower (pp. 220–21) and Leadenhall Tower by Richard Rogers Partnership, it has a relatively modest impact on the skyline, in order to preserve distant views of the Tower of London. FOA envisages the development as "a small campus where the built and the unbuilt are equally important and carefully

co-ordinated". Public space, it says, is central to the proposal: a T-shaped glazed galleria up to 20 metres wide connects the three office buildings, providing a new pedestrian connection across the site. The existing bus station, a dismal structure and a conspicuously wasteful use of land, is moved and replaced by a covered facility, and a new entrance to Aldgate Underground station, fully accessible to the disabled, is provided. A winter garden and viewing gallery, open to the public, are provided at the top of the tallest of the three blocks.

Public benefits of this sort have to be funded, and to this end the scheme offers big, efficient office floorplates of up to 2000 square metres around central cores. Deep floors have to be day-lit and a curtain-walled glass envelope is traditionally the way to achieve this. Recent increases in the stringency of building regulations, and guidelines on renewable energy laid out by Mayor Ken Livingstone for major London developments, mean that the envelope

must have exemplary environmental credentials. The cladding consists of double-glazed units with an argon-filled cavity, baffling solar gain without significantly reducing the quality of the natural light. Responding to the Mayor's policies, the project uses boreholes and a heatpump to extract groundwater and use it as a means of heating and cooling the buildings in all but extreme weather conditions.

The glazed prismatic forms of the buildings are critical to the aesthetic impact of the scheme, challenging the tediously orthogonal character of the post-war developments in the Aldgate area. This project exemplifies the way in which developers are taking the lead in progressive architectural patronage in London, and in the creation of new public spaces and transport connections.

Above and opposite, top right and bottom
A glazed galleria at the heart of the building provides a new pedestrian route across the site, which was previously occupied by a drab bus station.

Left
The Trinity development's varied context includes the historic church of St Botolph's, Aldgate.

Opposite, top left
The complex occupies a critical site where the City meets the East End.

FURTHER READING

Allinson, Ken, *London's Contemporary Architecture: A Visitor's Guide*, 4th edn, London
    (Architectural Press) 2006
Allison, Peter (ed.), *David Adjaye: Houses*, London (Thames & Hudson) 2005
Allison, Peter (ed.), *David Adjaye: Making Public Buildings*, London (Thames & Hudson) 2006
Bennetts Associates: Four Commentaries, London (Black Dog Publishing) 2005
Bradley, Simon, *St Pancras Station*, London (Profile Books) 2007
Building the BBC: A Return to Form, London (Wordsearch Communications) 2004
Chapman, Tony, *The Stirling Prize: Ten Years of Architecture and Innovation*, London (Merrell) 2006
Davies, Colin, *Hopkins 2*, London (Phaidon) 2001
Foster + Partners, *Foster Catalogue 2005*, Munich (Prestel) 2005
Jackson, Alan A., *London's Termini*, Newton Abbot (David & Charles) 1969
Jones, Edward, and Woodward, Christopher, *A Guide to the Architecture of London*, 3rd edn,
    London (Seven Dials) 2000
Kerr, Joe, and Gibson, Andrew (eds), *London, from Punk to Blair*, London (Reaktion Books) 2003
Long, Kieran, *New London Interiors*, London (Merrell) 2004
McKean, John, *Royal Festival Hall*, Buildings in Detail, London (Phaidon) 1992
Nairn, Ian, *Modern Buildings in London*, London (London Transport) 1964
Nairn, Ian, *Nairn's London*, Harmondsworth (Penguin) 1966
Eric Parry Architects, vol. 1, London (Black Dog Publishing) 2002
Powell, Kenneth, *30 St Mary Axe: A Tower for London*, London (Merrell) 2006
Powell, Kenneth, *City Reborn: Architecture and Regeneration in London, from Bankside to Dulwich*,
    London (Merrell) 2004
Powell, Kenneth, *Richard Rogers: Complete Works, III*, London (Phaidon) 2006
Sheard, Rod, *The Stadium: Architecture for the New Global Culture*, Sydney (Pesaro) 2005
Schumacher, Patrik, and Fontana-Giusti, Gordana (eds), *Zaha Hadid: Complete Works*, London
    (Thames & Hudson) 2004
Sudjic, Deyan, *Future Systems*, London (Phaidon) 2006
Summerson, John, *Georgian London*, London (Pleiades Books) 1945, and subsequent edns
Watkin, David, *Radical Classicism: the Architecture of Quinlan Terry*, New York (Rizzoli) 2006
Wilkinson, Chris, and Eyre, James, *Bridging Art and Science: Wilkinson Eyre Architecture*, London
    (Booth-Clibborn Editions) 2001
Wright, Herbert, *London High*, London (Frances Lincoln) 2006

The illustrations in this book have been reproduced courtesy of the following copyright holders:

Avanti Architects: 177 (top right); © Sue Barr/VIEW: 212, 213; Hélène Binet: 113 (bottom left and right); © James Brittain/VIEW: 13; © Nigel Carr/VIEW: 145 (bottom), 180, 181 (bottom); © David Chipperfield Architects: 48 (top); Cityscape: 189; Keith Collie: 62 (middle and bottom); © Peter Cook/VIEW: 48, 49 (bottom), 64 (top), 65 (top right), 68, 69 (bottom left and right), 81 (middle and bottom), 88, 89, 100, 101, 110 (top), 111, 120, 121 (bottom), 122 (middle and bottom), 123, 130 (bottom), 131, 134 (right), 135, 136 (left), 137; de Rijke Marsh Morgan Architects: 104, 105; Fletcher Priest Architects: 30; © Foster + Partners: 8, 80 (top), 92, 93, 114, 218, 222; © Chris Gascoigne/VIEW: 66 (middle and bottom), 67, 170 (left and middle), 171; © Dennis Gilbert/VIEW: 2, 14, 22 (middle and bottom), 34 (bottom), 35, 54 (bottom), 55, 60 (middle and bottom), 61, 70, 80 (bottom left, middle and right), 103, 115, 140 (bottom left and right), 141, 158 (bottom left and right), 159, 162 (middle and bottom), 163, 201, 215, 233; Nigel Greenhill: 145 (top left and right); Robert Greshoff: 177 (top left); Grimshaw: 128, 129; © Nick Guttridge/VIEW: 12, 54 (middle), 168 (bottom), 169, 179; Zaha Hadid Architects: 86, 87, 173; Hayes Davidson: 32 (bottom), 33; Hayes Davidson and John Maclean: 227 (top); Hayes Davidson and John Maclean © RPBW: 227 (bottom right); © Alex Hill/VIEW: 28, 38, 39 (middle and bottom), 76 (bottom), 77, 126 (top), 127, 182, 183 (bottom left and right); HOK Sport Architecture: 83 (top left, middle and right); © Hufton & Crow/VIEW: 65 (top left, top middle and bottom), 83 (bottom); Kandor Modelmakers/ Photography – Andrew Putler: 31 (top); © Nicholas

Kane 2006: 177 (bottom); Kohn Pedersen Fox: 220 (bottom); Kohn Pedersen Fox/Cityscape: 220 (top), 221; © Raf Makda/VIEW: 190 (bottom left and right), 191; © Ioana Marinescu/VIEW: 113 (top), 160 (bottom), 161, 199 (bottom left and right); Images by Miller Hare: 40, 41; © Kilian O'Sullivan/VIEW: 124, 125 (bottom left and right), 133 (right, top and bottom), 175, 186 (middle and bottom), 187; Peabody Trust, London: 181 (top); © Renzo Piano Building Workshop: 226, 227 (bottom left); Andrew Putler: 188 (right); © Christian Richters: 230, 231; © Paul Riddle/VIEW: 132 (top and bottom right), 193, 202, 203 (right); Richard Rogers Partnership: 32 (top), 148, 149; Richard Rogers Partnership/ Cityscape: 6; © Tom Scott/VIEW: 91, 156–57; Ian Simpson Architects: 188 (left); © Grant Smith/VIEW: 51, 106 (middle and bottom), 167, 185, 229; © Jefferson Smith/Arcblue.com: 204 (bottom), 205; © Andy Stagg/VIEW: 28, 72, 73, 98 (middle and bottom), 99, 107 (bottom left and right), 109, 194 (bottom), 195, 196 (middle and bottom), 197; Studio Daniel Libeskind: 110 (bottom left and right); © Edmund Sumner/VIEW: 44 (middle and bottom), 45, 52 (bottom left and right), 53, 63 (bottom), 95, 172, 225; Quinlan and Francis Terry: 150, 151; © Paul Tyagi/VIEW: 84 (left), 84 (middle left and right; bottom left and right), 147; V&A Images/Victoria and Albert Museum: 42 (bottom right); Morley von Sternberg: 43, 119; © Anthony Weller/VIEW: 15, 216, 217 (top left and right); West 8: 31 (bottom); © Nigel Young/Foster + Partners: 219, 223

The publisher has made every effort to trace and contact copyright holders of the illustrations reproduced in this book; they will be happy to correct in subsequent editions any errors or omissions that are brought to their attention.